AF477892

*Palgrave Macmillan Studies in Banking and Financial Institutions*

Series Editor: **Professor Philip Molyneux**

The Palgrave Macmillan Studies in Banking and Financial Institutions are international in orientation and include studies of banking within particular countries or regions, and studies of particular themes such as Corporate Banking, Risk Management, Mergers and Acquisitions, etc. The books' focus is on research and practice, and they include up-to-date and innovative studies on contemporary topics in banking that will have global impact and influence.

Titles include:

Yener Altunbaş, Blaise Gadanecz and Alper Kara
SYNDICATED LOANS
A Hybrid of Relationship Lending and Publicly Traded Debt

Yener Altunbaş, Alper Kara and Öslem Olgu
TURKISH BANKING
Banking under Political Instability and Chronic High Inflation

Elena Beccalli
IT AND EUROPEAN BANK PERFORMANCE

Paola Bongini, Stefano Chiarlone and Giovanni Ferri *(editors)*
EMERGING BANKING SYSTEMS

Vittorio Boscia, Alessandro Carretta and Paola Schwizer
COOPERATIVE BANKING: INNOVATIONS AND DEVELOPMENTS

COOPERATIVE BANKING IN EUROPE: CASE STUDIES

Roberto Bottiglia, Elisabetta Gualandri and Gian Nereo Mazzocco *(editors)*
CONSOLIDATION IN THE EUROPEAN FINANCIAL INDUSTRY

Alessandro Carretta, Franco Fiordelisi and Gianluca Mattarocci *(editors)*
NEW DRIVERS OF PERFORMANCE IN A CHANGING FINANCIAL WORLD

Dimitris N. Chorafas
CAPITALISM WITHOUT CAPITAL

Dimitris N. Chorafas
FINANCIAL BOOM AND GLOOM
The Credit and Banking Crisis of 2007–2009 and Beyond

Violaine Cousin
BANKING IN CHINA

Peter Falush and Robert L. Carter OBE
THE BRITISH INSURANCE INDUSTRY SINCE 1900
The Era of Transformation

Franco Fiordelisi
MERGERS AND ACQUISITIONS IN EUROPEAN BANKING

Franco Fiordelisi and Philip Molyneux
SHAREHOLDER VALUE IN BANKING

Hans Genberg and Cho-Hoi Hui
THE BANKING CENTRE IN HONG KONG
Competition, Efficiency, Performance and Risk

Carlo Gola and Alessandro Roselli
THE UK BANKING SYSTEM AND ITS REGULATORY AND SUPERVISORY FRAMEWORK

Elisabetta Gualandri and Valeria Venturelli (*editors*)
BRIDGING THE EQUITY GAP FOR INNOVATIVE SMEs

Kim Hawtrey
AFFORDABLE HOUSING FINANCE

Otto Hieronymi
GLOBALIZATION AND THE REFORM OF THE INTERNATIONAL BANKING AND
MONETARY SYSTEM

Munawar Iqbal and Philip Molyneux
THIRTY YEARS OF ISLAMIC BANKING
History, Performance and Prospects

Sven Janssen
BRITISH AND GERMAN BANKING STRATEGIES

Kimio Kase and Tanguy Jacopin
CEOs AS LEADERS AND STRATEGY DESIGNERS
Explaining the Success of Spanish Banks

M. Mansoor Khan and M. Ishaq Bhatti
DEVELOPMENTS IN ISLAMIC BANKING
The Case of Pakistan

Mario La Torre and Gianfranco A. Vento
MICROFINANCE

Philip Molyneux and Eleuterio Vallelado (*editors*)
FRONTIERS OF BANKS IN A GLOBAL WORLD

Anastasia Nesvetailova
FRAGILE FINANCE
Debt, Speculation and Crisis in the Age of Global Credit

Anders Ögren (*editor*)
THE SWEDISH FINANCIAL REVOLUTION

Dominique Rambure and Alec Nacamuli
PAYMENT SYSTEMS
From the Salt Mines to the Board Room

Catherine Schenk (*editor*)
HONG KONG SAR's MONETARY AND EXCHANGE RATE CHALLENGES
Historical Perspectives

Noël K. Tshiani
BUILDING CREDIBLE CENTRAL BANKS
Policy Lessons for Emerging Economies

**The full list of titles available is on the website:**
**www.palgrave.com/finance/sbfi.asp**

**Palgrave Macmillan Studies in Banking and Financial Institutions**
**Series Standing Order ISBN 978–1–4039–4872–4**

You can receive future titles in this series as they are published by placing a standing order. Please contact your bookseller or, in case of difficulty, write to us at the address below with your name and address, the title of the series and the ISBN quoted above.

Customer Services Department, Macmillan Distribution Ltd, Houndmills, Basingstoke, Hampshire RG21 6XS, England

# Consolidation in the European Financial Industry

Edited by

Roberto Bottiglia
Elisabetta Gualandri
Gian Nereo Mazzocco

# Contents

# List of Tables

# List of Figures

# List of Boxes

# Preface and Acknowledgements

*Roberto Bottiglia, Elisabetta Gualandri and Gian Nereo Mazzocco*

This book is the outcome of research undertaken by three groups of academics, from the universities of Modena and Reggio Emilia, Udine and Verona, as part of a National Research Project (PRIN) financed by the universities themselves and the Italian Ministry of Education, entitled 'Financial intermediaries cross-border and cross-sector concentration processes in Europe: regulatory, strategic and management issues and value creation'.

The central theme is the general process of consolidation, and the M&A operations in particular, widespread in the financial sector since the early 1990s of the last century, and responsible for a radical transformation of the structural characteristics of the banking and financial systems in both Europe and the United States. The main drivers of this process have been the liberalisation and integration of the European market and, in more general terms, the IT revolution and the globalisation of financial markets worldwide.

The subject of consolidation in the financial sector, the focus of attention for large numbers of academics and operators in many countries over a considerable period of time, has recently acquired even greater significance in the aftermath of the financial crisis. For a long time, favourable macroeconomic conditions meant that the positive aspects of these processes were most in evidence, in particular the new availability of financial services to the mass market, the expansion of the range of services benefiting more or less all categories of clientele and, probably, a tendency to an increase in the efficiency of both markets and systems. However, the resulting formation of very large banking and financial groups, operating at the cross-border level and subject only to constraints and controls which all proved to be more or less ineffectual and inefficient, generated huge concentrations of risks and levels of correlation responsible for the spread of the recent financial crisis across almost the entire globe.

On the one hand, the crisis revealed the obstacles to the success of banks' M&A-based growth strategies, while on the other it highlighted the pitfalls of the creation of very large, complex groups, certainly capable of achieving synergies and competitive advantages, but also generating negative effects with regard to operating efficiency, groups' governance and control, and the rationality of the structures themselves. Banking consolidation processes, and the body of M&A operations through which they have taken place, are thus being reviewed today in the light of utterly new facts and processes, which at the operational level have led to the largest mobilisation of public resources ever seen, and on the intellectual scene are catalysing the attention of vast numbers of analysts and academics all over the world.

This book focuses on the consolidation process that has taken place within the financial system of the European Union. One distinctive feature of this process in the case of Europe is the growing number of cross-border and cross-sector M&As, a key factor in the integration of the credit and financial markets. Unfortunately, this process has not been accompanied by the introduction of effective regulation and supervision for the groups formed, an asymmetry made all too clear at the peak of the financial crisis, by the implosion of two of Europe's largest cross-border, cross-sector groups, Fortis and Dexia, and the subsequent rescue operations.

The book consists of 12 chapters, which together cover the subject of consolidation in the banking, insurance and stock exchange sectors, with some specific discussions of topics relating to regulation and supervision. The strong focus on the banking sector reflects its central role in all of Europe's financial systems.

The first two chapters provide a general description of the phenomenon. Chapter 1 sets out to provide a general definition of the consolidation process in the banking-financial industry by outlining the course of events in both the European Union and the USA. It defines the types of operations carried out (cross-border and cross-sector) and then discusses their aims, motivations and drivers. This is followed by a survey of the main negative consequences of the banking consolidation process, and the body of M&A operations through which it has taken place, overlooked in the literature but made starkly obvious by the crisis. It is thus clear that the subject of consolidation is destined to remain at the centre of the debate on banking and finance for a considerable period to come. Chapter 2 offers a broad survey of the vast literature of theoretical and empirical studies on financial sector consolidation that has appeared since the mid-1990s, discussing findings for the US, European and international markets.

The two chapters which follow analyse the implications and consequences of financial sector M&As. Chapter 3 considers the measurement of a number of effects of consolidation operations in the financial industry, concentrating in particular on the degrees of internationalisation of systems and strategic diversification, and the measurement of value creation. Chapter 4 is an empirical analysis of the effects of banking consolidation operations in terms of shareholder value and risk, with an in-depth discussion of the role of the phenomenon's cross-border and cross-sector dimensions. The survey is conducted on a large, comprehensive and original list of M&A operations concluded between 1997 and 2007 by banks and insurance companies from EMU countries, with a focus on a sample of listed firms from this group.

The three chapters which follow basically cover consolidation amongst the large groups which form the top tier of banking systems. Chapter 5 reports on the dynamics of the consolidation of major European banking groups during the period 2000–8, and provides an overview of the expansion policies pursued by these groups in recent years. It also considers the impact of the subprime mortgage crisis. The study includes the top 15 European banking groups by stock market capitalisation and total assets, with two Spanish, three French, three British, two Swiss, one Dutch, two Italian and two German banks.

Chapter 6 studies a fairly recent aspect which is, however, of major of importance for the future evolution of the largest banking and financial groups in both Europe and North America, partly in the light of the crisis: the changes in their ownership structure, concentrating in particular in the role of the Sovereign Wealth Funds (SWFs), most of them from non-European states. This is done by analyzing the 44 most important global banking groups in terms of their capitalisation and total assets. Twenty-three groups are based in Europe, 18 in the United States and Canada, and three in Japan. One smaller bank, Standard Chartered, is also included following the massive recapitalisation of the group by SWFs.

Chapter 7 focuses on an equally specific topic which is also extremely important, especially for large banking groups: the possible links between growth, bank size and operational risk. The aim is to examine the dynamics of operational risk during consolidation by seeking to identify changes in the quality and quantity of operational risk in the newly merged group compared to the pre-merger situation. A case study is presented, dealing with the two largest Italian banking groups: UniCredit Group and Intesa SanPaolo.

The next two chapters are concerned with the subject of regulation and supervision, an urgent priority given the events of the financial crisis. Chapter 8 considers the insurance sector, and especially the outcomes of the geographical diversification of insurance companies and the implications of the capital regime to be introduced by the Solvency 2 framework, now being asked to bridge the gap between regulation and business operations. Europe's legislators are currently hard at work on this framework, which, although scheduled for implementation in 2012, is still struggling to achieve a standard approach for the financial requirements, supervisory review process and market conduct of European insurers and reinsurers. Chapter 9 discusses the regulation and supervision of cross-border groups operating in the EU in the light of the crisis. It outlines the existing regulatory and supervisory framework and highlights the imbalance between it and the development of cross-border groups and the inadequacies that have come to light, before discussing the cases of Dexia and Fortis, the two most dramatic European banking group collapses. It then moves on to a critical examination of the main reforms on the drawing board, especially those put forward by the de Larosière Report, with its proposals for the establishment of two pillars: micro-prudential supervision and macro-prudential supervision.

The two chapters which follow cover consolidation in the stock exchange sector. Chapter 10 studies the ongoing moves to merge the main markets, investigating their drivers and implications. The focus is on the European stock exchange consolidation process fostered by the new regulatory framework introduced by the Markets in Financial Instruments Directive (MiFID). The evidence is twofold: even though there is a continuous process of consolidation in the stock exchange industry, barriers to entry continue to fall and new competitors obtain authorisation to operate as Multilateral Trading Facilities (MTFs). However, the crisis has had a substantial effect on banks, the main shareholders of MTFs, thus slowing down the rate of start-ups. Chapter 11 concentrates on the effects on the market consolidation process in terms of the governance and value both of the markets themselves and of the companies which operate them. An empirical analysis is carried out on the valuation criteria adopted in the most recent stock exchange mergers (mainly NYSE Group and Euronext; London Stock Exchange and Borsa Italiana). Value drivers are examined, in particular the relationship between operational exchange volumes and economic-financial dynamics. Moreover, stock exchange pricing is related to the specific governance structure resulting from exchange mergers. Chapter 12 discusses the integration of systems and markets, with particular attention being given to the problems arising from the widespread obstacles to the regulation of international operations, and the possible solutions. The analysis reveals that the existing regulatory framework on matters affecting the regulation of cross-border transactions appears to be not only incomplete, but also incapable of providing a satisfactory level of certainty. At the European level, the problems posed by the crises hitting intermediaries working in a multiplicity of legal contexts require the adoption of the necessary reforms by member states, thus opening the way to truly international standards, complete solutions for the regulation of cross-border settlements.

The research findings were presented at a workshop at the University of Verona. The comments received and the subsequent discussions provided useful input for the final drafting of the various articles. Thanks in particular to Roberto Tedeschi and Prof. Francesco Vella.

# Notes on the Contributors

**Roberto Bottiglia** is a Full Professor in Banking and Finance and Director of the Business Administration Department at the University of Verona, where he teaches Bank Management. He graduated in Business Administration from the Bocconi University of Milan. Research topics include agricultural credit, financial marketing, IT in banking, the structure of financial systems and banks' strategies. He recently edited a book on the consolidation of financial systems and the crisis of major banking groups in Europe and the USA.

**Giusy Chesini** is an Associate professor in Banking and Finance at the Faculty of Economics of the University of Verona, where she teaches Financial Markets and Institutions and is Director and member of the Scientific Committee for postgraduate courses. She graduated in Business Economics from the University of Verona. Her research topics include the stock exchange industry, evolution of financial systems, banking and risk management.

**Laura Chiaramonte** is a PhD in Business Administration from the University of Verona, where she graduated in Business Economics. Research topics include hedge funds' strategies, the evolution of financial systems, the drivers and effects of bank acquisitions, and domestic and cross-border banking consolidation in Europe. She recently edited a book on banking mergers and acquisitions in the European Union.

**Simonetta Cotterli** is a Lecturer in Business Law at the University of Modena and Reggio Emilia. She graduated in Law at the University of Bologna and received a PhD in Banking Law from the European University Institute of Fiesole, EUI. Her main research interests are related to the regulation of banking activity and other financial institutions. She is a member of CEFIN, Center for Studies in Banking and Finance.

**Veronica De Crescenzo** is a Lecturer in Banking and Finance at the Faculty of Economics of the University of Verona, where she teaches Financial Markets and Institutions. She graduated in Economics from the University of Verona and received a PhD in Financial Markets and Institutions from the University of Udine. Her main research interests are related to firms' capital structures, the evolution of financial markets and operational risk.

**Alberto Dreassi** is a Research Fellow at the Faculty of Economics of the University of Udine, where he teaches Insurance Economics. He graduated in Banking Economics from the University of Udine, where he also obtained a PhD in Business Sciences. His research topics include the supervision and regulation of insurance companies and pension funds and cross-border supervision, solvency and market conduct in the insurance sector. He also peer reviews material for the journal *Transition Studies Review* (published by Springer).

**Riccardo Ferretti**, PhD in Capital Markets and Financial Management from the University of Bergamo, is a Full Professor of Banking and Finance at the University of Modena and Reggio Emilia and Director of CEFIN, Center for Studies in Banking and Finance. His research interests include the growth of banking firms, bank capital, the efficiency of financial markets, bank evaluation, the cost of capital, loan pricing, behavioural finance and financial communication.

**Josanco Floreani** is a Lecturer in Banking and Finance at the Faculty of Economics of the University of Udine, where he teaches Banking Operations. He graduated in Economics from the University of Udine and received a PhD in Business Sciences from the same university. His main research interests are related to the economics and governance of the securities industry, and the regulation of financial markets.

**Enrico Geretto** is a Lecturer in Banking and Finance at the Faculty of Economics of the University of Udine, where he teaches Asset Management and Financial Instruments. His main research interests are related to the economics of banking and other financial intermediaries, derivatives and asset management. He is the author of a number of articles in leading banking and academic journals.

**Elisabetta Gualandri**, MA in Financial Economics at the University College of North Wales, is a Full Professor of Banking at the University of Modena and Reggio Emilia, where she is a member of the governing council of CEFIN, Center for Studies in Banking and Finance. Recent research topics include regulatory guidelines and supervisory architecture in the European Union, the financing of innovative (small and medium-sized enterprises (SMEs) and public intervention programmes. She recently edited a book for Palgrave Macmillan on *Bridging the Equity Gap for Innovative SMEs*. She was appointed auditor of Banca d'Italia in 2007.

**Alessandro V. Guccione** is a Lecturer in Business Law at the Faculty of Law of the University of Modena and Reggio Emilia. He graduated in Law from the University of Bologna and received a PhD in Business Law from the Bocconi University of Milan. His main research interests relate to the regulation of financial markets, business law and corporate governance. He is author of a book on financial collateral arrangements regulation in Italian and EU law and is an editor of the Italian business law journal *Giurisprudenza Commerciale*.

**Gian Nereo Mazzocco** is a Full Professor in Banking and Finance and Dean at the Faculty of Economics of the University of Udine, where he teaches

Bank Management and Financial Instruments. He has been coordinator of the PhD in Business Studies at the University of Udine for many years. His recent research topics concern bank and corporate finance. He is council member of the local branch of Banca d'Italia.

**Stefano Miani** is a Full Professor in Banking and Insurance and director of the MA Course in Banking and Finance at the Faculty of Economics of the University of Udine, where he is the director of the governing council of CIWE, Interdepartmental Center for Studies in Welfare. Recent research topics include pension funds and pension systems, the regulation and supervision of financial markets and intermediaries, the regulation and monitoring of insurance companies, the New Basle Accord, and the financing of SMEs and the role of *'confidi'* (Italian mutual guarantee societies).

**Andrea Paltrinieri** is a PhD student in Business Administration at the University of Verona, where he graduated in Bank and Insurance Economics. Research topics include the evolution of financial systems, market efficiency, asset management and institutional investors, with a particular focus on sovereign wealth funds and hedge funds.

**Francesco Pattarin** is a Lecturer in Banking and Finance at the University of Modena and Reggio Emilia. He holds an MSc in Finance from Birkbeck College, University of London, and a Doctoral degree in Economics from the University of Rome 'La Sapienza'. He is a member of CEFIN, Center for Studies in Banking and Finance. His main research interests are in applied financial economics and econometrics, with a focus on portfolio selection and investment topics.

**Flavio Pichler** is an Associate Professor in Banking and Finance at the Faculty of Economics of the University of Verona, where he teaches Financial Markets and Institutions and the Economics of Insurance. He graduated in Economics from the University of Verona and received a PhD in Business Administration from the University of Venice 'Ca' Foscari'. Research topics include the theory, regulation and supervision of financial systems, the economics of insurance, banking and risk management.

**Maurizio Polato** is an Associate Professor in Banking and Finance at the Faculty of Economics of the University of Udine, where he teaches Securities Exchange Economics. He graduated in Economics from University of Venice 'Ca' Foscari' and received a PhD in Business Economics from the same university. His main research interests are related to the economics and governance of the securities industry, banking economics, and risk management.

**Valeria Venturelli** is a Lecturer in Banking and Finance at the University of Modena, where she teaches Financial Markets and Capital Budgeting. She graduated in Economics from the University of Modena and Reggio Emilia and received a PhD in Financial Markets and Institutions from the Catholic

University of Milan. Her main research interests are the economics of banking and other financial institutions, valuation methods and the cost of capital. She recently edited a book for Palgrave Macmillan on *Bridging the Equity Gap for Innovative SMEs*. She is a member of CEFIN, Center for Studies in Banking and Finance.

# List of Acronyms and Abbreviations

| | |
|---|---|
| ABN Amro | Algemene Bank Nederland Amsterdamsche-Rotterdamsche Bank |
| AEX 25 | Amsterdam Exchange Index 25 |
| AG | Assurances Générales |
| AIAF | Associazione Italiana degli Analisti Finanziari |
| AIG | American International Group |
| AMC | Asset Management Company |
| AMEV | Algemeene Maatschappij tot Exploitatie van Verzekeringsmaatschappijen |
| Amex | American Stock Exchange |
| AT | Austria |
| ATSs | Alternative trading systems |
| B | Belgium |
| Bar | Barclays |
| BATS | Better Alternative Trading System |
| BB&T | Branch Banking & Trust |
| BBVA | Banco Bilbao Vizcaya Argentaria |
| BCBS | Basel Committee on Banking Supervision |
| Benelux | Belgium, the Netherlands and Luxembourg |
| BIA | Basic Indicator Approach |
| BME | Bolsas y Mercados Espanoles |
| BNP | Banque Nationale de Paris |
| BOJ | Bank of Japan |
| CAC 40 | Cotation Assistée en Continu 40 |
| CAPM | Capital Asset Pricing Model |
| CaR | Capital at Risk |
| CARs | Cumulative Abnormal Returns |
| CBOE | Chicago Board Options Exchange |
| CBOT | Chicago Board of Trade |
| CDC | Caisse des Dépots et Consignations |

| | |
|---|---|
| CEA | Comité Européen des Assurances |
| CEBS | Committee of European Banking Supervisors |
| CEE | Central and Eastern Europe |
| CEIOPS | Committee of European Insurance and Occupational Pensions Supervisors |
| CEO | Chief Executive Officer |
| CESR | Committee of European Securities |
| CH | Switzerland |
| Citi | Citigroup |
| CLOB | Central Limited Order Book |
| CME | Chicago Mercantile Exchange |
| CN | China |
| CONSOB | Commissione Nazionale per le Società e la Borsa |
| CoS | Colleges of Supervisors |
| CPSS | Committee on Payment and Settlement Systems |
| CR5 | Concentration Ratio Five |
| CS | Crédit Suisse |
| CSD | Central Securities Depository |
| DAX 30 | Deutsche Aktienindex 30 |
| DB | Deutsche Bank |
| DE | Germany |
| DPS | Dividend per Share |
| DTCC | Depository Trust and Clearing Corporation |
| EBITDA | Earning Before Interest Taxes Depreciation and Amortization |
| EBS | Electronic Broking Services |
| Ec | Economic capital |
| EC | European Commission |
| ECB | European Central Bank |
| ECN | Electronic Communications Network |
| ECOFIN | Economic and Financial Affairs Council |
| EE | Eastern Europe |
| EEA | European Economic Area |
| EI | Ireland |
| EMCF | European Multilateral Clearing Facility |

| | |
|---|---|
| EMU | European Monetary Union |
| EP | Expected Profits |
| EPS | Earnings Per Share |
| ES | Spain |
| ESCB | European System of Central Banks |
| ESFS | European System of Financial Supervision |
| ESRC | European Systemic Risk Council |
| ETFs | Exchange Traded Funds |
| EU | European Union |
| EuroCCP | European Central Counterparty Limited |
| EV | Enterprise Value |
| EVA | Economic Value Added |
| FCD | Financial Conglomerates Directive |
| FDIs | Foreign Direct Investments |
| FE | Far East |
| FI | Finland |
| FOCF | Free Operating Cash Flow |
| For | Fortis |
| FR | France |
| FRS | Federal Reserve System |
| Fsa | Financial security assurance |
| FSA | Financial Services Authority |
| FSAP | Financial Services Action Plan |
| FSeA | Financial Services Agency |
| FTSE 100 | Financial Times Stock Exchange 100 |
| G10 | Group of Ten |
| GDP | Gross Domestic Product |
| GIC | Government of Singapore Investment Corporation |
| GR | Greece |
| Gvt | Government |
| HBOS | Halifax Bank of Scotland |
| HHI | Herfindahl–Hirschman Index |
| HSBC | Hong Kong and Shanghai Banking Corporation |
| HVB | HypoVereinsbank |

| | |
|---|---|
| IAIS | International Association of Insurance Supervisors |
| IC | Invested Capital |
| ICAP | Intercapital |
| ICT | Information and Communication Tecnology |
| ID | Internationalization Degree |
| IGD | Insurance Groups Directive |
| IMF | International Monetary Fund |
| ING | Internationale Nederlanden Groep |
| IOSCO | International Organization of Securities Commissions |
| IRB | Internal Rating Based |
| ISE | International Stock Exchange |
| ISVAP | Istituto per la Vigilanza sulle Assicurazioni Private e di Interesse Collettivo |
| IT | Information Technology |
| It | Italy |
| ITG | Investment Technology Group |
| IWG | International Working Group of Sovereign Wealth Funds |
| JP Morgan | John Pierpont Morgan |
| KBC | Koepelwebsite van de van oorsprong Belgische |
| KPMG | Klynveld Peat Marwick Goerdeler |
| KR | Korea |
| KW | Kuwait |
| L | Luxembourg |
| LCH. | London Clearing House |
| LIBOR | London Interbank Offered Rate |
| LSE | London Stock Exchange |
| LY | Libya |
| M&A(s) | Merger(s) and Acquisition(s) |
| ME | Middle East |
| Merr | Merrill Lynch |
| MiFID | Markets in Financial Instruments Directive |
| Morg | Morgan Stanley |
| MoU | Memorandum of Understanding |
| MPS | Monte dei Paschi di Siena |

| | |
|---|---|
| MTFs | Multilateral Trading Facilities |
| MTS | Mercato telematico dei titoli di stato |
| NASDAQ | National Association of Securities Dealers Automated Quotation |
| NCB | National Central Bank |
| NL | Netherlands |
| NO | Norway |
| NOPAT | Net Operating Profit After Taxes |
| NYBOT | New York Board of Trade |
| NYMEX | New York Mercantile Exchange |
| NYSE | New York Stock Exchange |
| OECD | Organisation for Economic Co-operation and Development |
| OLS | Ordinary Least Squares |
| OMX | Optionsmäklarna/Helsinki Stock Exchange |
| OTC | Over the Counter |
| OTD | Originate to Distribute |
| PSE | Pacific Securities Exchange |
| PT | Portugal |
| QA | Qatar |
| RBS | Royal Bank of Scotland |
| RMs | Regulated Markets |
| ROA | Return On Asset |
| ROE | Return On Equity |
| ROIC | Return On Investment Capital |
| RORAC | Return On Risk Adjusted Capital |
| RWA | Risk Weighting Asset |
| SA | Standardised Approach |
| SaA | Saudi Arabia |
| SBU | Strategic Business Unit |
| SE | Shannon Entropy |
| SEC | Securities and Exchange Commission |
| SG | Singapore |
| SIs | Systematic Internalisers |
| SMEs | Small and Medium-sized Enterprises |

| | |
|---|---|
| SoFFin | Financial Markets Stabilisation Fund |
| SPS | Senior Preference Shares |
| St.Ch. | Standard Chartered |
| SWF | Sovereign Wealth Fund |
| TD Bank | Toronto Dominion Bank |
| TE | Tracking Error |
| TNI | TransNational Index |
| TSB | Trustee Savings Bank |
| UAE | United Arab Emirates |
| UBS | Union Bank of Switzerland |
| UFJ | United Financial of Japan |
| UK | United Kingdom |
| Unic | UniCredit |
| US Bancorp | United States Bancorp |
| USA | United States of America |
| USD | United States Dollar |
| VaR | Value at Risk |
| VSB | Verenigde Spaarbank |
| WACC | Weighted Average Cost of Capital |
| Wach | Wachovia |
| WE | Western Europe |
| WFE | World Federation of Exchanges |

# 1
# Consolidation in the Financial Industry

*Roberto Bottiglia, Elisabetta Gualandri and Gian Nereo Mazzocco*

## 1.1   Introduction

Especially in the highest band of production systems, merger and acquisition (M&A) operations are the main means of growth, and are usually intended to expand the corporate structure through policies of both production integration and strategic diversification.

M&A operations have been widespread in the financial sector since the early 1990s, and have led to a radical transformation of the structural characteristics of the banking and financial systems, in both Europe and the United States. In particular, this mass of mergers and acquisitions has led to an increase, across the board, in the degree of concentration of the credit supply, and in the availability of financial services on a vast scale, targeting different types of clientele and markets.

The formation of extremely large groupings of intermediaries and the demolition of the barriers to the mobility of the supply and demand for financial services are further effects of the rush by banks, insurance firms and other categories of financial players to engage in mergers and takeovers amongst themselves, both on a national scale, and, subsequently, at the cross-border level.

Recently, the grave financial crisis which originated on the American market and spread rapidly across the world has highlighted a number of critical aspects of financial consolidation and globalisation processes, leading observers to consider the possible limits to this process and the role public authorities may play in guiding systems' structures towards a balanced mix of efficiency and stability.

In view of its significance, the phenomenon of M&A operations in the banking and financial industries has been studied extensively and has been the subject of a large number of empirical investigations, intended to measure its impacts from two main points of view: the first is macroeconomic and deals mainly with the effect of these operations on the structure of the financial system and the relative implications (competition mechanisms, access to credit for various types of clientele and relative costs), while the second is more strictly corporate in nature and focuses on strategic factors and an analysis of the potential benefits, especially in terms of value creation. Within these two types of approach, a very large number of studies have set out to examine specific or partial aspects of the phenomenon, such as the extent to which it has affected the various countries or different types of intermediaries (in terms of size or area of business), the reasons, causes and implications of financial consolidation operations, their impact on external supervision and/or internal governance and control systems, and so on.

In the following pages we will attempt to provide a general definition of the phenomenon, many specific aspects of which will then be analysed in the contributions of the various chapter authors.

## 1.2    M&A operations in the banking sector

In view of banks' centrality to the structure of financial systems everywhere, it is useful to begin by providing a few brief data on the concentration process that has taken place in the banking sector, mainly by means of M&A operations. As can be seen in Tables 1.1, 1.2, 1.3 and 1.4, which summarise the main aspects of the phenomenon, the rate of M&A operations has been very high, in both Europe and the USA. Therefore, as well as a continuous reduction in the number of banks, which has been ongoing for at least two decades in both areas, there has also been an across-the-board increase in the industry's levels of concentration. When it comes to the number of consolidation operations, on the other hand, although the figure is constantly high, the trend is uneven, with phases of particularly intense growth alternating with periods of relative decline. This is substantially in line with the cyclical nature of M&A processes and the key importance of the unit size of

*Table 1.1*    Rates of concentration of the credit market in the USA and Europe – market share of five largest banks as % of total assets (CR5), 2003–8

| Year | CR5 USA[1] | CR5 Europe[2] |
| --- | --- | --- |
| 2003 | 36.0 | 39.7 |
| 2004 | 42.2 | 40.9 |
| 2005 | 45.0 | 42.1 |
| 2006 | 46.9 | 42.1 |
| 2007 | 49.0 | 44.4 |
| 2008 | 49.2 | – |

*Notes:* 1 USA: Large commercial banks with total assets of more than $300 million.
2 Europe: 27-member EU 27.
*Sources*: Own processing of Federal Reserve Board (2008) and European Central Bank (2008b), p. 38.

*Table 1.2*  Rates of concentration of the credit market in the main European states – market share of five largest banks as % of total assets (CR5), 2003–7

| Country | 2003 | 2004 | 2005 | 2006 | 2007 |
|---|---|---|---|---|---|
| Germany | 21.6 | 22.1 | 21.6 | 22.0 | 22.0 |
| Spain | 43.1 | 41.9 | 42.0 | 40.4 | 41.0 |
| Belgium | 83.5 | 84.3 | 85.3 | 84.4 | 83.4 |
| France | 46.7 | 49.2 | 51.9 | 52.3 | 51.8 |
| Italy | 27.5 | 26.4 | 26.8 | 26.2 | 33.1 |
| Netherlands | 84.2 | 84.0 | 84.5 | 85.1 | 86.3 |
| United Kingdom | 32.8 | 34.5 | 36.3 | 35.9 | 40.7 |

*Source*: Own processing of European Central Bank (2008b), p. 38.

*Table 1.3*  Number of M&A operations in the US banking sector, 1998–2003

| Year | Number of operations | % of assets | % of deposits | % of branches |
|---|---|---|---|---|
| 1994 | 475 | 3.8 | 4.4 | 5.1 |
| 1995 | 475 | 4.9 | 5.5 | 6.5 |
| 1996 | 446 | 7.5 | 8.4 | 8.5 |
| 1997 | 422 | 5.3 | 6.1 | 7.3 |
| 1998 | 493 | 13.3 | 14.7 | 14.3 |
| 1999 | 333 | 4.2 | 4.6 | 4.3 |
| 2000 | 255 | 2.8 | 2.2 | 3.3 |
| 2001 | 231 | 4.6 | 5.0 | 6.0 |
| 2002 | 203 | 1.8 | 1.8 | 2.3 |
| 2003 | 184 | 1.0 | 1.2 | 2.1 |
| TOTAL | 3,517 | | | |

*Source*: Own processing of Pilloff (2004), p. 2 and following pages.

*Table 1.4*  Number of M&A operations in the European banking sector, 2000–6

| | 2000 | 2001 | 2002 | 2003 | 2004 | 2005 | 2006* |
|---|---|---|---|---|---|---|---|
| **M&A operations** | | | | | | | |
| 12-State Euro Area | 58 | 45 | 69 | 68 | 45 | 58 | 16 |
| 25-State EU | 70 | 65 | 74 | 73 | 61 | 65 | 21 |
| 12-State Euro Area | 27 | 17 | 19 | 18 | 18 | 21 | 9 |
| 25-State EU | 54 | 32 | 36 | 27 | 28 | 31 | 13 |

(*Continued*)

*Table 1.4 (Continued)*

|  | 2000 | 2001 | 2002 | 2003 | 2004 | 2005 | 2006* |
|---|---|---|---|---|---|---|---|
| **M&A operations from non-EU states** | | | | | | | |
| 12-State Euro Area | 1 | 5 | 2 | 3 | 1 | 8 | 3 |
| 25-State EU | 4 | 7 | 5 | 8 | 2 | 12 | 6 |

*Note*: *2006 data relate to the first six months.
*Source*: Own processing of European Central Bank (2006), p. 66.

the operations undertaken, which means that in some periods an apparently small number of operations actually involve very large volumes, reflecting just a few large or very large mergers.

Leaving aside their structural differences, the drivers behind M&As in the two systems were very similar: the start of a phase of far-reaching deregulation in the financial sector, a wave of intensive innovation in technology and financial instruments, the consequent growth of competitive stresses between operators, the rising financial integration of the domestic and international markets and, finally, the general trend towards globalisation. In the case of Europe, a significant role was also played by the introduction of the single currency and the gradual integration of the credit and financial markets, encouraged by the painstaking, hard-won harmonisation of the relative regulatory systems. Overall, the consolidation process took place initially at the domestic level, creating large, sometimes very large, banking groups strongly rooted in their countries of origin, appropriately known as 'national champions'. Subsequently, the role of cross-border operations increased, also involving companies operating in sectors adjoining that of banking itself: insurance, investment banking, asset management, wealth management and private banking. This generated a further dimension of the process, which can be defined as cross-sector consolidation. Specifically, banks have increasingly extended their areas of interest to include an ever-expanding range of activities (such as global custody, cash management operations and pensions) and states (especially the emerging nations of the Far East and South America). Similarly, the types of operations carried out have also increased and become more complex, through the adoption of alternative models better suited to the individual contexts and markets (development of joint-ventures, acquisition of minority holdings and retail distribution agreements).

The crisis was inevitably followed by a slowdown in the rate of M&A operations, which in some cases took the form of a drastic review of growth polices and the substantial destructuring of some large banking groups. However, the serious difficulties in which some large groups found themselves actually provided a significant spur to M&A activities, giving rise to genuine mega-mergers, in which various national governments and supervisory authorities were involved in different ways. Another factor tending to favour further market consolidation was the disappearance of a large number of small banks, probably destined to become parts of larger groups.

As things now stand, since relatively little time has passed since the start of the processes triggered by the crisis, it is difficult to assess the extent and mechanisms of its influence on M&A activity in the financial sector, and, above all, what its definitive legacy might be in terms of concentration of the systems and changes in balances of competition.

In short, considering a long enough time-scale and accepting the uncertainties deriving from the extraordinarily difficult period generated by the recent crisis, we can state that on the one hand M&A activity has been the most significant phenomenon affecting the structure of the credit and financial systems during the last two decades, while on the other, it has also been the core process in the strategic growth of financial institutions, first and foremost those largest in size. This also raises a number of questions concerning the factors underlying the development of growth strategies based on operations of this kind.

## 1.3   Cross-border and cross-sector consolidation operations: types and impediments

As we have just seen, the growth in the number of M&A operations has been a significant, ever-present feature of the international financial scene. After a lengthy initial phase, during which they were confined to the banking sector itself and the domestic stage, these operations began to expand in scale, acquiring a cross-border and cross-sector dimension. On one side, this reflects the growing importance of international and strategic diversification within the development policies of international and banking groups, while on the other it underlines the contribution of M&A operations to globalisation processes in the financial sector. In the mass of studies on this subject, the large amount of attention paid to these aspects reflects the use of these characteristics as distinguishing features, a key pointer to identifying operations' strategic aims, by which their success can then be measured. To assist in this, Table 1.5 provides an overview of the various types of M&A operations in relation to the contexts, or, if we prefer, the outcomes, in which they take place (or from which they derive). M&A operations between banks create new domestic or international groups which largely maintain the same operating characteristics, and are simply a means for expanding the size or operational range of the organisations involved. Cross-sector mergers and acquisitions, on the other hand, create a financial conglomerate. In this case, the range of activities in which the new entity deriving from the operation is able to engage is significantly different and much larger, ranging from traditional banking business to highly specialised

*Table 1.5*   Types and outcomes of M&A operations in the financial sector

|  | Domestic | Cross-border |
|---|---|---|
| **Between banks** | The merger and acquisition operation involves banks which operate within the same country. Operational outcome: **domestic bank** | The merger and acquisition operation involves banks which operate in different countries. Operational outcome: **international bank** |
| **Cross-sector** | The merger and acquisition operation involves banks and firms of other kinds (such as insurance or asset management companies) operating in the same country. Operational outcome: **domestic conglomerate** | The merger and acquisition operation involves banks and firms of other kinds (such as insurance or asset management companies) operating in different countries. Operational outcome: **international conglomerate** |

activities such as investment banking and asset and wealth management, or even areas of business outside the banking sector itself, such as insurance and pensions services.

It is easy to identify operations of this kind at the origins of most of the biggest banking groups in both Europe and the USA. In these cases, the original business model (commercial banking) was extended substantially, with a shift towards either models with a very broad offering (universal banking), or more focused/specialised business structures, which, however, still feature globalised organisations and the prioritisation of strong synergies between areas of business.

It is also important to note that the complexity intrinsic to the various strategies outlined in the chart is a common feature, to a varying extent, of the history of all the large banking and financial groups, since the four categories mentioned in the individual cells (domestic bank, cross-border bank, domestic conglomerate, cross-border conglomerate) are typical stages in the development path they have all trodden, mainly by means of M&A operations. From domestic consolidation within the traditional commercial banking sector, intended to increase geographical coverage and win leadership on the national market, the next step is to move on to a broader, more complex economic context by accessing foreign markets and countries, in a process which continues, in the most extreme cases, up to the attempt to achieve absolute leadership at the international level. More or less simultaneously, there is a transition from a clearly defined strategic approach to a huge expansion in the spread of activities, providing the basis for entry into new, promising areas of business, implying, to a greater or lesser degree, a fairly significant change in the nature of the organisation itself. The end product of this process, which naturally has not affected all the various types of banks and the different natural systems in the same way, are the large banking groups, with their high degree of diversification and internationalisation, and the major financial conglomerates operating on a global scale.

In actual fact, these paths to growth have often intersected and overlapped. While it is true that the move into cross-border operations generally follows recognition as 'domestic champion' in the traditional core business, there have also been plenty of cases in which internationalisation and diversification have taken place hand-in-hand over time. Certainly, the formation of large cross-border groups or vast global conglomerates is usually the outcome of development policies increasingly directed at expanding the organisation's areas of operation and strategic portfolio, but examples can easily be found in which M&A activity (often even just one large merger operation) has been both the driving force behind and the founding event of new, complex groupings. At the same time, in many cases there have also been radical reviews of apparently irreversible strategic decisions, with the abandonment of areas of business or geographical markets leading to a refocusing on the core business in terms of both market and type of operations.

Overall, M&A activities have played a decisive role in phases of both growth and diversification and also of rationalisation and retraction, allowing groups to modify their perimeters and strategic-structural approach in response to stimuli from the surrounding environment. At some times, consolidation operations have led to major breaks with the past, as for example in the case of mega-mergers, but at others they have allowed the gradual implementation of policies of expansion into new areas of business and geographical-territorial areas, in coordination with the more conventional, organic growth mechanisms: the opening of new branches, the direct foundation of subsidiaries, and the decentralisation of operations developed internally, all still actively present in the financial sector.

Moving on, we can see that the various types of M&A operations, as defined earlier, also encounter different types of obstacles; in view of the average size and critical importance of the banks involved, these factors may be exceptionally complex.

Table 1.6 lists the types of factors which may impede or hold up the realisation of banking groups in the financial industry, subdivided into macro and firm-specific factors (leaving aside the complex question of the values or prices at which the operations are carried out, the result of a combination of contingent factors difficult to classify in general terms).

Overall, it appears that in terms of impediments, as in other ways, the transition to cross-border and/or cross-sector M&A operations is a decisive one, since the move from domestic or intra-sectoral operations to cross-border and cross-sector ones generates a considerable increase in levels of complexity, and imposes serious limits on the number of organisations able to contemplate strategic choices of this kind.

*Table 1.6*   Main obstacles to M&A operations

| | Domestic | Cross-border |
|---|---|---|
| **Between banks** | Macro factors:<br>– Antitrust intervention<br>– Regulation<br><br>Firm-specific factors:<br>– IT systems<br>– Production-distribution organisation<br>– Human resources<br>– Disappearance of the brand<br>– Management motivations<br>– Shareholder motivations | Macro factors:<br>– Political interference<br>– Legal-regulatory systems<br>– Taxation systems<br>– Accounting systems<br>– Cultural-linguistic barriers<br>– Geographical distance<br>– Demographic-economic factors<br>– Fragmentation of domestic markets<br><br>Firm-specific factors:<br>– Lack of overlapping of fixed costs<br>– Information costs<br>– Decision-making processes<br>– IT systems |
| **Cross-sector** | Macro factors:<br>– Regulation<br><br>Firm-specific factors:<br>– Sales process<br>– IT integration<br>– Production-distribution organisation<br>– Conflicts of interest<br>– Managerial motivations and skills | Combination of cross-border and cross-sector factors. |

More specifically, the factors which may place obstacles in the way of deals between banks at the domestic level relate above all to regulatory frameworks intended to ensure free competition on the markets, which thus restrict banks' growth in the context of geographical areas of varying size. Excessively high market shares arising from mergers or acquisitions may lead to the intervention of the antitrust authorities, which are well established in all countries with modern financial sectors. And these authorities' activities are focused largely on the review of banking consolidation operations, which inevitably create groupings with large volumes of assets and big market shares. However, it should be remembered here that over the lengthy development of the M&A phenomenon, and in contrast to the experience from other periods and/or sectors, there have been only a few cases in which antitrust regulations have had really decisive effects, although they do exercise partial, indirect influence (as a restricting factor to be considered ex ante). In future, it will be interesting to see the outcomes of the current discussion on the possibility of setting regulatory limits on banks' absolute size, or their structural and organisational complexity.

Other factors which tend to limit M&A operations include operational and organisational difficulties, such as the integration of IT networks and distribution channels and the rationalisation of human resources, often cited as the reason for the disappointing outcomes of specific consolidation operations. At the higher levels, significant obstacles may also derive from the integration of management hierarchies, and the stability of the corporate ownership structure deriving from the consolidation. It is no coincidence that large banking sector M&A operations often meet with widespread resistance from specific categories of investors or shareholders, who fear that the operation will be damaging to their interests. This attitude is also reflected by the markets' generally negative response to announcements of large M&A operations in the sector, although there have been significant exceptions.

In cases where the consolidation generates considerable diversification of the bank's business (cross-sector M&As), additional obstacles tend to arise. On the one hand, there may be regulatory constraints, such as bans or restrictions on the development of activities across the various sectors of the financial industry (mainly banking and insurance), while, on the other, there may be difficulties involved in the bidder bank's entrance into a previously unexplored or at least partially unfamiliar operating segment. The lack of specific management expertise, conflicts in the sale to the clientele of old and new products with similar functions and contents, the low level of knowledge of the products for sale within the distribution network, the difficulties in IT integration, the reconfiguration of process and product lines, and so on and so forth, are all problems widely encountered during cross-sector mergers. Usually, the degree of difficulty and complexity of operations of this kind is considerably greater than for the M&As in the previous category, leading banks to proceed with caution in projects of this type, which are often highly selective and focused.

Moving on to our next category, the potential barriers to cross-border M&A operations, apart from those already discussed for domestic projects, include technical and regulatory factors (asymmetries in regulatory or supervisory systems, difference in taxation systems and legal and accounting procedures), the lack of knowledge and experience of the local markets and clientele (contrasts between the basic mentalities of the different systems), and political interference arising from the desire to protect the national character of banking institutions (especially the largest ones). This form of nationalistic interference comes in many shapes and forms, sometimes blatant and sometimes subtle and intangible, but no less incisive; it has also been strongly reinforced by the financial crisis and the large transfusions of public funds into banks' capital.

This combination of factors becomes even more decisive in the case of M&A operations with both cross-sector and cross-border connotations, which almost always involve particularly large players. The influence of these obstacles is reflected in various ways: in Europe, the general failure of the largest operations aimed at the creation of huge banking-insurance conglomerates; in the USA, the small number of M&A operations of this kind, except for the integration between commercial and investment banking (itself under observation after the crisis); in both systems, the recent trend towards the 'separation' of large business sectors from the banking model as such, as in the case of asset management operations.

## 1.4   Drivers, aims and risks of banking sector M&A operations

Given the many obstacles to M&A operations, the fact that they have become so widespread in the financial industry reflects their high level of potential benefits for the individual players, basically, the speed with which banks can increase their size and modify their strategic and structural nature to achieve their chosen aims. At this point, therefore, it is useful to take a quick look at the objectives which can be pursued by means of M&A operations. Table 1.7 lists the main reasons cited for activities of this kind, subdivided on the same principle as before (domestic or cross-border, in-sector and cross-sector operations).

In view of the number of drivers and their overlapping nature, it may also be useful to examine a few ways in which they might be grouped or classified.

*Table 1.7*   Main drivers/aims of an M&A operation

| | Domestic | Cross-border |
|---|---|---|
| **Between banks** | <u>Small and medium-sized banks:</u><br>– expansion of area of operations<br>– economies of scale<br>– rationalisation of the distribution, accounting, IT and risk management structures<br>– avoidance of hostile takeovers<br><br><u>Large banks:</u><br>– achievement of leadership in terms of size<br>– economies of scale<br>– exercise of market power<br>– creation of shareholder value | – leadership in terms of size<br>– development of new market areas<br>– international economies of scale<br>– development of operations with an international clientele |
| **Cross-sector** | – economies of scope<br>– diversification of risk-return profile<br>– complementary use of distribution networks<br>– possible rationalisation of the production structure | – leadership in terms of size<br>– overall strategic-geographical diversification |

We may start by making the distinction between value-maximising and non-value-maximising drivers. The first group includes motives such as the creation of shareholder value, the achievement of economies of scale, and the generation of market power, while the second comprises the management's personal motivations and the decisions of the industry's supervising bodies. Overall, this line of interpretation tends to distinguish between operations on the basis of the extent to which they are intended to achieve aims relating to earnings or size.

A second approach sets out to identify the specific factors underlying the decision to undertake a consolidation process, summarised in Box 1.1. In this interpretative model, which groups these factors into categories, the accent is placed mainly on the synergies an M&A operation is expected to generate as a result of higher levels of efficiency, due in turn to economies of scale or scope, on the acquisition of market power (deriving both from the size of the organisation created in relation to the structural characteristics of the market, and perhaps from the acquisition of too big to fail status), and on a combination of essential subjective factors which determine and guide the management's attitudes.

## Box 1.1 Factors that affect the decision-making process

- Economies of scale:
  - based on costs
  - based on brand recognition
  - based on earnings
  - based on the presence of safety nets
  - based on protection against hostile takeovers
- Economies of scope:
  - based on costs
  - based on earnings
  - based on financial diversification
- Market power
- Search for a quiet life or hubris behaviour

Another way of classifying the drivers of mergers and acquisitions between financial institutions distinguishes between the various factors on the basis of membership of one of the following five categories:

- secular: long-term factors, including economies of scale, technology, competition, profitability, pressure from the financial markets;

- strategic or defensive: factors relating to active or defensive strategies implemented by the bank, such as strategic diversification, the 'too big to fail' principle, the achievement of critical mass, the consolidation of market shares and managerial ambitions;
- crisis: motives relating to systemic rather than individual crises;
- catalyst: these may include factors such as regulatory changes, the creation of the single European currency, the deregulation process, etc., which speed up consolidation processes already ongoing or provide fresh stimuli for such operations;
- herd factor: banks' tendency to behave in the same way as their competitors.

In real life, however, the various drivers of a merger overlap to a large degree and form a complex blend of motivations/aims, to the extent where every single operation has its own specific nature, also considering the influence of a large number of contingent factors, both macroeconomic and geographical.

It should also be borne in mind that, although useful in giving us a general understanding of what really occurs, all analysis frameworks and classification procedures are actually simplifications of reality, even if every operation (or group of operations, of any size) may contain drivers, underlying factors, aims and effects which can be summed up with the aid of one of the categories defined.

As well as the aims or drivers of M&A operations, we must also remember the risks involved. They affect the parties to operations in different ways, and depending on the operation's strategic importance and size, they may have far-reaching effects on the subsequent life of the banks concerned and the groups to which they belong. These risks occur partly during the period immediately prior to the deal, partly while the operation is actually taking place, and partly after its conclusion, with effects which may be extended well beyond the short term.

Table 1.8 informs us that in the phase prior to the conclusion of the negotiations, the main factors to be considered are those relating to the price of the operation (including the agreement of the technical procedures by which the operation is to be carried out) and the basic soundness of the strategy pursued; the definition of the managerial and control structure of the institution created by the operation could be added to these. During this phase, and in the one immediately afterwards, the input of the advisors of the financial institutions involved is usually highly significant.

There are also major risk factors during the actual realisation of the M&A operation, when difficulties may arise from the interaction between the corporate structures involved and the system of stakeholders, who include investors and the financial markets in general, the staff of the banks involved, and even competitors, who may oppose the operation or apply pressure to the banks' clientele and shareholders.

*Table 1.8*  Potential risks of an M&A operation

|  | Domestic | Cross-border |
|---|---|---|
| **Between banks** | <u>Ex ante:</u><br>– strategic<br>– pricing<br><br><u>During:</u><br>– competitive pressure<br>– relations with clientele<br>– human resources management<br>– relations with the financial market<br><br><u>Ex post:</u><br>– operational<br>– resources allocation<br>– loss of clientele – market shares | <u>Ex ante:</u><br>– strategic<br>– pricing/exchange rate<br>– regulatory differences<br>– differences in environmental and cultural factors<br>– political interference<br><br><u>During:</u><br>– competitive pressure<br>– relations with domestic clientele<br>– human resources management<br>– relations with the financial market<br><br><u>Ex post:</u><br>– operational<br>– resources allocation<br>– loss of clientele – market shares<br>– problems of integration with regard to regulatory, fiscal, accounting and administrative aspects<br>– reputational risks |
| **Cross-sector** | <u>Ex ante:</u><br>– strategic<br>– pricing<br><br><u>During:</u><br>– competitive pressure<br>– relations with clientele<br>– human resources management<br>– relations with the financial markets<br><br><u>Ex post:</u><br>– operational<br>– resources allocation<br>– loss of clientele – market shares<br>– reputational risks | Combination of the risks listed for cross-border and cross-sector operations, for all three phases considered |

In the next phase, over a time-scale of varying length, a wide variety of risks occur, generally involving difficulties in or the impossibility of achieving the aims initially pursued. Conceptually, the risks of this phase therefore merge with those of the initial period, since it is now that any errors in the planning of the operation will be revealed.

Two further comments can be made: firstly, the type of risks is intrinsically broader and more complex in cross-border and cross-sector operations, due to the increased complexity of the risk and contextual factors. Secondly, the consequences of the recent crisis clearly reveal an obvious link between M&A-based growth strategies and crises, starting from some of the biggest European and US financial groups. Although no wide-ranging analyses are available as yet, there are evident causal relationships between the intensity of growth processes carried out by means of acquisitions, the achievement of large or very large size, expansion of geographical context and strategic diversification, on the one side, and the incidence of crises on the other.

It is no coincidence that the groups hardest hit include players which, in the period immediately before the crisis, had implemented processes of intensive growth through external lines and a massive diversification of activity, mainly in the investment banking and mortgage lending sectors, as well as rapid expansion into new geographical areas. Similarly, as we have already seen, the way out of these difficulties is to be sought, apart from the essential recapitalisation, in processes of refocusing on the more stable core business (usually retail & commercial banking) and a reduction in geographical coverage, abandoning marginal markets, including some recently acquired ones.

## 1.5   Effects and implications

We have already seen that M&A operations produce events that impact strongly on the companies involved, the human resources they employ, and the clientele they serve; we have also already examined their potential impact on the structure of financial systems and the functioning of the credit markets. In the approach followed in the vast literature on the subject, this aspect has received a particularly large amount of attention, probably due to the widespread acceptance of a model of capitalism well established over time and hinged on the centrality of the financial market and the figure of the shareholder/investor (and their expectations) – the very model that has now been thrown into doubt by the evidence of the processes of instability it tends to produce and spread on a global scale.

The studies of the interrelations between mergers and value creation fall into this category: they aim either to define the market's reactions to the announcement of M&A operations, or to examine the effects on the efficiency and profitability of the banks involved in or formed by such operations over the longer term. Leaving aside the differences between these two approaches, it must first be pointed out that neither is immune to criticism, which concentrates, on the one hand, on the group of hypotheses that underlie the evaluation models (including, above all, the presumed efficiency of the financial markets), and, on the other, on the need to make the right decisions as to the type of data and time horizons to be used.

The way in which M&A operations affect the market's structure is generally studied in relation to the change in its degree of concentration, and the consequent possible effects on competition in the sector and its efficiency and stability. One of the aspects which receives the most attention in this regard is that of the possible consequences for the competitiveness of the credit market, on which depends the access to credit itself, a resource of crucial importance for economic growth, and the cost of which has a decisive influence on the overall efficiency and competitiveness of the entire production system. Other studies, closely linked to those described above, aim to assess the implications of banking sector consolidation processes on the general efficiency of the credit and financial systems. In general terms, the two contrasting hypotheses focus on the one hand on the potential positive effects of the M&A operation in terms of cost reduction, and on the other on the possible abuse of market power deriving from the survival of a small number of competitors, potentially tempted to engage in forms of market-fixing it is not always possible to detect and punish under the relevant legislation.

Overall, the studies conducted in various geographical contexts and on various time-scales do not appear to have identified significant negative effects; in fact, they often find that the consequences of M&A operations are positive overall. However, the potential for general application of many of the results obtained is limited both by the specific nature of the context studied and by the 'historic' nature of the process of banking sector consolidation, which only began very recently, has no historic precedents as such, appears still to be ongoing (or at least incomplete in many countries), and for which it is difficult to identify a space-time framework of reference for definition and measurement of the relative differential effects.

With regard to the stability of the system, the consequences of financial sector consolidation processes are potentially very clear. While on the one hand their larger size tends to protect individual banks or intermediaries from the risk of financial difficulties, due to risk diversification and more efficient management methods, on the other, the development of large financial groups with a high degree of diversification and globalisation, created through cross-border and cross-sector M&A operations, tends to give rise to contagion and systemic risk. The truth of this second hypothesis was demonstrated, beyond all possible doubt, by the events triggered by the bankruptcy of Lehman Brothers and the consequent spread of the crisis to different countries and contexts in the international financial system, saved from general collapse only by the prompt but extremely expensive intervention of the national governments and central banks. As a result, it is certain that the entire topic under discussion is destined for an in-depth review in the light of recent events, the implications and consequences of which are still far from clear.

We are left with the impression that the stability of the interconnected, globalised international financial system has been seriously undermined by the final outcome of the consolidation process in the banking and financial sector, and especially by its most obvious consequence: the formation of a small group of huge financial players with assets and risks on a scale so large they are more than able to destabilise entire economic systems. Emblematically, this is represented by the switch in emphasis from the discredited 'too big to fail' formula, a definition that came to be axiomatically assigned to financial intermediaries not even particularly large in size, to the new 'too large to save', an expression more representative of today's status quo, that summarises the impact major bank rescues may have on the prosperity of the societies involved.

## 1.6  Conclusions

In conclusion, the concentration processes that have drastically changed the structure of the financial and credit systems over the last two decades are certainly amongst the most significant events of the period which began with the major geopolitical changes that began at the end of the 1980s, and evolved in symbiosis with the IT revolution. They have wrought lasting transformations on the financial scene, fuelling international and globalisation processes and affecting many aspects of the operation of the financial markets and credit systems. For a long time, favourable macroeconomic conditions meant that the positive aspects of these processes were most in evidence, with the new availability of financial services to the mass market, the expansion of the range of services benefiting more or less all categories of clientele and, probably, a tendency to an increase in the efficiency of market and systems. However, the resulting formation of very large banking and financial groups, operating at the cross-border level and subject only to constraints and controls which all proved to be more or less ineffectual and inefficient, generated huge concentrations of risks and levels of correlation responsible for the spread of the recent financial crisis across almost the entire globe. The negative effects of the market concentration were thus on just the same globalised scale as the benefits enjoyed previously, but unfortunately much stronger and more dramatic. Banking consolidation processes, and the body of M&A operations through which they have taken place, are thus being reviewed today in the light of utterly new facts and processes, which on the operational level have led to the largest mobilisation of public resources ever seen, and on the intellectual scene are catalysing the attention of vast numbers of analysts and academics all over the world.

In view of its complexity, the concentration of the banking sector and its outcomes (the formation and development of large groups, the globalisation of financial business, the spread of innovation, and the impact on supervision and control systems) are destined to remain in the centre of the debate on banking and finance for a long time to come.

# 2
# M&As in Banking: A Literature Review

*Enrico Geretto*

## 2.1  Introduction

Mergers and acquisitions (M&As) have been analysed extensively by a large number of studies, from both the theoretical and the empirical points of view, during the last 30 years. At the beginning, most studies were focused on the American market, because of the number and volume of operations in that area. Later on, researchers gradually extended their analyses to the European market, with a special focus on the period following the introduction of the euro. The results vary greatly, since they depend on not only the historical period and the market analysed, but also the methodological approach (event study vs operating performance), the objectives (cost efficiencies, profit efficiencies, value creation, and so on) and the specific type operation considered (domestic or cross-border, national or international cross-sector M&As). Therefore, it still seems difficult to define a clear, stable taxonomy about the results of banking consolidation operations. Nevertheless, a complete review of the literature is considered worthwhile, on the one hand to identify any common findings and, on the other, to establish a large bibliographical basis for the development of further research on the topic.

## 2.2  Literature review

M&As produce effects on several different aspects of banks' performance. The aim here is to survey these effects by reviewing the relevant literature. The analysis mainly considers papers which appeared starting from the mid-1990s, when the general conditions of the international financial system could be considered similar to those of today.[1] The study analyses findings for American, European and international operations separately. The papers referred to below can be considered the most important empirical studies about M&A operations' effects on bank performance, while some context surveys about the banking industry are included to reconstruct the evolution of the background scenario.[2]

*Table 2.1*   Results of the main US studies

| Authors | Results |
| --- | --- |
| Berger–Humphrey (1994) | The findings confirm that merger operations do not have clear a effect on the future efficiency of the new company (some mergers generate more efficiency, others reduce it). Nevertheless, potential recoveries of operating efficiency (X-Efficiency) and the feasibility of scope/scale economies, for small size banks only, are suggested. |
| Rhoades (1994) | 39 M&A operations, in the period 1980–1993, are considered. In general, results do not show a significant increase in performance levels because of merger operations: only studies conducted with the event study technique point to gains for target banks' shareholders. |
| Peristiani (1996) | The new bank's post-merger performances are analysed. The buyer bank does not improve its X-Efficiency, although both profitability and economies of scale improve. The main factor affecting these results is the ability of the management to improve the quality of the bank's assets. |
| Siems (1996) | The study analyses the results of mega-mergers. Positive CARs can be observed for target banks and negative CARs for bidder banks, which, however, can achieve better results if there is territorial overlapping. The findings suggest that the market evaluates M&As in a positive manner and expects them to generate cost reductions and improved efficiency, rather than an increase in market power. |
| Akhavein–Berger–Humphrey (1997) | Mega-mergers' effects in terms of efficiency and results on prices are studied. The results show a significant increase in the profit efficiency of target banks after M&As. This is mainly due to a shift in investment strategy (from securities portfolio investments to market loans), and the low efficiency performance observable before the merger operation. |
| Berger (1998) | The paper suggests an increase in profit efficiency, but not in cost efficiency. Benefits are mainly achieved by banks not showing significant efficiency levels pre-merger, and there are no benefits for banks that had above average efficiency levels before the M&A operation. Merger benefits arise from a remodelling of the investment portfolio towards loans to customers and greater risk diversification. |

(Continued)

*Table 2.1*   (*Continued*)

| Authors | Results |
| --- | --- |
| Berger–Saunders–Scalise–Udell (1998) | This study considers the effects of banking M&As on SMEs' access to credit. Results show a reduction in the availability of credit to firms in this class, although this effect tends to be mitigated by competitors' behaviour and the reallocation of business goals by the new bank created. |
| Boyd–Graham (1998) | The sample considered by the survey consists of mergers between small banks. In general, positive results are observed, in terms of cost reduction and improved efficiency. |
| Rhoades (1998) | Here nine different merger cases, studied by different authors, are used to verify the effect of M&A operations on efficiency. Increased efficiency can be provided by operations involving medium-sized banks with some market overlapping. Cost cutting commonly occurs, although cost efficiency is not always observed: this is assumed to be due to unexpected difficulties in IT integration and in the operational sector. |
| Scott-Frame–Lastrapes (1998) | The study reveals that the M&A operations studied led to transfer of a wealth from bidder banks' shareholders to those of target banks. Bidder banks can achieve better results in case of interstate mergers, and if the purchase method, which includes the goodwill and its amortisation in the financial statement, is used. |
| Berger–Demsetz–Strahan (1999) | The results of more than 250 different studies are presented in this survey. The main consequences of mergers between financial intermediaries are increase in market power, higher profitability, risk diversification, slight improvement in the offer of services to SMEs, improvement in payment system efficiency, and costs for the financial system due to the increase in systemic risks and the creation of safety tools by supervisors. |
| Calomiris (1999) | The paper attempts to measure the efficiency arising from merger operations taking place within a merger wave. In a market where a high and growing number of M&As are taking place, the advantages generated by operating cost reduction, diversification and broadening of the customer base can only be assessed through cross-comparison of data. |

(*Continued*)

*Table 2.1   (Continued)*

| Authors | Results |
| --- | --- |
| Hadlock–Houston–Ryngaert (1999) | The survey assesses the probability that a bank will be an acquisition target on the basis of its management incentives, corporate governance and the performance achieved. The findings reveal that the most important factor influencing a bank's likelihood of being an M&A target is the proportion of its equity held by its managers. The more shares they have, the lower the probability that the bank will become an M&A target. |
| Kwan–Laderman (1999) | The article aims to examine the effects of M&As in terms of performance and value creation. The results of the research are not completely clear: CARs and the effects of efficiency on profitability are insignificant. This applies even in the many cases where banks that originate M&A operations have high pre-merger efficiency levels. |
| Kwan–Wilcox (1999) | This study considers the possible effects of incorrect accounting of financial statement items may have on the evaluation of an M&A operation. Once the operating costs have been cleared of possible accounting distortions, it can be seen that the values concerned decline in the post-merger phase. |
| Berger–De Young (2000) | This study evaluates the effects of geographical and cross-border expansion. The data suggest that the impact of geographical expansion is limited in terms of the bank's efficiency. An efficient bank tends to maintain this efficiency level even after the expansion. |
| Brewer III–Jackson III–Jagtiani–Nguyen (2000) | This article studies the factors that influence the bid premium offered by M&As, examining abnormal returns during the operation announcement period. In general, the premium offered is positively correlated with the target bank's profitability, and is influenced by the bank's capitalisation level. CARs are found to be affected by the size of the target bank and its market share; abnormal returns are significantly lower in mergers between large banks than in those between different sizes banks. |
| Kane (2000) | The study analyses mega-mergers. It is demonstrated that in general large banks (buyers) increase their value if the target bank is large in size and/or located in the same country as the bidder bank. 'Too big to fail' status seems to be significant for the outcomes of these mergers. |

*(Continued)*

*Table 2.1   (Continued)*

| Authors | Results |
| --- | --- |
| Rhoades (2000) | The analysis considers all data referring to M&A transactions on the American market. Thorough restructuring of the market, in terms of concentration, can be traced, especially with reference to metropolitan areas. |
| Zollo–Leshchinskii (2000) | The main goal of this study is to analyse the factors that may explain the variance in the distribution of post-merger performances, and to verify whether markets are efficient in incorporating all the public information related to merger announcements into the prices of bidder banks. The findings indicate that: banks that have carried out M&A operations do not improve their performances, unless they have implemented specific procedures and tools for the proper management of integration processes; long-term performances are influenced by a significant degree of integration between the partner banks; the short-term market does not respond effectively to the information available. |
| Bliss–Rosen (2001) | The research focuses on the relationship between M&As and managers' salaries. In general, there is a direct link between salary levels and consolidation, even if the share values of the acquirer bank fall. Managers paid by means of stock options have less incentive to undertake M&A operations. |
| DeLong (2001a) | This paper shows that the market rewards mergers that provide productive and geographical concentration. Long-term efficiency increases when the merger operation involves a buyer bank that is not so efficient and payment for the operation is not made in cash only. |
| DeLong (2001b) | A series of M&A operations are divided into value-creating and value-destroying categories, and the abnormal returns at the time of the announcement are measured for these two clusters. Mergers that generate a strong productive and geographical focus create value on average, while others do not. The aggregate revenues of the banks involved in these operations are positively correlated to the ratio between the size of the bidder and target. |

(Continued)

*Table 2.1   (Continued)*

| Authors | Results |
| --- | --- |
| Hart–Apilado (2002) | This study considers banks undertaking their first interstate merger operations, with reference to the period before and after the changes in the relative legislation (Riegle-Neal Interstate Banking and Branching Efficiency Act, 1994). Results show that, in terms of abnormal returns, target banks have an advantage over bidders: however, the new entity proves capable of creating value. The comparison between the two different time periods reveals that mergers have tended to generate higher returns since the changes to the regulatory framework. |
| DeLong (2003a) | This study analyses the ability of long-term post-merger performances to meet market expectations. In general, this is not the case, because of the difficulty that operators face when making forecasts and the complexity of M&As. The main factor that seems to positively affect long-term performances is the source and amount of revenues. |
| Anderson–Becher–Campbell II (2004) | This study considers how an M&A operation affects the CEO's salary. The findings are as the literature suggested: higher post-merger salaries are linked to higher managerial productivity and not to larger company dimensions. |
| Pilloff (2004) | The analysis considers all data referring to American M&A operations. The results show that deals mainly involved small credit institutions operating close to the buyer bank. The rate of M&A activity was definitely higher in urban than rural markets. The majority of mergers were between a target operating in a single state and a bidder with at least one office in the same state. |
| Hannan–Pilloff (2005) | The study analyses the possibility that capital adequacy provisions (so called Basel II) could influence M&A activities. Although the level of statistical significance is low, the tests performed seem to support the idea that the banks most active in mergers are the ones with capital adequacy in excess of the regulatory requirements, and that their high degree of activity is due to a surplus of capital. |
| Mayer-Sommer–Sweeney–Walker (2005) | This paper studies the different effects, in terms of shareholders' returns, produced by three mergers undertaken by the same bank. Value creation is only observed in one case, and this seems to be due to the large numbers of shares in the target bank held by its managers and employees. |

*(Continued)*

*Table 2.1   (Continued)*

| Authors | Results |
| --- | --- |
| Brewer III–Jackson II–Jagtiani (2007) | This analysis attempts to discover whether the presence of independent directors in the bidder bank's management is able to protect shareholders' interests in the event of M&A operations, with regard to the potential conflict of interest with the management. The findings show that the presence of outsiders is an important governance mechanism that protects shareholders' positions. |
| Gupta–Misra (2007) | The study tests the hypothesis that the relationship between the earnings from mergers and the characteristics of the deal is affected by management motivation. Two different samples of M&As are created (creators and destroyers of shareholder value), subdivided on the basis of the supposed management motivations (value enhancing vs value reducing). In the first case (value enhancing), it can be observed that target banks earn a lot, while bidder banks do not lose; in the second case (value reducing), the target banks still benefit financially, but to a lesser extent, and bidder banks register a significant loss of value. |
| Al Sharkas–Hassan–Lawrence (2008) | The study's findings demonstrate that post-merger banks have lower operating costs than banks not involved in M&A processes, thanks to access to better technology (operating efficiency) and the minimisation of cost due to a better mix of inputs used in production (allocation efficiency). |

*Table 2.2   Results of the main European studies*

| Authors | Results |
| --- | --- |
| Vander Vennet (1996) | The study examines the effects of M&A operations on the performance of credit institutions. The findings show that domestic mergers between similar size partners can guarantee better results; an improvement in cost efficiency levels in cross-border operations is also observed. The main drivers of domestic mergers are found to be defensive strategies, personal motivations of the management and maximisation of company size. |
| Giorgino–Porzio (1997) | Efficiency indicators improve in the case of mergers through acquisition, but fall for mergers of equals. CARs are positive only for a small period of time, and continue to be very significantly negative for a long period after the merger. |

*(Continued)*

*Table 2.2*   *(Continued)*

| Authors | Results |
| --- | --- |
| Focarelli–Panetta–Salleo (1999) | The main findings of this study of the Italian market are as follows: mergers are the result of strategies aimed at increasing the revenues from services of the bidder bank, while acquisitions are driven by the desire to increase the value of the target bank by improving the quality of its loans portfolio. Banks involved in M&A operations achieve an increase in ROE, but not in ROA. |
| Punt–Van Rooij (1999) | This study sets out to find out whether there is a relationship between market share and its concentration and ROE – ROA in the European banking sector. The improvement of X-Efficiency and profitability, obtained through consolidation processes, are considered two of the most important factors for a successful M&A. It cannot be confirmed that higher market power leads to less favourable price levels for consumers. |
| Cybo-Ottone–Murgia (2000) | The findings show that domestic M&A operations between banks and acquisitions of insurance companies generate abnormal positive returns. The same results do not derive from mergers with securities firms or foreign institutions. |
| Beitel–Schiereck (2001) | This study considers domestic, international, intra-sector and cross-sector M&A operations. The impacts in term of value creation are analysed: these impacts are very considerable for the target bank and combined entity, while the returns for the bidder are lower. However, the results tend vary depending on the period considered: acquirer banks have mainly registered negative abnormal returns since 1998. Cross-border operations tend to destroy value. |
| Cavallo–Rossi (2001) | This analysis aims to discover whether consolidation processes promote economies of scale and scope for the banks involved in the merger. Results show improvements in the aspects considered, provided by the regulatory changes and technological progress. Economies of scale and scope are typically the main aim of small banks, while large banks seek economies of diversification. |
| Huizinga–Nelissen–Vander Vennet (2001) | After proving the potential for significant economies of scale and operating inefficiencies (X-Inefficiencies) in the European banking sector, |

(*Continued*)

*Table 2.2   (Continued)*

| Authors | Results |
| --- | --- |
| | this study examines the effects of M&A operations. The findings indicate a significant improvement in efficiency on the costs side, but only a small improvement in profit efficiency. This could mean that most of the benefits arising from merger operations are enjoyed by consumers and not by the merged banks. |
| Franchini (2002) | This paper analyses the M&A operations of Italian banks. Results show that bidder banks are more efficient and profitable than target banks, M&A operations lead to a small improvement in short-term cost efficiency, efficiency of scale deteriorates during the post-merger period, ROE generally increases while the effects on ROA are more ambiguous, and the new bank's capitalisation decreases considerably. |
| Malavasi (2002) | The aim of this study is to analyse the changes in the efficiency of Italian banks involved in merger operations. Average cost levels tend to deteriorate due to the merger during the year after the operation, followed by an improvement during the next two years, returning to the pre-merger level. Increases in revenues are generally compensated by the rise in operating costs. In general, there is no change in profit efficiency. |
| Vander Vennet (2002) | This study analyses the benefits that can be obtained through cross-border mergers. When a very efficient buyer is involved in an operation where the target is a low performing bank, the merger leads to the elimination of most operating inefficiencies. The majority of improvements in efficiency are related to revenues rather than costs. |
| Abraham–Van Dijcke (2003) | This study investigates the results of single-country and cross-border M&A operations. On average, the performance of domestic operations is better than that achieved by cross-border operations. |
| Berger (2003) | The study considers the effects on efficiency of the single European market in banking services, concentrating in particular on consolidation through cross-border and cross-sector mergers. On the cost side, diseconomies of scope are suggested, arising from organisational problems, while on the revenue side it is considered that increases can be achieved through source diversification, brand reputation and one-stop shopping. |

*(Continued)*

*Table 2.2   (Continued)*

| Authors | Results |
| --- | --- |
| Pesic (2003) | The survey aims to assess the effectiveness of banking mergers with reference to the six largest Italian players. The study suggests that the effectiveness of the processes can only be understood over the long term. The initial level of efficiency of those operators involved in the M&A is identified as a key factor. In the banks considered, improved performance profiles achieved through the acquisition were transformed into increased value for shareholders. |
| Altunbas–Marqués Ibàñez (2004) | In general, the M&A operations studied led to an improvement in ROE. The analysis assesses the degree of similarity between banks involved in mergers, in terms of strategic focus. Domestic deals appear to be expensive when strongly dissimilar institutions are involved, while cross-border operations generate higher financial returns if all other conditions are equal. |
| Beitel–Schiereck–Wahrenburg (2004) | With reference to 13 variables, useful in explaining the success of an M&A operation, the analysis studies stock market reactions after merger announcements. The study suggests that the stock market prefers mergers that involve banks operating in the same sector and territory. Banks which have not been involved in M&As as bidders in the past are indicated as better able to generate value than those with previous experience in the field. This is explained by the market's assessment of M&As, which seems to focus not so much on the creation of shareholder value as on specific management goals. |
| Cummins–Weiss (2004) | The study examines the value creation effects of M&A operations between insurance companies (both domestic and cross-border). On average, CARs are negative for bidders and positive for targets, thus using different event windows. Cross-border operations are value-neutral for buyers, while domestic ones destroy value. Both can generate positive returns for target companies. The findings seem to indicate that international consolidations are beneficial. |
| Diaz–Olalla–Azofra (2004) | This research analyses intra and cross-sector mergers. The results show an increase in acquirers' long-term profitability, in particular in M&As between banks. This effect is less significant with reference to cross-sector operations. |

*(Continued)*

*Table 2.2   (Continued)*

| Authors | Results |
| --- | --- |
| Goergen–Renneboog (2004) | The analysis identifies a high level of creation of abnormal returns for target banks but a value close to zero for bidders. Hostile takeover operations have similar results, but amplified in both cases. The results for M&As involving companies operating in the UK are better than for other European countries. If payments are in cash the returns are higher than those generated with other means of payment. The size ratio of the two banks or their past performances, as assessed by the market, do not seem to affect their capability for value creation. Generally, domestic operations create higher value than cross-border operations: the same applies for targets located in Austria, Germany, the United Kingdom and Switzerland, compared with banks acquired in other countries. The main drivers of European M&A operations are the creation of synergies, agency problems and management motivations. |
| Lepetit–Patry–Rous (2004) | The findings show large benefits in terms of abnormal returns for the target bank group. On average, positive performances can be obtained from domestic and cross-border merger operations. Furthermore, the market assigns a higher risk to bank-insurance combinations. |
| Ayadi–Pujals (2005) | The study makes a separate analysis of cross-border and domestic merger operations to measure their profitability and efficiency. Domestic mergers generate a significant cost cutting effect for both banks involved. In both kinds of operations, profitability arises mainly from revenue diversification. |
| Ayala (2005) | The study aims to combine several aspects linked to the success of a bank merger: synergies; potential combinations; organisational integration; employees' resistance; similarities in management style. The greater/lower impact of the factors listed seems to have a positive/negative influence on the final outcome of the M&A. |
| Caruso–Palmucci (2005) | The analysis is focused on the creation or distribution of value for listed Italian banks involved in M&A operations during 1994–2003. The results show that the market considers the creation of value through mergers possible, but prices are sometimes too high due to private benefits. The final effect suggested is |

*(Continued)*

*Table 2.2   (Continued)*

| Authors | Results |
| --- | --- |
|  | that value creation only favours the shareholders of the acquired bank and the management of the buyer bank. |
| Campa–Hernando (2006) | The study's findings reveal that a merger announcement generates an increase in value for the target bank's shareholders but no significant effects for those of the bidder institution. One year after the announcement, excess returns are not significantly different from zero. In general, M&A operations involve target institutions with an operating performance below the average for their sector. Acquired banks show a significant improvement in terms of efficiency, visible on average two years after the operation. |
| Campbell–Kraussl (2006) | The study applies a real options pricing model to a set of M&A operations to evaluate the premium prior to announcement of the acquisition price. The factors that appear to influence the option price are the bidder bank's size and the debt to equity ratio of the target bank. |
| Fricke (2007) | The study considers mergers between banks during the year 2002 to measure any changes in efficiency levels after the merger. An increase in technical efficiency and efficiency of scale is observed for all countries examined except Germany. In general, improvements in efficiency appear to depend mainly on the size of the banks involved and economic conditions in the country concerned. |
| Fritsch–Gleisner–Hozhauser (2007) | The analysis refers to M&A operations involving target banks in Central and Eastern European countries (while bidders were mainly West European institutions). The findings do not reveal any specific 'announcement effect' on the acquirers' share value. The factors on which abnormal returns for bidder banks seem to depend are the target country's level of economic freedom, regulatory level and GDP growth rate. |
| Lorenz–Schiereck (2007) | This study examines the effects of deals that fail to go through after announcement, compared to deals that are announced and concluded. If an M&A operation falls through, there are negative returns for the bidder bank, alongside a major increase in the target bank's share price. |

*(Continued)*

*Table 2.2   (Continued)*

| Authors | Results |
| --- | --- |
| Affinito–Piazza (2008) | The study aims to identify the factors that constitute barriers to integration for the retail banking sector. An econometric analysis identifies them as information asymmetries (connected to cultural and linguistic differences and the economic structure), national supervisory practices and corporate governance rules. |
| Beccalli–Pascal Frantz (2008) | The analysis considers 714 M&A operations between European bidder and target banks operating worldwide. The study analyses the impact of the acquisition on the fluctuation of several performance indicators: the results suggest that the new bank's results may be worse in terms of ROE and cash flow creation. The study indicates that improvements in cost efficiency can be achieved 5–6 years after the operation. |
| Fiordelisi (2008) | This empirical analysis studies the efficiency and value creation (estimated by an EVA model) deriving from M&A operations in France, Germany, Italy and the UK. No significant effects are observed with regard to efficiency: bidder banks marginally improve their efficiency level over a five-year horizon, while target banks reduce it. Acquisition operations have a slight value-creation effect, with more positive results in the case of merger operations. Outcomes are different for specific countries. |
| Kohler (2008) | The analysis examines the influence that controls on cross-border mergers can have on their success. The data show that a bank's probability of being the subject of an international take over is directly linked to its characteristics, economic conditions in the target country and the transparency of the M&A authorising process there. |
| Ekkayokkaya–Holmes–Paudyal (2009) | The analysis studies the effects of merger operations on shareholder value, considering the introduction of the monetary union and the reduction of barriers to cross-border operations. The findings show that after the monetary unification shareholders' returns decreased because of the higher level of competition among market operators. |

*Table 2.3*   Results of the main international studies

| Authors | Results |
| --- | --- |
| Becher (2000) | Using the event study technique, this analysis demonstrates that bank mergers created value for shareholders during 1980–1997. Target banks earn more than 20%, bidder banks break even and the combined entity generates a positive return of 3%. Bidder bank results are sensitive to the length of the event window: with shorter windows, results tend to become significantly negative. |
| Berger (2000) | The analysis compares the efficiency achieved from integration processes in the US with that in Europe. The results suggest that the potential gains in efficiency are large, but this is only achieved in a small number of cases. Most returns are in the form of revenue efficiency rather than cost efficiency. The main driver is risk diversification. |
| Berger–De Young–Genay–Udell (2000) | The study reviews the results of a large number of works analysing cross-border M&A operations. The findings suggest that domestic banks have higher profit efficiency than foreign banks. In general, US banks have higher efficiency both at the foreign level in general and at the single foreign country level. |
| Ferretti (2000) | This research measures the American, European and Italian stock exchange reactions to bank acquisitions. Initially, the market does not consider target bank evaluations excessive, but in a later period, due to the increase in the price-book value ratio, market reaction becomes negative, especially in Italy. It seems that the stock exchange prefers larger acquisitions to those where small banks are involved. |
| Focarelli–Pozzolo (2000) | The analysis examines the drivers of banks' foreign expansion decisions. These are found to be the presence of international shareholders with international experience and head office in a country with an efficient banking market. |
| Floreani–Rigamonti (2001) | The study analyses the value creation of mergers between insurance companies. The results show large returns for bidder firms' shareholders, where the higher the value of the operation, the higher the expected result. In general, value creation is higher where the operation involves one European institution and one non-European firm. |
| Focarelli–Pozzolo (2001) | The study examines the reasons why cross-border growth in the case of banks is less common than in other sectors. This could be due to information asymmetries and regulatory constraints. International |

*Table 2.3   (Continued)*

| Authors | Results |
| --- | --- |
| | expansion appears to be encouraged by the presence of foreign investors in the shareholder base, rather than the size of the banks involved. |
| Houston–James–Ryngaert (2001) | This study, which considers a large number of cases over a long time period, examines the results generated by M&A operations in relation to the expectations of the management and external analysts, and stock exchange reactions. Operations in the second half of the 1990s succeeded in generating value through cost cutting, in line with managers' expectations. |
| Amihud–DeLong–Saunders (2002) | This study examines the transfer of risk between the different countries to which bidder and target banks belong. Investors react in a positive way when the risk increases in the country of the buyer bank and negatively in case of worldwide risk increase. This seems to suggest that the market expects rescue intervention by domestic banking regulators for national banks, but not for foreign banks and investments. |
| DeLong (2003b) | The article considers market reactions to merger operation announcements in the USA and the rest of the world. In general, non-American buyers earn more, but target banks benefit less than in the US sample. The effects observed in the US and non-US samples are similar in countries with efficient stock markets. |
| Evenett (2003) | This review examines the wave of cross-border M&A operations in different economic sectors during the late 1990s. Cross-border banking sector M&As generated benefits for clients operating in non-European economies, but in many cases these were nullified by deleterious strategic alliances with institutions in the target country. |
| Amel–Barnes–Panetta–Salleo (2004) | The study examines the main findings of the principal surveys on this subject, with the distinction between banks, insurance firms and asset management companies. Consolidation seems to bring evident benefits to small companies involved in M&A operations, while results in terms of economies of scale or better managerial efficiency are low. |
| Buch–DeLong (2004) | This study analyses almost 3,000 cross-border M&A operations worldwide in the period 1985–2001. The obstacles to these deals are found to be the cost of information and the regulatory framework: while the latter factor can be dealt with over time, the former will be particularly difficult to eliminate. |

*(Continued)*

*Table 2.3*  (*Continued*)

| Authors | Results |
| --- | --- |
| Resti–Galbiati (2004) | The study compares the share price trend of banks involved in M&A operations in Italy, Europe and the United States. In general, target companies are rewarded, while bidder companies are penalised at the announcement. Data for bidders improve if the observations cover a longer period and if the acquired bank is small in size. The premium for the target bank is higher when the nationality of the bidder bank is different and its relative size is larger. The combined CARs of the two merged banks are not significantly different from zero. |
| Scholtens–De Wit (2004) | The study considers the effects of a merger announcement on the stock exchange prices of the banks involved. It considers two different samples of operations, for the USA and Europe. For the former, negative abnormal returns for bidder banks and positive returns for target banks are recorded; in the second case, lower excess returns are reported than in the USA. In general, differences between the returns for the buyer and acquired banks are small in Europe. |
| Hijzen–Gorg–Manchin (2006) | The research examines the impact of trade costs on cross-border M&A operations, making the distinction between intra-sector (horizontal integration) and cross-sector (vertical integration) deals and considering further factors such as geographical distance and other barriers. The results suggest that negotiation costs are less significant in horizontal than in vertical integration. |
| Buch–DeLong (2008) | The analysis considers three aspects related to cross-border mergers: drivers, influence on efficiency levels and risks. Drivers are often ambiguous. With reference to the influence on efficiency levels, foreign banks outperform national ones. The study suggests slight effects on systemic risk. |
| Focarelli–Pozzolo (2008) | The analysis examines the different level of internationalisation of banks and insurance companies deriving from cross-border M&A operations. 'Follow the client' strategies are common in both sectors, while the risk diversification profile is more important for the insurance companies. Barriers to international growth have major impact for banks but not for insurance companies. |

(*Continued*)

*Table 2.3   (Continued)*

| Authors | Results |
| --- | --- |
| Williams–Liao (2008) | The studies considers the effects of cross-border M&As targeting emerging countries. Overall, there is value creation for the shareholders of target institutions, with negative abnormal returns for bidder banks' shareholders. The drivers of the shareholders' returns are the institutional – economic environment of the country of the target bank, the profitability of the target bank and the method of payment for the acquisition. |

## 2.3   Main results

The provision of a comprehensive analysis and a synopsis of the literature outlined above is a daunting task, because of the variety of research aims and analysis techniques and the lack of a clear distinction between genuine mergers and acquisitions of controlling interests (Nail and Parisi, 2005, pp. 3–10).

It is equally difficult to identify the main effects of M&A operations on the banks involved. In general, a transfer of wealth from bidder bank to target bank shareholders is identified, a finding obtained through two different approaches. The first (event study) evaluates the effects produced on the share quotation of the banks involved in the merger by estimating the Cumulative Abnormal Returns (CARs), or estimating the excess returns of the individual banks over a period of time of varying length (event window) starting before and ending after the M&A operation. Abnormal returns are calculated daily, using the difference between the partners' share returns and the hypothetical returns (calculated using econometric models, such as the market model) that the same institutions would have booked if the merger had not been announced. The second approach (operating performance) considers the effects of M&A operations on profitability and efficiency, by analysing pre and post-merger value difference; in this case, the typical time horizon is medium-term.[3]

The wealth transfer between shareholders seems to confirm that the consolidation is an opportunity for improving the performance of the acquired institution, compared to expectations in the case of further stand-alone management. Both partner institutions can achieve positive results mainly where there are high overlap levels; in other words, when M&As generate an increase in the level of productive and geographical focus: this seems to suggest that the operating complexity typical of cross-sector diversification processes leads to increased costs, not sufficiently compensated by risk reduction. The effects of the relative size of the parties are unclear: sometimes, mergers between equals are rewarded, while in other cases the market prefers operations where small and medium institutions are acquired. In Italy, M&As between small cooperative banks show major post-merger benefits in terms of revenue diversification and cost cutting, similar to those of US community banks (Emmons et al., 2001).

The method of payment that seems to have a positive effect on banks' share price trends is the cash purchase, presumably because it is thought to be an indicator of a well-planned operation. The market seems to recognise when an operation is undertaken due to personal motivations on the part of the management, and gives a negative response. The post-merger level of organisational integration influences the performance of the new credit entity; abrupt replacement of the target bank's top management has negative effects. These two findings may be explained, on the one hand, by the better organisation of administration and production, and, on the other, by the loss of know-how and effective management. Economic improvements are mainly achieved in terms of revenues and only marginally in costs, because no major economies of scale or scope, or operating economies, are seen; with reference to the European situation, the studies do not appear to identify any advantages in this area.[4]

Some studies have been conducted on the effects of market concentration on banks' clients, (companies with credit lines and depositors). Small enterprises do appear to experience some curtailing of their access to credit, although shortfalls seem to be covered by the involvement of other banks. Market consolidations tend to produce a slight reduction in the cost of borrowing, perhaps due to the competitive pressure felt during the deal process. Savers experience a reduction in interest rates immediately after the M&A operation, but rates subsequently rise to a level higher than that pre-merger. Probably, the reduction of interest costs is intended to cover the higher costs deriving from the merger, after which gains in efficiency allow conditions to be brought back into line with market standards.

The drivers of domestic mergers appear to be strategies aimed at increasing the revenues from services of the bidder bank, while the main goal of acquisitions is to increase the quality of the loan portfolio through restructuring. In both cases, equity profitability (ROE) but not asset profitability (ROA) improves after the operation, probably reflecting improvements in terms of the cost income ratio but not allocation efficiency. The analyses of European cross-border operations do not provide unambiguous results, but some studies suggest higher cost reductions compared with those obtainable from local operations. Other analyses stress that shareholder value creation is higher for domestic operations than for those on an international scale, which typically have very high information costs. The same conclusions can be drawn from an examination of studies of interstate M&A operations in the United States. The non-transparent control procedures applicable to cross-border merger operations seem to significantly reduce their feasibility.

Our review provides some interesting findings both from the theoretical and the operative points of view. At the theoretical level, some of the advantages considered to arise from M&A operations must not be assumed to be permanent: the empirical results are conflicting, with no clear rules emerging (Bianchi, 2001, pp. 3–4). For operators, the conclusions point to the importance of coming up with the correct growth strategy, which must lead to the right choice of partner: the positive returns expected from the consolidation will only be achieved if there is a perfect 'match'. On the basis of this survey, further research could be addressed in two different ways. On the one hand, it is believed that the choice of period, sector, geographical area and sample size (in other words, the definition of a homogeneous cluster) is an essential prerequisite for significant analyses, that have to be conducted over lengthy time intervals. On the other hand, one interesting line of research could be an investigation of the changes in the rating assigned by international agencies to the parties to mergers, in both the pre-merger and the post-merger phases.

## 2.4  Conclusions

The literature review offered provides a specific analysis of the main research into the topic, with a particular focus on studies of American, European and international M&A operations. The studies are considered in a chronological order, to highlight any effects of the historical context of the operations examined, such as the influence of specific regulatory and market factors at the time when the deal was finalised.

The papers' findings underline the high degree of complexity of the operations studied, and observe a wide variety of effects. This is mainly due to the specific characters of the companies involved, market conditions and regulatory constraints. These factors make it extremely difficult to draw up a set, stable series of effects generated by consolidation processes between banks, at both the domestic and international levels. The factor constant and common to all findings is the absolute uncertainty regarding short-term benefits for the partner companies. Moreover, the lack of a consolidated method for measuring the outcomes of the various forms of M&A operations is noted. The ongoing recent production of a large number of research works on this topic seems to confirm how deeply the lack of surveying techniques and measuring instruments for M&A processes is felt.

# 3
# M&As in Banking: Measurement of Some Effects[1]

*Enrico Geretto and Gian Nereo Mazzocco*

## 3.1  Introduction

There are several key factors underlying bank mergers:[2] important objectives include geographical expansion, aimed at controlling new markets, the diversification of areas of business and sources of revenue, and the creation of value for shareholders. The relative importance of these determinants of banks' strategies has changed gradually: M&As have evolved from a means of achieving domestic or international external growth to an attempt to stabilise revenues through the diversification of strategic segments and, finally, to a mechanism for the creation of shareholder value.

Nevertheless, measurements of the effects of M&As on the banks involved have chosen to monitor changes in the two companies' share values (the event study approach), through estimation of the Cumulative Abnormal Returns (CARs), that is, the excess return over a wide time interval before and after the acquisition. Alternately, studies have considered the merger's effects on profitability and efficiency levels, by observing the pre- and post-merger variations identified by a number of indicators taken as proxies of the profile to be evaluated (the operating performance approach) (Rhoades, 1994; Pilloff and Santomero, 1997, pp. 8–10; Franchini, 2002, pp. 66–98).

Recognising that international growth, diversification and value creation are the typical core goals of financial sector M&As, this study proposes a set of indicators capable of measuring the cross-border and cross-sector expansion they generate, together with the economic benefits for the players involved (bidder and target banks).

## 3.2  Measurement of some effects of M&A operations

### Indicators of internationalisation

Generally, the degree of internationalisation of a banking system, or a single bank, is measured by the volume of foreign investments (Foreign Direct Investments, FDIs). At an aggregate level, they are strongly influenced by

M&As.[3] It is quite easy to see the limitations of an indicator of this kind for a specific intermediary, since it is incapable of considering all the aspects of a growing operating presence on foreign markets. To better understand this aspect, the literature proposes a sort of percentage 'meta-indicator', the Transnational Index (TNI), the simple average of three different values;[4] assets invested abroad to total assets; gross intermediation margin generated by foreign activities to total gross intermediation margin; foreign employees to total employees. It thus considers three fundamental data covering an intermediary's international development. Although this 'meta-indicator' is more effective in expressing an intermediary's internationalisation profile, it is not able to properly consider the fact that technological development seems to significantly reduce the number of employees posted abroad to assist non-resident customers. The TNI can naturally be subdivided into its constituent three ratios, and several other ratios can be calculated, with reference to loans, securities, deposits, number of clients, and so on.[5] By studying these figures, it is possible to analyse a particular aspect of a bank's geographical diversification, but not to gather information about its overall international presence.

An alternative measurement model for a bank's degree of internationalisation is the Herfindahl–Hirschman Index (HHI) (Choi et al., 2006). By using the percentages of assets invested domestically and abroad to total assets, rather than the incidence of interest and dividend revenues on this figure, it is possible to obtain a measure of the geographical diversification of business. For example, an intermediary operating in two different countries with its business split equally between them (50 per cent on the domestic market and 50 per cent abroad) would have an HHI index of 0.5; with business spread evenly over four countries, the index would be 0.25, lower than the previous case, indicating a higher level of diversification. Here again, as for the TNI index, there is the lack of a specific measure able to reveal the strength of the bank's roots in the various areas, and the degree of coverage of the markets served.

Given these limitations, the need is observed for a different kind of indicator, better able to define the variations in an intermediary's worldwide presence in the aftermath of cross-border M&A operations. Analytically, $\Omega$ represents a set consisting of all the countries in the world, and thus of a finite number of elements, and $Y_\alpha$ is a subset of $\Omega$, containing all the countries where bank $\alpha$ or financial conglomerate $\alpha$ operates. $\psi(.)$ is the counter function, defined in $\Omega$ with real values $\psi : \Omega \rightarrow \Re$, such that, given a domain to a set, it returns the number of elements as a result. In these conditions, the Internationalisation Degree (ID) is defined as the ratio between the counter function applied to the subset $Y_\alpha$ and the same function applied to $\Omega$, that is:

$$ID = \frac{\psi(Y_\alpha)}{\psi(\Omega)} \tag{3.1}$$

It can be observed that the function ID is included within the range $(0;1]$. Its value will be close to 1 if bank $\alpha$ is operating worldwide, or close to 0 if bank $\alpha$ operates in only a few countries. The information that can be inferred from the analysis of ID is not precise, since all countries are given the same importance within the set $\Omega$, so the same result will be obtained when comparing two institutions operating in countries of different financial importance.[6] To discriminate between two financial institutions operating in regions with different importance on the basis of the ID value, we introduce an importance function $\phi(.)$, defined in $\Omega$ at real values $\phi : \Omega \rightarrow \Re$, based on items such as GDP, geographical size, population, financial balances, and so on. This function links the corresponding weight to each item within $\Omega$.[7] In these conditions, the new version of the internationalisation index (second level ID) is given by the following equation:

$$ID_{II^\circ level} = \frac{\sum_{i:\omega \in Y_\alpha} \phi(\omega_i)}{\sum_{i:\omega \in \Omega} \phi(\omega_i)} \tag{3.2}$$

where the numerator represents the sum of the weight linked to all countries in subset $Y_\alpha$, while the denominator represents the sum of all the weights in set $\Omega$. The acceptability condition requires the sum of all the weights has always to be equal to 1 and, as a consequence, the indicator can be written as follows:

$$ID_{II^\circ level} = \sum_{i:\omega \in Y_\alpha} \phi(\omega_i) \tag{3.3}$$

The proposed refinement does not allow an assessment of an increase in market share in a country where the bank is already present, and in the case of cross-border mergers between companies already present in the same foreign markets, but with different market shares, the operation will not be able to generate a change in the ID index pre- and post-merger. This is mainly due to the fact that the operation does not involve an entrance into new geographical areas. An additional modification was thus introduced. To consider variations in the share of a specific foreign market and obtain more information about the possible increase in market shares, it is necessary to use a presence attribution mechanism functioning not only in absolute but also in relative terms. The formalisation of the index is as follows (third level ID):

$$ID_{III^\circ level} = \sum_{i:\omega \in Y_\alpha} \left( \phi(\omega_i) \times \Theta_i \right) \tag{3.4}$$

Where $\Theta_i$ represents the measure of the market share held in the i-th country.[8]

The solution suggested allows more information to be obtained than with the previous solutions. This allows static and dynamic comparisons to be made between banks or conglomerates, considering both the importance of the countries involved and the market shares held in these geographical areas.[9]

## Diversification indicators

The techniques for measuring a bank's degree of product diversification have been extensively analyzed from both the theoretical and the empirical points of view.[10] The typical fields of research are the diversification of the loans portfolio across the various borrower categories, or of revenue sources, with reference to their nature (based on interest or on commissions).[11] The main analytical measurement techniques, in both cases, are the HHI or, alternatively, loan or revenue composition ratios generated in different ways. Several studies, focused on the connections between listed banks' size and degree of diversification (Roll, 1988, pp. 541–66; Demstez and Strahan, 1997, pp. 300–13; Gascon and Gonzalez, 2000), have chosen the $R^2$ coefficient as a product diversification indicator. If systematic risk is eliminated from the total earnings variance, only the firm-specific risk is left: low levels of firm-specific risk indicate a greater diversification of business, because the regression of the bank's share returns compared to market returns provides an explained variance that is very close to the overall variance; that is, a determination coefficient close to 100 per cent. In other words, the actual values of the dependent variable are extremely close to the characteristic line and they indicate high homogeneity between company data and the aggregate market, which represents the maximum achievable level of diversification (Fuller and Farrell, 1993, pp. 239–46; Resti, 2001, pp. 168–76).

Some studies attempt to use the determination coefficient principle to measure the difference between the portfolio composition of a specific intermediary and a benchmark, based on a sort of market loans portfolio, to measure the degree of diversification (Pfingsten and Rudolph, 2002; Behr et al., 2007). The measure used in these cases is the normalised sum of the absolute differences. This sum explains the proportion of the portfolio that would need to be reallocated to replicate the benchmark, and the average relative difference, able to express the deviation of a single segment compared to its own dimensions. The lower the values observed, the higher the bank's degree of diversification. An additional indicator, borrowed from industrial organisation studies, defines the level of diversification as an inverse measure of the degree of concentration and it is obtained by adding the sums of the products of the share of the total business of each activity to the logarithm of their reciprocal.[12] This ratio, known as the entropy index, has values close to zero for the highest levels of specialisation, and values equal to the logarithm of the number of activities, when all activities have the same weight in all the sectors considered: the information capacity of the entropy index is similar to that of the HHI.

To measure the degree of diversification of the activities of a financial conglomerate created by a cross-sector M&A operation, it is assumed that it has the structure of a controlling entity with holding functions, and holds equity investments in controlled entities operating in banking, insurance, asset management and other markets.[13] To measure the level of operative diversification, the quantitative set provided by the HHI is used, as a sum of the squares of different activities' shares of the total portfolios managed: this method is considered to provide the best quality information in the shortest times. Formally:

$$HHI = \sum_{i=1}^{n} X_i^2 \qquad (3.5)$$

where:
n = categories of companies belonging to the group;
$X_i$ = share of the i-th activity of conglomerate's total business.

The output of the Herfindahl–Hirschman function is in the interval (0;1], assuming the value 1 if the intermediary considered engages in only one area of business, and decreasing in proportion to the increase in a number of activities, each of which accounts for a similar percentage share of total business. The proxy parameters, considered to be relevant for banking, insurance, asset management and other activities, can be obtained from balance sheet aggregates, such as interest-bearing assets, financial investments, the volumes of wealth managed by asset management companies and, for other companies, from the sum of the operating financial portfolios.[14] The proposed correction lies in the consideration that the single companies within a conglomerate belong to it by a share equal to the share held by the controlling entity in each. With reference to this aspect, the final version of the product diversification index, considering the relative contributions of the controlled entities, is as follows:

$$HHI = \sum_{i=1}^{n} \left( X_i \times p_i \right)^2 \qquad (3.6)$$

where:
n = categories of companies belonging to the group;
$X_i$ = share of i-th activity of total business of controlling entity;
$p_i$ = controlling entity's holding in i-th company to total investment.

It could be interesting to combine the index obtained with the HHI value, not weighted by share of equity, calculated with reference to the revenues of the different companies within the conglomerate, in order to estimate the contribution of the diversification to income. Here again, some proxies representing the various activities' contributions to the overall economic result need to be defined. For the banking sector, one possibility is the interest margin, representing the returns on lending after elimination of any adjustments on credits and other revenues, especially those obtained from other services of various kinds. For the insurance sector, the margin considered could be premiums collected less the costs of claims (for both life and non-life insurance), to which investment earnings have to be added. In the case of asset management companies, the aggregate should consist of net commissions earned from wealth management services provided to the market and the revenues from financial portfolios. For other companies, the earnings from the core business should be considered.[15] Naturally, these figures should be expressed as a proportion of the total value.

To measure the changes generated by M&A operations that modify the conglomerate's structure, the HHI for the areas of business engaged in at any time before the change is calculated. Analytically:

$$\Delta HHI = HHI_{post\ merger} - HHI_{pre\ merger} \tag{3.7}$$

If the delta obtained has negative values, the M&A operation involved heterogeneous players, increasing the degree of diversification degree; if the delta is positive, the opposite holds true.

Measurements of a conglomerate's product diversification could also be obtained by examining the number of products and services offered, or rather their variation over time. This could reveal the intensity of cross-selling, and also the degree of product integration between single companies, in terms of market offering.

## Value creation indicators

The Economic Value Added (EVA) model is used to define the M&A's ability to generate or destroy value for shareholders.[16] Under this method, company performance is not measured on the basis of economic results pure and simple; the relative capital charge is first deducted. In general:

$$EVA = NOPAT - (IC \times WACC) \tag{3.8}$$

where:
    NOPAT = Net Operating Profit After Taxes;
    IC = Invested Capital;
    WACC = Weighted Average Cost of Capital.

One alternative formula that expresses the economic value generated, as the product of the invested capital and the spread between the return on the capital and its cost, is as follows:

$$EVA = (ROIC - WACC) \times IC \tag{3.9}$$

where:
    ROIC = Return On Invested Capital.

Analytically, the second equation is obtained by dividing both members of the first EVA formula by the invested capital (ROIC = NOPAT/IC).

While the EVA method can be applied to industrial companies without any particular precautions in the definition of its components, a large number of adjustments are required when calculating the index for financial intermediaries.[17] Specifically for banks, the Net Operating Profit After Taxes (NOPAT) is obtained from the net profit, less extraordinary items and items of no financial impact (for example, provisions for risks and taxes).[18] For the Invested Capital (IC) the main variation from the ordinary formula is that the subordinated liabilities only are considered together with the net assets:[19] operating debt items (customers' deposits) are not considered because their costs are implicitly measured by NOPAT. The Weighted Average Cost of Capital (WACC) is obtained from the following equation:

$$WACC = \left( k_e \times \frac{E}{IC} \right) + \left[ k_d \times (1 - t) \times \frac{D}{IC} \right] \tag{3.10}$$

where:
   $K_e$ = cost of equity;
   $K_d$ = debt cost;
   t = tax shield;
   E = equity;
   D = debts.

The main problem here is evaluating the cost of equity (Ferretti, 1995, pp. 201–30; Sironi, 1996, pp. 278–93; Saita, 2000, pp. 332–5). In attempting to do this, four main techniques can be used. Using the dividend yield technique, the cost of equity is taken as equal to the rate of return at which the sum of the current values of expected dividends is the same as the current share price: some difficulties in determining the value of future dividend values should be noted with reference to this method, and further problems arise when evaluating unlisted banks.

A second criterion is the price/earnings ratio: the cost of capital is calculated as the reciprocal of this ratio. In this case, the future return required by shareholders, obtained as the ratio between earnings per share (EPS) and the shares' market price is considered as proxy of the cost of capital: the main limitations of this method are, on the one hand, the relationship between book values (net profit) and market values (share price) and, on the other hand, the possible distortions deriving from market expectations concerning future profits (high profit expectations tend to increase share prices, and this reduces the EPS/P ratio. Paradoxically, at the same level of net profit, the cost of equity decreases).

One alternative to the previous two methods is to estimate the cost of equity by calculating the sum of the risk-free return and the historical excess return of the company's shareholders, calculated as the average of the differences between past returns and the relative current rates on free risk investments. There are several problems linked to this approach: the use of historical data means that large data series are required, and the method presupposes that all factors affecting the risk premium are stable over time.

The most widely used method for calculating the cost of capital is the Capital Asset Pricing Model. Although not without its critical assumptions (efficient markets, lack of transaction and fiscal costs, rational operators with uniform expectations, and so on),[20] it is the most commonly applied method of evaluating $K_e$, assumed to be equal to the risk-free rate increased by a certain risk premium depending on the level of systemic risk level (expressed by the share's beta, meaning the ratio between the covariance of the return on the share with the market return and the share's variance). In mathematical terms:

$$K_e = R_{free} + \beta \times \left( R_{mkt} - R_i \right) \tag{3.11}$$

where:
 $R_{free}$ = risk-free rate;
 $\beta$ = beta of share i;
 $R_{mkt}$ = market rate of return;
 $R_i$ = rate of return of share i.

For banks, an alternative technique for calculating Economic Value Added for shareholders measures the difference between ROE and the cost of capital, multiplied by the bank's equity (E) (Sironi, 2005, pp. 709–12). In symbols:

$$EVA = \left( ROE - K_e \right) \times E \tag{3.12}$$

The difference compared to the method described previously is that this technique defines a spread between ROE and $K_e$, instead of ROIC, and relates this difference to the bank's equity, or rather to the capital consistent with the risk faced, instead of the invested capital.[21] Here again, it is possible to propose a formulation of EVA in absolute terms, as the difference between net profit (NP) and capital charge.

Analytically:

$$EVA = NP - \left( K_e \times E \right) \tag{3.13}$$

This is a sort of simplified version of the standard method, consistent with the main aim of EVA calculation. It is intended to assess the excess value for shareholders only, considering opportunity costs, or rather the return they require on the capital shares they have underwritten and which are absorbed by the overall risks (credit, market and operating risks) faced by the bank. The two methods of defining EVA are very similar, the first more general and in line with common practice, and the second more operative and focused. Which approach is more appropriate in any specific case will depend on the aim of the evaluation and the input data available.

The value creation – destruction measurement method can now be applied to two scenarios, the first a bank M&A operation between banks, and the second a cross-sector consolidation operation intended to create a conglomerate structure.

In the case of the M&A between banks, the changes in value could assessed by comparing the ex-ante data of the two individual companies with the ex-post data of the new institution. If this last figure is higher than the sum of the data of the two stand alone companies, Economic Value Added may have been generated.

However, this measurement is not sufficient, since shareholders can only really be considered to have benefited if the EVA after the merger is higher than the EVA they would have enjoyed if the banks had not merged. To measure this aspect, a measurement of the Tracking Error (TE) compared to a sample of banks similar to those examined[22] has to be introduced; this peer group of banks provides the basis for the construction of a hypothetical benchmark bank that represents the average of the sample. Therefore, pre-merger EVAs have to be calculated for the meta-bank as well as for the bidder and target banks.

Then their divergence from the benchmark has to be analysed:

$$TE_{bidder\ pre} = EVA_{bidder\ pre} - EVA_{benchmark\ bidder\ pre} \qquad (3.14)$$

$$TE_{target\ pre} = EVA_{target\ pre} - EVA_{benchmark\ target\ pre} \qquad (3.15)$$

The tracking error obtained, for both the bidder and the target bank, does not express a value but only an initial figure that depends on the methods followed for the construction of the benchmarks: clearly, the influence of a different choice from a dimensional point of view on the results could be large. After the merger, the TE has to be measured as the difference between the EVA of the new institution and the sum of the EVAs of the previous benchmarks:

$$TE_{new\ bank} = EVA_{new\ bank} - EVA_{benchmark\ bidder\ post} - EVA_{benchmark\ target\ post} \qquad (3.16)$$

This measurement, compared to the simple sum of $TE_{bidder\ pre}$ and $TE_{target\ pre}$, represents the overall result achieved by the merger in terms of differential value creation, and indicates whether the new institution is able to generate better, worse or unchanged results for the merged banks, compared to their previous stand-alone condition.

In analytical terms, if:

- $TE_{bidder\ pre} + TE_{target\ pre} = TE_{new\ bank}$, the merger does not achieve any value creation or destruction; $\qquad$ (3.17)
- $TE_{new\ bank} > TE_{bidder\ pre} + TE_{target\ pre}$, the merger generates a total increase in value; $\qquad$ (3.18)
- $TE_{new\ bank} < TE_{bidder\ pre} + TE_{target\ pre}$, the operation destroys value. $\qquad$ (3.19)

The implicit assumption of the proposed model is that the tracking error of the EVA of the stand-alone bank compared to the benchmark would remain constant. The main problem, since the model uses book values, is related to the consequences of an M&A process for the new bank's balance sheet, where items like goodwill and other book value adjustments that modify the values of the parameters used to calculate the EVA are often included, creating a distortion in comparisons with the ex-ante data. To overcome this problem, specific normalisation procedures have to be adopted to eliminate the items strictly connected to the merger operation from the new bank's EVA.

All the same, the overall result obtained cannot be split between the two institutions involved in the M&A process. This information could be provided by a tracking error related to the spreads between ROE and $K_e$ of the banks involved (bidder and target), compared to the peer bank sample: in this case, the measure provided is not an absolute value, easily influenced by factors such as size, but a comparison between indicators obtained from ratios between parameters. The outcome informs us whether the differential returns of the bidder and target companies (ROE – $K_e$) are higher or lower than those attributable to a similar peer group.

Analytically:

$$TE_{bidder\ pre} = Spread_{bidder\ pre} - Spread_{benchmark\ bidder\ pre} \qquad (3.20)$$

$$TE_{target\ pre} = Spread_{target\ pre} - Spread_{benchmark\ target\ pre} \qquad (3.21)$$

In this case, TEs can also provide information about the ex-ante income situation of the two banks. The comparison with post-M&A TEs shows the effect of the operation for both the bidder and the target company. Post-TEs are as follows:

$$TE_{bidder\ post} = Spread_{new\ bank} - Spread_{benchmark\ bidder\ post} \qquad (3.22)$$

$$TE_{target\ post} = Spread_{new\ bank} - Spread_{benchmark\ target\ post} \qquad (3.23)$$

Similarly, the spread of the new bank has to be calculated by sterilising the effects of the M&A operation on the equity.

In the case of a financial conglomerate generated by an acquisition, the previous considerations with regard to M&As between banks apply only partially. The value creation/destruction assessment has to be divided into two parts, relating respectively to the shareholders of the target company and the conglomerate. In the first case, the measurement approach is similar to the tracking error method suggested for banks, taking care to adapt the EVA measurement to the specific company (insurance or asset management firm, bank, etc.), with appropriate choice of the items included in the NOPAT, IC and related costs.[23] The problems are greater with reference to the benefits for the shareholders of the controlling entity arising from the integration of a new intermediary into a conglomerate: the varied nature of the companies which make up the group, both ex-ante as well as ex-post, means that any variations in value cannot be measured effectively using the methods described. The model accepted as methodologically correct in these cases is derived from portfolio evaluation theory, where it is used to assess the impact of a change in composition on risk levels. It is believed that value creation should be measured by the Return on Risk Adjusted Capital index (so-called RORAC), because only when this indicator, calculated by considering the variation in the risk level due to the merger, is higher than the cost of equity $K_e$, do the conglomerate's shareholders benefit.[24] The RORAC index derives from the ratio between estimated net profits and risk capital, taken as the maximum loss an intermediary may incur given a specific confidence level and time horizon. The measurement of the overall risk capital for the conglomerate should consider all the correlations between the returns of the different companies, both current and at the time of the merger. Analytically, if we suppose that an insurance company is about to join a group comprising a bank and an asset management company, the risk capital should be calculated as follows:

$$CaR_t = \sqrt{\begin{aligned}&CaR_{bank}^2 + CaR_{amc}^2 + CaR_{ins}^2 + 2CaR_{bank}CaR_{amc}\,\rho_{\,bank,\,amc}\\&+2CaR_{bank}CaR_{ins}\,\rho_{\,bank,\,ins}+2CaR_{amc}CaR_{ins}\,\rho_{\,amc,\,ins}\end{aligned}} \qquad (3.24)$$

where:

   $CaR_t$ = overall risk capital;
   $\rho$ = correlation index.

Therefore, it is possible to measure the variation in the risk capital resulting from the diversification of the conglomerate's activities. By measuring marginal CaR (also known as incremental VaR), or rather the changes in the risk values of the single business units due to the merger, it is possible to obtain the value to which the overall expected profits should be compared.[25]

This kind of RORAC (so-called marginal RORAC) provides an accurate assessment of the risk-adjusted return, to which the cost of capital is then compared: only when the former exceeds the latter does the merger operation create value for the conglomerate's shareholders.

## 3.3   Conclusions

For a considerable period mergers and acquisitions have been the subject of analysis by experts and managers, from many points of view. This abundant literature suggests that the key factors of these processes are not always generated by company strategies aimed at protecting shareholders' interests, and the objectives set during the planning of the operation are often only achieved in part or by accident, if at all. To measure some meaningful effects arising from M&A operations, this study suggests a number of indicators considered suitable for expressing the degree of internationalisation, the level of diversification and the value creation capability, innovatively and in full. In view of the number of aspects considered in every ratio and their complexity, it may be that not all of them have been fully discussed here: nevertheless, we believe that our analysis has helped to clarify some aspects of interest in the field of external company growth in the financial sector.

# 4
# M&As and Equity Risk in the EMU Financial Sector

*Riccardo Ferretti, Francesco Pattarin and Valeria Venturelli*

## 4.1 Introduction

Over the past decade mergers and acquisitions (M&As) in the financial sector have been very frequent. In Europe the pace of M&As has been rapid. This process has been driven by the consolidation of market-oriented policies in the EU member countries, as well as by the expansion of the common market environment and the introduction of the euro since 1999. The opening of new markets in former Communist countries has also played a prominent role.

We survey a large, comprehensive and original list of M&A operations concluded from 1997 to 2007 by banks and insurance companies from EMU countries; a selection of exchange-listed firms is then examined to assess whether M&As changed the market risk profile of the acquirers, and to investigate whether any variations can be traced to the cross-border or cross-industry character of the operation. To this purpose, we first estimate market risk differentials between different segments of the financial sector and across EMU countries over several different periods of the decade, and make an assessment of the opportunities for risk reduction. Then, we use daily data to estimate market risk for individual acquirers before and after the completion of M&A operations and we test for any variations induced by the characteristics of the deal.

In section 4.2 we provide a review of the empirical evidence on the effects of M&As on shareholders' value and risk; we emphasise the results of research about M&As in the financial sector, with a further focus on the European market. Section 4.3 offers an account of M&A activity originated by Euro area financial intermediaries from 1997 to 2007, as it emerges from the analysis of the list we have assembled; in particular, we describe the phenomenon with respect to the location and the nature of acquiring and target companies. In section 4.4 we provide evidence of rising opportunities for reducing shareholders' market risk through cross-border and, to a lesser extent, cross-sector M&As after the introduction of the euro. In section 4.5 we present the results of our analyses about the effects of M&As on market risk based on a sample of individual operations completed by exchange-listed financial intermediaries domiciled in EMU countries from 2000 to 2007. Concluding remarks are made in section 4.6.

## 4.2  Evidence on stock market reactions to M&As

Mergers and acquisitions have been scrutinised widely in academic research according to two main perspectives: (1) the detection of equity value creation, or destruction, mainly through event studies about the stock market performance of acquiring and target firms; (2) the analysis of the consequences for the shareholders of the bidder and the target companies in terms of systematic risk. The identification of the key characteristics of the companies or deals that distinguish value-creating from value-destroying mergers is also a matter of interest to many studies.

In this section, we offer a brief review of the existing evidence about these research questions, in general and with specific focus on cross-border and cross-industry M&As in the financial sector.

### Value creation for shareholders

There is a quite extensive literature concerning the value creation potential of M&As. By and large, existing studies conclude that around the announcement day: (1) the shareholders of the target company earn positive and statistically significant abnormal returns,[1] that sometimes come from price run-ups before the announcement date (Jensen and Ruback, 1983; Datta et al., 1992; Bruner, 2002; Campa and Hernando, 2004); (2) the shareholders of the acquirer do not earn abnormal returns and may suffer share price losses (Bruner, 2002; Campa and Hernando, 2004); (3) abnormal returns of the combined entities are usually not statistically different from zero (Campa and Hernando, 2004); (4) diversifying mergers have detrimental effects on the value of equity (Mørck et al., 1990); (5) the bidder stock price has a better performance when the deal is announced during a 'hot' merger market (Rosen, 2006).[2] With respect to point (4) the evidence is not clear-cut. A study by Campa and Hernando (2004) conducted on European markets provides evidence of better performance of the acquirers' stocks in domestic and in-industry M&As against, respectively, cross-border and cross-industry ones, but Goergen and Renneboog (2004) cannot find any significant difference by type of operation.

Studies on bank M&As also show mixed results (Chapter 2). Beitel and Schiereck (2001) survey a hundred papers and report that a quarter of them do find, on average, positive abnormal returns for the stocks of both acquirers and targets, but in most instances bank mergers do not enhance the acquirer equity value – as is common among M&As involving non-financial firms. The same conclusion is reached by studies that focus on Europe too. In Beitel et al. (2004) abnormal returns are zero for the acquirers, but positive and statistically significant for both the targets and the combined entities; similar results are reported in Lepetit et al. (2004), Resti and Galbiati (2004), Petrella (2008). Cybo-Ottone and Murgia (2000) find positive and significant value creation for the combined entities in a sample of M&As involving various types of financial institutions.

Studies on M&As among insurance companies provide mixed results as well: if Madura and Picou (1993) find evidence of value creation, Kusnadi and Sohrabian (1999) do not, except for target firms.

According to many researchers, activity and the geographical degree of diversification influence market reactions to M&A deals. Specialising M&As, that is consolidation among banks with similar products or activity focus, are more beneficial to acquirers (Cornett et al., 2003) and to the joint entity (DeLong, 2001b) than M&As that diversify the scope of the business. M&As that focus geographically produce higher abnormal return for both the acquiring bank and the joint entity (DeLong, 2001b; Houston et al., 2001) than deals with geographic diversification; also, Amihud and co-authors (2001) find negative and statistically significant abnormal returns for acquirers in a sample of cross-border mergers.

Nor is there any evidence that the equity value of insurance companies benefits from diversifying M&As. Elango (2006) shows that US insurers seeking international acquisitions are neither rewarded nor penalised by the stock market; however, the shareholders' reaction is negatively related to differences between merging firms in terms of culture, environment, legal system, and geography, but depends positively on the size of the foreign market and on the intensity of the commercial activity between the domicile countries, assessed with respect to bilateral trade volumes.

Among European banks, Campa and Hernando (2004) and Petrella (2008) find that the stock performance of target companies is higher for cross-border than for domestic mergers, while returns are lower for acquirers and negative for the joint entity; Beitel and co-authors (2004) as well as Resti and Galbiati (2004) report similar results for both acquirers and targets, but negligible abnormal returns for the joint entity. Value creation in domestic M&As is not rejected either in the analyses by Lepetit and co-authors (2004) or in those by Cybo-Ottone and Murgia (2000). Considering the business focus of the banks involved in the deals, Beitel and co-authors (2004) find statistically significant and opposite stock-market performance for acquirers and targets depending on their respective specialisations: the equity value of the acquirer increases when the deal is focused, while the stockholders of the target earn higher returns when the deal reduces specialisation; but Petrella (2008) argues that focusing benefits the latter as well. Lepetit and co-authors' (2004) analysis controls for variations in exposure to market risks over time: their results partially confute common evidence since they reveal a positive and statistically significant market reaction to activity-diversifying M&As, while activity specialisation does not have any influence on stock prices. In Cybo-Ottone and Murgia (2000) the value creation of cross-industry deals is limited to banks acquiring insurance companies.

It is worth cautioning that the aforementioned results may conceal a high degree of variability among individual operations, because the returns of both targets and acquirers often show a broad range of responses, from very positive to very negative.

## Effects on market risk

The prevailing explanations of the poor performance of M&As for the share-holders of the acquiring company point to higher than expected merger costs (for example, organisational burden and bid-premium paid for the target) that hinder cost saving and, to a lesser extent, revenue enhancement (Houston et al., 2001). Since these obstacles are probably greater when the merging firms belong to different countries or industries, it is not surprising to see domestic and activity-focused deals usually producing better returns than diversifying ones.

However, it may be the case that the market risk of the acquirer changes after the M&A is concluded, thus altering the shareholders' expected return.[3] While Agrawal and co-authors (1992) argue that the poor stock market per-formance of acquirers should not be attributed to estimation biases induced by post-merger changes in market risk, others find a significant degree of sensitivity of abnormal returns to the estimation period (Connell and Conn, 1993; Kiymaz and Mukherjee, 2001). Diversifying M&As may then have positive effects on the risk profile of the acquiring firms that compensate – or even outweigh – integration costs by reducing the cost of capital. From this perspective, what is the evidence on the risk impact of diversifying mergers? Do we observe a reduction in market risk?

The prevailing evidence from empirical studies is that M&As induce sig-nificant changes in the risk of the acquirer, often resulting in its reduction (Connell and Conn, 1993; Davidson et al., 1987; Langetieg et al., 1980; Lubatkin and O'Neill, 1987; Mandelker, 1974). In a recent study of domes-tic US mergers, Hackbarth and Morellec (2008) find changes in the beta of the bidder both before and after the merger is announced. The direc-tion of the shift depends on the relative risk of the companies involved: the firm-level beta increases before the announcement and then decreases when the beta of the bidder's core assets exceeds the beta of the target's core assets; the opposite happens when the bidder's assets are safer than the target's. This finding may help to explain the contrasting evidence on the benefits of diversification. For a sample of large UK companies, Thompson (1983) concludes that diversifying mergers tend to increase risk, rather than reduce it, and to produce larger beta changes than focused deals. Kiymaz and Mukherjee (2001) analyse a sample of cross-border mergers completed by US acquirers and show a significant decline in beta over the post-event period; domicile affects the size of the variation but not its sign. Amihud and co-authors (2001) use a multi-index approach to study cross-border mergers involving commercial banks. The beta of the acquirers on the world market index increases after the deal, especially when targets are outside the European Union, while the beta on the domestic market does not change on average: this is often because the risk-load shifts between the acquirer and target countries.

## 4.3   M&A activity in the EMU financial sector: 1997 to 2007

In this section we provide a picture of the M&A activity of EMU financial intermediaries from 1997 to 2007. Our account is based on an original data set of M&A deals where banks, insurance companies and financial conglomerates resident in the EMU area appear as acquirers; the targets of the selected operations are from EMU as well as non-EMU countries worldwide.

We first state the composition criteria of the list of deals that we have examined and then present our main findings.

### Composition of the M&A deals list

Data on M&A operations were collected from Bureau-van-Dijk's 'Zephyr' database, which cover deals involving European companies going back to 1997. Each record in the database includes information about the target and the acquiring companies, such as the country of residence, the sector (or sectors) of business activity, whether the involved companies are listed and on what exchanges, the deal value, several relevant dates (such as the announcement date and the date when the deal is completed) and the stake acquired by the bidder – if the conditions and terms of the deal were disclosed.

We selected deals where acquirers and targets are in one of the following Zephyr database categories: bank, building society, bank holding company, life and non-life insurance company. The selection period is from 1997 to 2007; any deals where the acquirer is not resident in the EMU area were excluded. Also, since Zephyr records lack details for deals with more than one party on either side, these were removed from the sample. The resulting list totals 1,526 M&A operations.

We subdivided the companies on the list into three main sectors: banks, insurers and financial conglomerates. The Zephyr classification was used as a benchmark for allocating companies to either of the first two sectors. To identify entities that can be classified as 'financial conglomerates', we cross-referred to the lists compiled by the relevant authorities of each member country under Article 3 of European Commission Directive 2002/87; since the lists are updated almost every year, they provide up-to-date information. Unfortunately, the first lists of financial conglomerates appeared in late July 2005 and refer to year 2004; therefore, for the period 1997–2003, we define as 'financial conglomerates' any entities whose principal business sector is 'Banks and insurance companies' in the Zephyr database.

We define a deal as 'cross-border' when the target and the acquirer are domiciled in different countries; a deal is 'cross-sector' when the parties belong to different sectors as defined above (for example, a bank acquiring an insurance company).

## M&A activity from 1997 to 2007

M&As have been quite frequent in the European financial sector since the end of the 1990s because of the reshaping of the market environment driven by the removal of intra-EU barriers to competition and by the rising demand for financial services from former Communist countries in Eastern Europe and the Balkans. The resulting integration process has been supported by deregulation policies in EU member countries, both in domestic arenas and internationally.

Table 4.1 provides a synthesis of the major features of M&A activity originated by EMU banks, insurers and financial conglomerates as they emerge from our data set.

While half of the deals over the whole period are focused on the same country and sector as the acquirer, cross-border M&As have a 45 per cent share and their number increases steadily over time. Most cross-border operations do not diversify by sector. Cross-sector M&As account for only 15 per cent of the total; while their share is quite stable at the domestic level, for cross-border operations it increases almost threefold over the period.

An examination of M&As by sector of both acquirer and target reveals that most activity involves banks (Table 4.2); insurers come second and financial

*Table 4.1*   M&A deals originated in the EMU area: annual average by type and period

| Type of deal | Period | | | |
|---|---|---|---|---|
| | 1997–2000 | 2001–4 | 2005–7 | 1997–2007 |
| Domestic / In-sector | 67 | 75 | 56 | 67 |
| (%) | 49.6 | 55.6 | 41.5 | 49.6 |
| Domestic / Cross-sector | 10 | 11 | 10 | 10 |
| (%) | 7.4 | 8.1 | 7.4 | 7.4 |
| Cross-border / In-sector | 51 | 44 | 52 | 49 |
| (%) | 37.8 | 32.6 | 38.5 | 36.3 |
| Cross-border / Cross-sector | 8 | 14 | 19 | 13 |
| (%) | 5.9 | 10.4 | 14.1 | 9.6 |
| Total | 135 | 144 | 137 | 139 |
| (%) | 100.0 | 100.0 | 100.0 | 100.0 |

*Source*: Own processing of Zephyr Database.

*Table 4.2*    M&A deals by acquirer and target sectors: 1997–2007

| Acquirer sector | Target sector | | | Total |
|---|---|---|---|---|
| | **Banks** | **Insurance companies** | **Financial conglomerates** | |
| Banks | 901 | 70 | 1 | 972 |
| (%) | 92.7 | 7.2 | 0.1 | 100.0 |
| Insurance companies | 36 | 366 | – | 402 |
| (%) | 9.0 | 91.0 | | 100.0 |
| Financial conglomerates | 106 | 43 | 3 | 152 |
| (%) | 69.7 | 28.3 | 2.0 | 100.0 |
| Total | 1,043 | 479 | 4 | 1,526 |
| (%) | 68.3 | 31.4 | 0.3 | 100.0 |

*Note*: A dash indicates the absence of any cases.
*Source*: Own processing of Zephyr Database.

conglomerates are involved in the minority of operations. However, while banks and insurers are acquirers and targets with more or less the same frequency, a financial conglomerate is seldom a target.

In both banking and insurance, over 90 per cent of M&As aim to consolidate the presence of the acquirer in its own sector. Financial conglomerates have a 10 per cent share of total acquisition activity, directed mainly at banks (70 per cent) and insurers (28 per cent); therefore, they are the only sector that is a net acquirer.

In Table 4.3 deals are classified by the geographical area of targets and detailed by the sector of acquirers. In general, most deals are inside the EMU area; more than 85 per cent of all targets are domiciled in Europe. Insurance companies are the least active acquirers outside the EMU – with the minor exceptions of the Asia-Pacific basin and North America. M&As initiated by banks are relatively frequent in Eastern Europe and Latin America; the former are mainly concluded by Austria, Belgium, Greece and Italy, while the latter involved Spanish and French acquirers. As expected, financial conglomerates are the most active players outside the EMU area, concluding a large share of operations in the rest of Europe and North America.

Further examinations reveal that cross-border transactions are mostly initiated from smaller EMU countries, particularly Austria, Belgium, Ireland and the Netherlands; this may be explained by the maturity and the high concentration of banking and insurance markets in these countries, which may drive intermediaries to look for new business opportunities abroad – as

*Table 4.3*   M&A deals by acquirer sector and domicile of the target, 1997–2007

| Domicile of target | Acquirer sector | | | Total |
|---|---|---|---|---|
| | Banks | Insurance companies | Financial conglomerates | |
| EMU country | 677 | 294 | 73 | 1,044 |
| (%) | 69.7 | 73.1 | 48.0 | 68.4 |
| Other EU country | 9 | 8 | 6 | 23 |
| (%) | 0.9 | 2.0 | 3.9 | 1.5 |
| Eastern Europe | 166 | 55 | 46 | 267 |
| (%) | 17.1 | 13.7 | 30.3 | 17.5 |
| Other European country | 18 | 9 | 4 | 31 |
| (%) | 1.9 | 2.2 | 2.6 | 2.0 |
| North America | 21 | 13.7 | 13 | 47 |
| (%) | 2.2 | 3.2 | 8.6 | 3.1 |
| Latin America | 53 | 8 | 5 | 66 |
| (%) | 5.5 | 2.0 | 3.3 | 4.3 |
| Asia | 15 | 9 | 3 | 27 |
| (%) | 1.5 | 2.2 | 2.0 | 1.8 |
| Australia and New Zealand | 2 | 4 | – | 6 |
| (%) | 0.2 | 1.0 | | 0.4 |
| Africa | 11 | 2 | 2 | 15 |
| (%) | 1.1 | 0.5 | 1.3 | 1.0 |
| Total | 972 | 402 | 152 | 1,526 |
| (%) | 100.0 | 100.0 | 100.0 | 100.0 |

*Notes*: A dash indicates the absence of any cases.
*Source*: Own processing of Zephyr Database.

suggested by Campa and Hernando (2006). Also, while cross-border M&As are mostly directed towards non-EMU countries, there is some variability of this pattern depending on the country of origin: Luxembourg, Belgium, Portugal and France are more likely operate within the EMU area, while Greece, Finland, Austria and Ireland often make acquisitions outside the region.

Since M&As within the EMU area are our main focus, we provide some detail about them. The pattern of M&As over the period 1997–2007 is

*Table 4.4* M&A deals involving only EMU companies by domicile: 1997–2007

| Acquirer country | Target country | | | | | | | | | | | | Total | Domestic M&A share |
|---|---|---|---|---|---|---|---|---|---|---|---|---|---|---|
| | AT | B | DE | ES | FI | FR | GR | EI | It | L | NL | PT | | |
| Austria (AT) | 18 | – | 4 | – | – | 1 | – | – | 2 | – | – | – | 25 | 72.0% |
| Belgium (B) | – | 49 | 1 | 1 | – | 7 | – | 1 | 1 | 11 | 11 | – | 82 | 59.8% |
| Germany (DE) | 4 | 1 | 137 | 5 | 2 | 6 | – | 2 | 7 | 1 | 3 | 1 | 169 | 81.1% |
| Spain (ES) | – | – | 1 | 73 | – | 2 | – | – | 4 | – | – | 8 | 88 | 83.0% |
| Finland (FI) | – | – | – | – | 31 | – | – | – | – | – | – | – | 31 | 100.0% |
| France (FR) | – | 4 | 12 | 8 | – | 146 | 2 | 2 | 12 | – | 4 | 3 | 193 | 75.6% |
| Greece (GR) | – | – | – | – | – | – | 46 | – | – | – | – | – | 46 | 100.0% |
| Ireland (EI) | – | – | 2 | – | – | – | – | 8 | – | – | – | – | 10 | 80.0% |
| Italy (It) | 3 | – | 3 | 4 | – | 1 | – | 2 | 251 | 1 | – | – | 265 | 94.7% |
| Luxembourg (L) | – | 2 | | 3 | – | 9 | – | – | 2 | 23 | 2 | 1 | 42 | 54.8% |
| Netherlands (NL) | – | 7 | 7 | 1 | – | – | 3 | 1 | 3 | – | 37 | 1 | 60 | 61.7% |
| Portugal (PT) | – | – | – | 4 | – | – | 1 | – | – | – | – | 28 | 33 | 84.8% |
| Total | 25 | 63 | 167 | 99 | 33 | 172 | 52 | 16 | 282 | 36 | 57 | 42 | 1044 | 81.1% |

*Note*: A dash means absence of cases.
*Source*: Own processing of Zephyr Database.

characterised by its domestic nature, as only 20 per cent of the deals are cross-border (Table 4.4). Geographical proximity is the main feature of these operations; for instance, Belgian intermediaries mainly acquire companies in France, Luxembourg and the Netherlands; the reverse is also observed, since these countries are the host for most bidders for Belgian companies. The explanations commonly offered for this phenomenon include short intra-firm distance and homogeneity of domicile countries with respect to language, culture, business and saving habits, as well as the presence of historical links.[4]

Some countries can be labelled as 'net acquirers', because their acquisitions of foreign companies outweigh those of domestic ones by foreign entities; other countries are 'net targets', since the opposite is observed. Belgium, Germany, France, Luxemburg and the Netherlands are net acquirers, while Spain, Finland, Greece, Ireland, Italy and Portugal are net targets.

Italy is home to the largest amount of transaction activity, accounting for about 25 per cent of the total number of deals, followed by France (18.5 per cent) and Germany (16.2 per cent). The general geographical and industrial pattern of M&As in the EMU is consistent with the picture that emerges from Table 4.1. Nevertheless, there are some important differences by country. Belgium and the Netherlands have a large share of M&A activity across their borders oriented to cross-industry expansion, while Finland, Greece, Italy and Portugal are the four countries where domestic, in-sector operations are most frequent.

According to the evidence delivered by our examination, most M&A activity initiated by EMU financial intermediaries over the 1997–2007 period aimed at concentrating and consolidating rather than at diversifying; more than 85 per cent of the deals in our list are M&As concerning the main business activity of the acquirer. A 40 per cent share of in-sector M&As were directed at foreign companies. Overall, cross-border M&As increased their share from 43 to 53 per cent. Geographical diversification within the EMU area was, on average, 15 per cent of all recorded activity, sought mostly by banks and insurers from large countries, notably Germany and France, and by Benelux companies. A similar share of M&As was directed toward Eastern Europe. Financial conglomerates expanded internationally at the highest relative rate. Companies based in Mediterranean countries, Portugal, Ireland and Finland were exclusively domestic acquirers, with only a few exceptions.

## 4.4   Market risk of the banking and insurance sectors in EMU countries

The goal of the analyses presented in this section is to assess whether and to what extent there have been any opportunities for intermediaries in the EMU financial sector to reduce market risk through cross-border or cross-sector diversification. To this end, we first look for differences in market risk across countries for banks and insurance companies; then we compare the market risk across sectors within each country. The presence of any such differences would provide evidence of opportunities for risk reduction from cross-country or cross-sector M&As.

For our conclusions to be meaningful, we need to adopt a comparable definition of market risk for any country and any sector. Therefore, we define market risk as the beta coefficient of a simple (single) index model, where the EMU stock market is represented by the Dow Jones Euro Stoxx price index; consistently, the country-specific Dow Jones sector price indices for banking and for insurance are used as proxies for the respective market values.[5]

Classical regression estimates of banks' and insurers' beta over various time periods are displayed in Table 4.5 and Table 4.6, along with R-squared coefficients; all regressions have been run on monthly price relatives. Considering several periods allows checking for beta variability over time, especially before and after the introduction of the euro in 1999.

*Prima facie*, it is apparent that there are substantial cross-country differences in beta for both banks and insurers, which are often large enough to be economically relevant; in several cases, pair-wise *t*-tests lead us to reject

*Table 4.5*   Banks market risk by period and domicile: index model estimates

| Acquirer country | Period | | | | | | | |
|---|---|---|---|---|---|---|---|---|
| | 1997–2007 | | 1995–8 | | 1999–2002 | | 2003–7 | |
| | Beta | $R^2$ | Beta | $R^2$ | Beta | $R^2$ | Beta | $R^2$ |
| Germany | 1.30 | 62.9% | 1.24 | 60.0% | 1.21 | 60.1% | 1.54 | 63.7% |
| Netherlands | 1.20 | 52.6% | 1.23 | 51.7% | 1.24 | 52.0% | 1.06 | 45.7% |
| Spain | 1.12 | 66.2% | 1.29 | 61.4% | 0.98 | 69.6% | 1.09 | 62.1% |
| Greece | 1.08 | 26.2% | 1.41 | 23.6% | 0.55 | 14.2% | 1.64 | 57.6% |
| France | 1.07 | 60.0% | 1.43 | 70.3% | 0.89 | 50.6% | 1.08 | 61.1% |
| Italy | 1.04 | 62.3% | 1.4 | 63.0% | 0.9 | 61.5% | 0.81 | 46.6% |
| Ireland | 1.01 | 4.8% | ... | ... | 1.26 | 2.60% | 0.8 | 36.8% |
| Belgium | 0.8 | 44.2% | 0.92 | 56.6% | 0.57 | 27.9% | 1.1 | 55.8% |
| Portugal | 0.77 | 34.6% | 1.11 | 50.1% | 0.47 | 25.0% | 0.86 | 23.1% |
| Austria | 0.54 | 12.7% | 1.03 | 31.1% | ... | ... | 0.85 | 33.0% |
| Finland | – | – | 1.13 | 27.8% | – | – | – | – |
| Average | 0.99 | 42.6% | 1.22 | 49.5% | 0.9 | 40.4% | 1.08 | 48.5% |

*Notes*: OLS estimates with significance tests based on Newey&West robust standard errors.
A dash means that estimation has not been performed for lack of data.
Dots indicate that beta estimates are statistically indistinguishable from zero.
*Source*: Own processing of Dow Jones indices provided by Datastream.

*Table 4.6*   Insurance companies market risk by period and domicile: index model estimates

| Acquirer country | Period | | | | | | | |
|---|---|---|---|---|---|---|---|---|
| | 1997–2007 | | 1995–8 | | 1999–2002 | | 2003–7 | |
| | Beta | $R^2$ | Beta | $R^2$ | Beta | $R^2$ | Beta | $R^2$ |
| Germany | 1.37 | 49.7% | 0.99 | 45.8% | 1.11 | 54.10% | 2.54 | 57.6% |
| Netherlands | 1.35 | 53.6% | 0.97 | 51.3% | 1.18 | 45.0% | 2.11 | 70.9% |
| France | 1.29 | 59.4% | 1.03 | 46.6% | 1.34 | 56.20% | 1.48 | 71.2% |
| Italy | 0.92 | 52.4% | 1.17 | 57.5% | 0.85 | 51.10% | 0.79 | 32.4% |
| Finland | 0.91 | 28.1% | 1.45 | 40.0% | 0.57 | 13.70% | 0.97 | 36.2% |
| Spain | 0.77 | 23.8% | 1.37 | 57.4% | … | … | 1.22 | 48.2% |
| Ireland | 0.62 | 13.5% | 0.64 | 22.9% | 0.47 | 5.0% | 0.88 | 22.4% |
| Portugal | – | – | 1.09 | 39.0% | – | – | – | – |
| Belgium | – | – | 1.07 | 54.7% | – | – | – | – |
| Average | 1.03 | 40.0% | 1.09 | 46.1% | 0.92 | 37.5% | 1.43 | 48.4% |

*Notes*: OLS estimates with significance tests based on Newey&West robust standard errors.
A dash means that estimation has not been performed for lack of data.
Dots indicate that beta estimates are statistically indistinguishable from zero.
*Source*: Own processing of Dow Jones indices provided by Datastream.

the hypothesis of identical sector-specific beta for two countries. We have set the significance threshold for every test to the conventional value of 5 per cent.

Over the whole period (1997–2007) there is a remarkable variability in beta by country. For banks, the ratio of the highest to the lowest beta is 2.4, for insurance companies it is 2.2; pair-wise *t*-tests for the difference are statistically significant in 26 per cent and 39 per cent of cases respectively – much more than the 5 per cent random rejection rate implied by the significance level of the tests. German banks and insurance companies are first in the ranking by beta, with values well above unity, while Dutch intermediaries come second and have the same level of market risk. The banking sectors of Spain, Greece, France, Italy, and Ireland have mid-ranking beta, in the range from 1.00 to 1.10, and are not statistically distinguishable from each other; it is worth remarking that, with the excepion of Italy, *t*-tests for all these countries against Germany are not significant either. At the lowest level, Portugal, Belgium and Austria have beta below unity that are statistically different from those of the top-three countries (Germany, the Netherlands and Spain). In the insurance sector, the beta of Germany, the Netherlands and France are in the range from 1.29 to 1.37, and much higher than the mid- and low-ranking beta of Italy, Finland, Spain and Ireland. These cases are all below unity; nevertheless statistically significant differences are limited to Spain and Ireland – and to Italy, but only against the Netherlands.

From the comparison of beta estimates by periods (1995–8, 1999–2002 and 2003–7) it emerges that beta change over time; the ranking of intermediaries from different countries by market risk is also different from period to period. The comparison of the pre-(1995–8) and the post-changeover (1999–2002) beta reveals that, on average, the transition to the euro has generally reduced market risk at the country level for both banks (by 0.30 points) and insurers (by 0.15 points); insurance companies in Germany, the Netherlands and France are the only cases of increasing beta values.

From 1999 to 2007 beta are quite unstable. With the exception of Italian intermediaries and Dutch banks, beta increase in all countries and sectors during the last five-year period (2003–7); this trend is stronger in the case of insurance companies. In addition, market risk diversity widens across countries. For banks, rejections in $t$-tests rise from 4 per cent in the pre-EMU period (1995–8) to 20 per cent after the changeover (1999–2002) before jumping to 35 per cent over the last five years (2003–7); for the insurance sector, rejection frequencies in the same periods are 11 per cent, 12 per cent and 47 per cent respectively.

Table 4.7 illustrates differences between beta of the banking and the insurance sectors in each country; values of standard significance $t$-tests are also shown. Over the whole period (1997–2007) banks appear riskier than insurance companies in Ireland, Spain and Italy, while the opposite holds in Germany, the Netherlands and France. During the pre-changeover period (1995–8) the banking sector was riskier in four out of five countries,

*Table 4.7*   Cross-sector differences in market risk by country and period: banks vs insurance companies

| Acquirer country | Period | | | | | | | |
| --- | --- | --- | --- | --- | --- | --- | --- | --- |
| | 1997–2007 | | 1995–8 | | 1999–2002 | | 2003–7 | |
| | Beta | t-test | Beta | t-test | Beta | t-test | Beta | t-test |
| Ireland | 0.38 | 1.408 | – | – | 0.79 | 1.208 | −0.08 | −0.362 |
| Spain | 0.35 | 1.732 | −0.08 | −0.28 | – | – | −0.13 | −0.645 |
| Italy | 0.12 | 1.047 | 0.23 | 0.972 | 0.05 | 0.34 | 0.03 | 0.157 |
| Germany | −0.08 | −0.296 | 0.25 | 0.901 | 0.1 | 0.347 | −1 | −1.437 |
| Netherlands | −0.14 | −0.559 | 0.26 | 0.986 | 0.06 | 0.139 | −1.06 | −3.005 |
| France | −0.22 | −0.908 | 0.40 | 1.347 | −0.45 | −1.109 | −0.4 | −2.554 |

*Notes*: OLS estimates with significance tests based on Newey&West robust standard errors.
A dash means that estimation has not been performed for lack of data.
*Source*: Own processing of Dow Jones indices provided by Datastream.

but afterwards the relative risk profile of the two industries has progressively changed, so that in the most recent five year period (2003–7) the beta of insurers are the highest everywhere – Italy being the only exception. Even if differences in beta are not small in absolute terms, we cannot confidently reject homogeneity among sectors within most countries and periods.

To sum up, from 1997 to 2007 there may have been opportunities for EMU banks and insurers to reduce risk through cross-border M&As and, perhaps, through cross-sector operations – but our evidence is statistically weak in this respect. Moreover, the potential benefits for acquirers belonging to a particular country or to a particular sector were not constant over time. Specifically, such benefits were likely to be higher from 2003 to 2007 than before, as the magnitude and statistical significance of beta differentials suggest.

Comparing these results to the account of M&A operations presented in the previous section, the coincidence of market risk reduction in both banking and insurance after 1999 with the peak period of M&A activity (2001–4) is apparent. In addition, two important analogies emerge. First, the number of cross-border M&As, either in- or cross-sector, was highest from 2005 to 2007, when significant differences in beta (and consequently the potential for risk-reduction) were most evident. Second, domestic cross-sector aggregations involving banks and insurance companies were, in general, a minority of M&A activity; our estimates of the risk-reduction potential within countries also show it to be poor or absent.

These findings do not conflict with the claim that cross-border M&As (could) have had an effect on market risk reduction in the EMU financial sector. A closer inspection of cross-border deals by sectors reveals that countries with high beta banks or insurers tend to be net acquirers, while the opposite holds for mid- and low-beta countries. In the banking sector, Belgium, Germany, the Netherlands and Spain are net acquirers and have an average beta of 1.10, while France, Greece Ireland, Italy and Portugal are net targets, with an average beta of 0.99. As for insurance companies, Germany, the Netherlands and France have beta averaging 1.33 and are net acquirers, while Finland, Ireland, Italy and Spain are net targets with an average beta of 0.80. Therefore, high levels of equity market risk may have represented an incentive for some EMU financial intermediaries to diversify through cross-border M&As, and not a hindrance to external growth.

## 4.5   The effect of M&As on shareholders' market risk

In this section we try to assess whether and to what extent M&As among EMU financial intermediaries have had any effect on shareholders' market risk. We have carried out our analyses over an eight-year period – from 2000 to 2007 – on a sample of deals performed by exchange-listed acquirers. The sample selection criteria and main features are described in the first paragraph; methodology and results are discussed in the second paragraph.

### Description of the M&A sample

To analyse the effect of M&A operations on the market risk borne by the equity holders of the acquiring companies, we selected a sample from the list of deals commented on in section 4.3. Because our analyses have shown that most opportunities for risk reduction appeared after the changeover to the euro in 1999, we focused on operations concluded from 2000 to 2007 that involved only companies domiciled in EMU countries.

As a first criterion for selection of the sample, we excluded all transactions where the acquired stake was lower than 10 per cent unless complete control over the target was gained; the motivation for applying this filter to the list is that we do not expect to find any meaningful changes in market risk when the share acquired in the target company was minor.

Our preliminary selection comprises 73 listed acquirers that concluded 217 deals over the period of interest; each company was thus involved in three M&A operations on average, while the actual number of deals per company spans a range from one to nine.

A feature of this data subset, which is inherited from the parent list, is that target companies are seldom listed on stock exchanges; this is so in less than 8 per cent of cases. This is unfortunate, since we are *de facto* unable to perform any meaningful comparison of the acquirer and the target market risk on these data, as time-series of market price relatives do not exist for most target companies. Therefore, our analyses are based on market risk estimates of the acquirers only.

One quarter of the 217 deals that we initially selected (55 cases) were excluded because of the absence of sufficient time-series data for estimating risk before and after the conclusion of the deal. This left 162 M&A operations performed by 67 companies available for the analyses.

Deals are evenly distributed over the eight years of the sampling period, with a single peak in 2006 (17 per cent) preceded and followed by years of lower levels of activity (9 per cent in 2005 and 2007).

In the sample 75 per cent of cases are in-sector deals, of which two-thirds are domestic (Table 4.8). In contrast to our finding for the complete M&A list, several cross-sector deals in the sample are domestic (15 per cent) and less than 10 per cent are cross-border. Furthermore, there are relatively more financial conglomerates (18 per cent) and fewer banks (53 per cent) among acquirers in the sample than in the list; the former are the only intermediaries engaged in cross-border and cross-sector M&As.

The distributions of target companies by sector for each type of acquirer are very close to those shown in Table 4.2. The similarity to the M&A list also holds with respect to the domicile country of acquirers, except for

*Table 4.8*  Sampled M&A deals by type and acquirer sector

| Type of deal | Acquirer sector | | | |
| --- | --- | --- | --- | --- |
| | Banks | Insurance companies | Financial conglomerates | Total |
| Domestic / In-sector | 65 | 26 | 1 | 92 |
| (%) | 75.6 | 55.3 | 3.4 | 56.8 |
| Domestic / Cross-sector | 7 | 4 | 13 | 24 |
| (%) | 8.1 | 8.5 | 44.8 | 14.8 |
| Cross-border / In-sector | 14 | 17 | – | 31 |
| (%) | 16.3 | 36.2 | | 19.1 |
| Cross-border / Cross-sector | – | – | 15 | 15 |
| (%) | | | 51.7 | 9.3 |
| Total | 86 | 47 | 29 | 162 |
| (%) | 100.0 | 100.0 | 100.0 | 100.0 |

*Note*: A dash indicates the absence of any cases.
*Source*: Own processing of Zephyr Database.

Italy and Greece, which are under-represented, and Belgium, Germany and Luxembourg, which have a larger share in the sample than in the list.

For all the sample cases we have been able to retrieve or calculate the percentage equity stake acquired – except for two deals by banks; descriptive statistics by acquirer sectors are displayed in Table 4.9.

The average stake, in the range of 60 to 70 per cent depending on the sector, is well above the majority-holding threshold; also, in at least three-quarters of cases the deal was an acquisition of all the target's equity. The dispersion of data, either measured by the standard deviation or assessed by the interquartile range, is not high and is almost the same across sectors; most cases concentrate towards the upper values. Stakes acquired by banks and financial conglomerates have very similar distributions, with half of cases above 50 per cent and a minimum value of 10 per cent. Insurance companies' acquisitions were of larger stakes, 10 or 20 per cent above the values recorded in the other sectors; in a few cases, the acquired stake was lower than 4 per cent.[6]

## M&As and changes in market risk

We have examined variations in market risk that could have been induced by M&As on the acquirers' equity by comparing the individual beta values before and after operations were completed. Since a large body of empirical research provides evidence that beta fluctuate over time, so is not safe to assume that beta estimates taken over long periods are unbiased, we have computed beta over three month spans using daily data.[7]

*Table 4.9*   Percentage acquired equity stake by sector of the acquirer

| Statistics | Acquirer sector | | | |
|---|---|---|---|---|
| | Banks | Insurance companies | Financial conglomerates | Total |
| Mean | 63.7 | 70.6 | 63.5 | 65.7 |
| Standard deviation | 32.4 | 32.1 | 34.2 | 32.6 |
| Minimum | 10.0 | 4.0 | 10.2 | 4.0 |
| 25th percentile | 39.8 | 49.0 | 30.1 | 41.0 |
| Median | 51.0 | 78.6 | 50.0 | 66.6 |
| 75th percentile | 100.0 | 100.0 | 100.0 | 100.0 |
| Maximum | 100.0 | 100.0 | 100.0 | 100.0 |
| Number of cases | 82 | 47 | 29 | 158 |

*Note*: Two values are missing among banks' deals.
*Source*: Own processing of Zephyr Database.

Table 4.10 displays statistics for beta values by sector for all deal types. Beta have been estimated on closing-price relatives recorded over the quarter before the M&A operation was concluded (for example, the first quarter if the acquisition was completed any day from the beginning of April to the end of May) and retrieved from Thomson-Reuters Datastream. A general feature that is apparent from the table is that beta values have a wide range of variability, from slightly less than zero to about two. Market risk was remarkably similar for banks and insurance companies: average beta are in the 0.60 range for both sectors; also, the median and quartiles values

*Table 4.10*   Beta estimates before M&A conclusion

| Statistics | Acquirer sector | | | |
|---|---|---|---|---|
| | Banks | Insurance companies | Financial conglomerates | Total |
| Mean | 0.63 | 0.67 | 1.02 | 0.71 |
| Standard deviation | 0.49 | 0.51 | 0.45 | 0.51 |
| Minimum | −0.36 | −0.1 | 0.17 | −0.36 |
| 25th percentile | 0.28 | 0.27 | 0.70 | 0.32 |
| Median | 0.54 | 0.57 | 1.08 | 0.65 |
| 75th percentile | 0.97 | 0.95 | 1.32 | 1.20 |
| Maximum | 1.97 | 1.83 | 2.05 | 2.05 |
| Number of cases | 86 | 47 | 29 | 162 |

*Source*: Own processing of Datastream Database.

are barely distinguishable. With not many exceptions, market risk for these sectors is mid- to low-grade: three-quarters of beta are below unity. As should be expected from their typical diversification of business activities, financial conglomerates' beta are closer to unity than those of banks and insurers. The overall proportion of statistically significant beta values is about 65 per cent, and the average R-squared level is 70 per cent.

In order to assess the impact of M&As on risk, we have estimated quarterly beta after the deals were concluded using the same method. We have then computed the difference between the post- and the pre-operation beta for each individual M&A (that is, price data recorded over the quarter when operations were concluded were not considered);[8] the distributions of estimated beta changes by geographical and sector characteristics are described in Table 4.11.

Domestic M&As have a similar – and generally low – impact on market risk; average and median values of changes in beta are very close to zero and the central half of the distribution lies in the ±0.20 range for both in- and cross-sector operations. Cross-border M&As are quite diverse. In-sector cases have impacts similar to those of domestic M&As, albeit with values that are shifted slightly upwards. Cross-sector operations are the ones that seem to have had the largest effect on market risk, with an average drop in beta of −0.10; compared to all other deal types, the distribution is also shifted downwards. While these features may be suggestive of market risk reduction deriving from cross-border and cross-sector operations, there are some reasons for exercising caution. Firstly, only financial conglomerates performed this type of operation in our sample, and they were already quite diversified (Table 4.8 and Table 4.10); thus, further diversification is likely to have been less important to shareholders than in the banking and insurance sectors.

*Table 4.11*   Beta changes after domestic M&As by type of deal

| Type of deal | Statistics | | | | | |
|---|---|---|---|---|---|---|
| | Minimum | 25th perc. | Median | 75th perc. | Maximum | Mean |
| Domestic/ In-sector | −0.90 | −0.19 | 0.02 | 0.19 | 1.57 | 0.03 |
| Domestic/ Cross-sector | −0.74 | −0.23 | 0.02 | 0.22 | 2.00 | 0.05 |
| Cross-bor- der/In-sector | −0.60 | −0.19 | 0.07 | 0.32 | 0.60 | 0.05 |
| Cross-bor- der/Cross- sector | −0.75 | −0.32 | −0.11 | 0.11 | 0.37 | −0.10 |

*Source*: Own processing of Datastream Database.

Secondly, the need for caution is reinforced by the small absolute amount of most changes. Thirdly, there are only 15 cross-border and cross-sector cases in the sample.

The picture emerging from the general examination of our estimates is that beta changes are not evidently oriented towards either risk reduction or enhancement, and that if any clear influence is to be found then it will be among outlying cases. Indeed, when variations in beta are tested for statistical significance at customary levels, the proportions of rejections are higher than they would be by chance alone: at the 5 per cent level, the number of significant changes is 22 out of 162 (13.5 per cent) and at the 10 per cent level the figure is 51 (31.5 per cent); this pattern also holds at the more conservative one per cent level and for each deal type.[9] In this regard, in Table 4.12 we display the average and count of 10 per cent significant beta variations by deal type, split into positive and negative cases.

The magnitude of significant changes is not negligible in both instances; positive variations averaged 0.52, negative ones –0.43. In line with the descriptive statistics in Table 4.11, the largest mean risk reduction is in cross-border and cross-sector operations (–0.59), while risk increases by 0.69 on average in domestic and in-sector operations. These types of deals are also the ones for which the absolute differences in (mean) positive and negative changes are the largest. However, the most striking aspect of these results is the balance between the number of positive and negative effects of M&As on beta for each type of deal; such that, if we average positive and negative values for each type, the results are in a range very close to zero (from –0.06 to 0.15).

The analyses of individual operations presented in this section lead towards two main conclusions. First of all, merger and acquisitions among financial intermediaries of EMU countries from 2000 to 2007 were not neutral with respect to the equity market risk exposure of the acquirers'

*Table 4.12*   Statistically significant beta changes by type of deal and sign

| Type of deal | Sign of Beta change | | | |
| --- | --- | --- | --- | --- |
| | Positive | | Negative | |
| | Cases | Mean | Cases | Mean |
| Domestic/In-sector | 12 | 0.69 | 15 | −0.42 |
| Domestic/Cross-sector | 5 | 0.32 | 5 | −0.44 |
| Cross-border/In-sector | 5 | 0.44 | 3 | −0.34 |
| Cross-border/Cross-sector | 3 | 0.35 | 2 | −0.59 |
| All operations | 25 | 0.52 | 26 | −0.43 |

*Note*: The table is based on cases significant at the 10 per cent level.
*Source*: Own processing of Datastream Database.

shareholders. The variations in single-index model beta are often statistically significant and have magnitudes that are such to affect average risk profiles, not only for stock shares of banks and insurance companies, but also for those of financial conglomerates. This is consistent with the potential for market risk variations in EMU countries discussed in section 4.4. However, it is not possible to clearly trace the effects on beta to any specific type of M&A, since negative and positive changes are evenly distributed within each type and, in general, of comparable magnitude. While we would not dispose of the evidence that domestic and in-sector M&As were more likely to increase risk, while cross-border and cross-sector ones might have reduced it, we are not strongly confident in these claims either.

Although difficult to explain, variations in market risk did happen in association with M&As. This is consistent with what predicates most of the existing literature on the topic. From a methodological perspective, this should be considered in any empirical research that uses CAPM-like approaches to assess the effects of M&As on shareholders' market value.

## 4.6   Conclusions

In this chapter we have examined M&A activity among financial inter-mediaries originated by companies domiciled in the EMU from 1997 to 2007. The period was marked by the introduction of the euro in 1999 and by the rising demand for financial services in Eastern European countries. Using an original list of M&A deals, we document an increase in cross-border M&A activity over the period, mainly within the EMU area and towards Eastern Europe. Albeit with a reduced share in overall activity, most aggregations continued to be domestic; in addition, banks and insurance companies mainly acquired targets in their respective sectors. With some exceptions, financial conglomerates were the only real international players in M&As.

According to our analyses, the opportunities for reducing shareholders' equity market risk, and the cost of capital likewise, through cross-border integration in the EMU increased significantly after the changeover to the common currency, while cross-sector diversification seems to have offered only minor risk reduction. We have then examined a sample of M&As undertaken by exchange-listed acquirers from 2000 to 2007, to assess whether and to what extent these opportunities were exploited.

Our results show that shareholders' market risk was indeed affected by M&A in several cases, potentially to a large extent; however, significant risk reduction was as frequent as an increase in risk after the conclusion of operations, and the average magnitude of changes was very similar in both instances. Moreover, it is not possible to clearly associate the direction of risk variations to the cross-border or cross-sector character of M&A deals. Therefore, we can argue that concerns about reducing shareholders' risk and, possibly, the cost of capital, were not a common determinant of external growth policies enacted by EMU intermediaries within their currency area. According to our results, any research investigating equity value creation through M&As in this environment will need to consider concomitant variations in stock price exposure to the market.

# 5
# M&A Activity Among Major European Banking Groups

*Roberto Bottiglia and Laura Chiaramonte*

## 5.1  Introduction

This chapter reports on the dynamics of the consolidation of major European banking groups during the period 2000–8, and provides an overview of expansion policies pursued by these groups in recent years. It also considers the impact of the subprime mortgage crisis.

The top 15 European banking groups by stock market capitalisation and total assets were included in the study. The panel comprised two Spanish, three French, three British, two Swiss, one Dutch, two Italian and two German banks.

The time horizon for the study was 2002 to 2008. There were two reasons for this choice: firstly, the desire to consider for each banking group the most recent phase of expansion, subsequent to incorporation; secondly, the difficulty in retrieving data on growth strategies for the period before 2000.

The source of data was the Zephyr database, from which it was possible to extract information on:

- deals completed by the banking groups in the study or their subsidiaries or associates, acting as bidders, with details of deal type (minority stake, majority stake, 100 per cent acquisition, acquisition to increase a stake to a given percentage, the acquisition of a remaining percentage, the acquisition of an unknown stake), deal value (in millions of euros) and deal status (completed, pending or announced). It was decided to exclude sales from deal type and to exclude rumours and withdrawn from deal status, even though such information was present in database records;
- M&A targets, with details of name, country (all countries in the world) and industry classification (banking and non-banking).

One limit of the study was information missing from the database, in particular data relating to deal value; this aspect was taken into due consideration during analysis.

Using data retrieved from Zephyr, a series of tables were created to shed light on the dynamics of external growth strategies pursued by the banking groups during the time horizon. Analysis of the tables highlighted the following aspects, at individual bank and aggregate level:

- time distribution of mergers;
- deal value and time distribution;
- deal type and frequency;
- the nature of the operation (domestic vs cross-border; sector vs cross-sector).

## 5.2  M&A activity: general aspects

On the basis of available data, a first step in the study was to consider a number of general aspects. Table 5.1 shows, for individual banks (acting as bidders) and at the aggregate level, the time distribution of M&As and deal values between 2000 and 2008.

During the construction of Table 5.1, it emerged that in many records deal values were missing; it was decided to specify, at individual and aggregate level, the number of M&As in database records with deal value shown, and the total value of such operations. It therefore became necessary to indicate in Table 5.1 for each year:

- the total number of deals (completed, pending and announced) from 2000 to 2008 involving banking and non-banking targets worldwide in which the banking groups in the study acted as bidder;
- the number of M&As with deal value shown (in brackets);
- total deal value in millions of Euros for transactions with deal value shown.

Table 5.1 indicates that the number of M&As completed by the leading European banking groups increased considerably during this period (+179 per cent), though the trend was variable rather than steady and progressive.

In particular, the number of external growth operations:

- remained virtually unchanged between 2000 and 2002 (fluctuating from a minimum of 142 to a maximum of 164 M&As per annum). The lull in activity was probably because the majority of banking groups in the study were still in the process of integrating previous acquisitions; this aspect contributed to postpone further rounds of consolidation;
- increased from 2002 to 2005 (+47 per cent). With the integration process completed, the banking groups were eager to expand into new business

sectors and geographical areas to ensure survival in an increasingly competitive environment;

- nearly doubled from 2005 to 2006 (+74 per cent). This substantial increase was due principally to the ascending importance of growth beyond national borders, and beyond the EU in particular (cross-border extra-EU M&As), in countries where the banks considered their presence inadequate;
- declined sharply in 2007 (−53 per cent compared to 2006), as a result of the subprime mortgage crisis that hit most leading European banking groups to a greater or lesser extent. Faced with a significant drop in market value and an associated reduction in potential, the banks focussed on routine management activities rather than external growth;
- made a remarkable recovery in 2008, registering the highest increase since the start of the 2000s (+134 per cent compared to 2007). Several banking groups in the study were responsible for this dynamism (BBVA, Banco Santander, BNP Paribas, Société Générale, Crédit Agricole, HSBC, Intesa SanPaolo, Deutsche Bank and Commerzbank). Despite the crisis, these groups conducted M&As at a remarkable rate, some deals in fact facilitated by the crisis. The market turmoil evidently fostered consolidation, principally in-sector acquisitions by solid, international, well-diversified institutions that were relatively unaffected by the crisis. In other cases the purpose of the deals was to stabilise the worst-hit groups, in tandem with or as an alternative to government recapitalisation plans. Of the banking groups in the study, the most adversely affected by the crisis were RBS, Barclays, Crédit Suisse and UniCredit, all forced by their well-known difficulties to reduce the pace of M&As and focus instead on rationalisation. Matters were a little different for two groups in the study, UBS and ING. Despite being seriously impacted by the subprime crisis, in 2008 these two banks successfully clinched a great number of deals, for the most part highly selective acquisitions with relatively low unit values. In this case, there was no evident link between the crisis and intensity of growth and expansion through M&As.

A final aspect revealed by analysis of Table 5.1 is the distribution and value of deals completed, pending and announced by the 15 banking groups.

Given that Zephyr does not report the deal value of all M&As, this aspect is not easy to interpret. The deal values indicated in Table 5.1 refer only to operations for which values were stated (in brackets).

Table 5.1 shows that the numerous acquisitions completed by the banking groups in the period 2000–8 were relatively low in unit value and very selective; in other words, the deals were designed to expand business in certain sectors and/or certain geographical areas. This type of behaviour was seen for most of the period, with the exception of 2000, 2004 and 2006.

*Table 5.1*  Number of M&As per year (number of M&As with deal value indicated) [deal value in millions of Euros] (2000–8)

| Groups (Country) | 2000 | 2001 | 2002 | 2003 | 2004 | 2005 | 2006 | 2007 | 2008* | Total |
|---|---|---|---|---|---|---|---|---|---|---|
| BBVA (ES) | 10 (5) [919] | 9 (8) [1,011] | 7 (6) [702] | 3 (3) [307] | 8 (3) [4,852] | 3 (1) [657] | 11 (4) [465] | 5 (2) [531] | 15 (9) [2,684] | **71 (41)** **[12,128]** |
| Banco Santander (ES) | 17 (10) [10,444] | 6 (5) [8,275] | 11 (7) [1,445] | 10 (6) [2,288] | 10 (6) [14,235] | 5 (4) [2,604] | 11 (7) [2,639] | 5 (2) [1,247] | 23 (10) [13,357] | **98 (57)** **[56,536]** |
| BNP Paribas (FR) | 9 (6) [1,363] | 8 (2) [2,867] | 20 (10) [6,333] | 16 (7) [176] | 15 (6) [1,414] | 12 (6) [360] | 27 (16) [9,219] | 5 (0) [–] | 17 (5) [296] | **129 (58)** **[22,028]** |
| Société Générale (FR) | 7 (3) [1,040] | 5 (3) [1,304] | 2 (2) [142] | 4 (1) [8] | 7 (4) [4,801] | 13 (3) [292] | 25 (5) [1,943] | 6 (2) [208] | 22 (7) [2,650] | **91 (30)** **[12,389]** |
| Crédit Agricole (FR) | 3 (2) [792] | 5 (3) [3,774] | 6 (1) [1,037] | 11 (7) [21,623] | 9 (4) [3,242] | 4 (2) [850] | 6 (2) [438] | 4 (4) [7,163] | 27 (13) [2,942] | **75 (38)** **[41,861]** |
| HSBC (UK) | 11 (5) [13,155] | 9 (8) [1,050] | 4 (3) [1,289] | 8 (7) [13,981] | 9 (5) [3,006] | 5 (2) [866] | 10 (5) [1,914] | 5 (2) [566] | 28 (12) [1,733] | **89 (49)** **[37,560]** |
| RBS (UK) | 7 (6) [4,971] | 13 (9) [2,264] | 7 (4) [234] | 8 (7) [3,036] | 10 (4) [4,719] | 9 (3) [3,200] | 5 (1) [1,376] | 6 (4) [912] | 10 (5) [1,406] | **75 (43)** **[22,117]** |
| Barclays (UK) | 2 (1) [9,344] | 4 (1) [8] | 7 (4) [1,173] | 10 (7) [1,905] | 28 (4) [3,561] | 55 (5) [1,598] | 122 (4) [1,129] | 17 (3) [226] | 18 (2) [431] | **263 (31)** **[19,375]** |
| Crédit Suisse (CH) | 12 (5) [13,885] | 9 (5) [1,071] | 4 (3) [80] | 4 (2) [3,036] | 1 (0) [–] | 5 (2) [131] | 11 (1) [399] | 22 (2) [309] | 24 (2) [64] | **92 (47)** **[18,976]** |

| | | | | | | | | | | |
|---|---|---|---|---|---|---|---|---|---|---|
| UBS (CH) | 9 (3) [37,421] | 9 (5) [611] | 6 (1) [3] | 4 (3) [82] | 7 (1) [246] | 15 (2) [27] | 33 (3) [309] | 31 (2) [70] | 56 (8) [1,077] | **170 (28)** **[39,847]** |
| ING (NE) | 17 (10) [37,119] | 18 (10) [3,049] | 18 (6) [3,455] | 12 (4) [583] | 11 (2) [258] | 16 (3) [822] | 17 (2) [29] | 12 (2) [1,609] | 40 (17) [8,648] | **161 (56)** **[55,572]** |
| Intesa SanPaolo (It) | 15 (5) [4,179] | 12 (9) [7,379] | 22 (9) [8,890] | 39 (18) [3,827] | 17 (9) [3,993] | 20 (8) [2,121] | 21 (10) [31,597] | 26 (14) [8,566] | 60 (32) [7,671] | **232 (114)** **[78,223]** |
| UniCredit (It) | 22 (14) [3,693] | 16 (11) [11,116] | 175 (14) [5,250] | 20 (11) [2,283] | 7 (1) [145] | 24 (6) [478] | 13 (7) [7,818] | 11 (2) [525] | 13 (6) [3,868] | **143 (72)** **[35,176]** |
| Deutsche Bank (DE) | 21 (11) [2,755] | 12 (4) [1,305] | 29 (13) [8,503] | 44 (21) [7,238] | 38 (6) [629] | 49 (8) [2,111] | 107(12) [2,620] | 40 (3) [2,140] | 88 (19) [8,796] | **428 (97)** **[36,099]** |
| Commerzbank (DE) | 2 (2) [1,771] | 7 (3) [39] | 4 (3) [932] | 9 (8) [1,668] | 5 (1) [28] | 7 (1) [212] | 3 (1) [124] | 1 (0) [–] | 18 (7) [2,033] | **56 (26)** **[6,808]** |
| **Total** | **164 (88)** **[142,854]** | **142 (86)** **[45,123]** | **164 (86)** **[39,468]** | **202 (112)** **[62,041]** | **182 (56)** **[45,130]** | **242 (56)** **[16,331]** | **422 (80)** **[62,019]** | **196 (44)** **[24,072]** | **459 (154)** **[57,657]** | **2,173 (787)** **[494,695]** |

* For 2008, completed, pending and announced deals were considered.
*Source*: Own processing of Zephyr Database.

These three years were characterised by mega-mergers concluded by a limited number of banking groups. Banco Santander, BNP Paribas, RBS, UBS, Intesa SanPaolo and UniCredit were involved in at least one such large-scale domestic or European cross-border deal.

## 5.3   Types of deal

A second factor to consider was the nature of the M&A operations in order to identify the most frequently used deal types and their intensity.

Table 5.2 compares, at the individual and aggregate levels, the different types of deal pursued by the banking groups to ensure growth between 2000 and 2008.

The deal types indicated in Table 5.2 refer only to modes of consolidation effectively used by the 15 banking groups in the deals analysed here. These include:

- minority stake;
- acquisition of a remaining percentage;
- 100 per cent acquisition;
- aquisition to increase a stake to a given percentage;
- majority stake;
- acquisition of an unknown stake.

From an analysis of Table 5.2 it becomes apparent that at the aggregate level, by far the most frequent deal type during the time horizon was minority stake. Of 2,173 M&As completed, pending and announced by leading European banking groups, nearly half (1,008) were minority stake deals. Lagging some way behind were: 100 per cent acquisitions (596); acquisitions to increase a stake to a given percentage (282); and majority stakes (197). Acquisitions of a remaining percentage (56) and acquisitions of an unknown stake (34) were the least common types of deal among the sample banking groups.

If the values in Table 5.2 for acquisitions to increase a stake to a given percentage (282) and acquisitions of a remaining percentage (56) are added to 100 per cent acquisitions (596), a slightly different result is obtained. In particular, the most common deal type becomes minority stakes (1008), closely followed by the other three deal types added together (934).

It is appropriate to group the three deal types given that on more than one occasion the banks gained full control of a target not through a 100 per cent acquisition but rather through a series of operations spread over a number of years designed to build up their stake to 100 per cent gradually. The same is true for acquisitions of a remaining percentage, used to gain 100 per cent control of a target.

*Table 5.2*   Deal type (2000–8)

| Groups (Country) | Minority stake | Acquisition of a remaining per cent | 100 % Acquisition | Acquisition to increase a stake to a given per cent | Majority stake | Acquisition of an unknown stake | Total |
|---|---|---|---|---|---|---|---|
| BBVA (ES) | 24 | 6 | 18 | 15 | 5 | 3 | **71** |
| Banco Santander (ES) | 32 | 6 | 26 (of which 3 mergers) | 20 | 12 | 2 | **98** |
| BNP Paribas (FR) | 47 | 6 | 38 (of which 1 merger) | 20 | 11 | 7 | **129** |
| Société Générale (FR) | 41 | 1 | 21 | 10 | 18 | 0 | **91** |
| Crédit Agricole (FR) | 32 | 1 | 17 | 16 | 9 | 0 | **75** |
| HSBC (UK) | 17 | 2 | 47 | 14 | 8 | 1 | **89** |
| RBS (UK) | 23 | 0 | 46 | 3 | 2 | 1 | **75** |
| Barclays (UK) | 209 | 0 | 39 | 9 | 5 | 1 | **263** |
| Crédit Suisse (CH) | 37 | 2 | 37 (of which 3 mergers) | 2 | 9 | 5 | **92** |
| UBS (CH) | 111 | 4 | 40 (of which 1 merger) | 10 | 4 | 1 (merger) | **170** |
| ING (NE) | 24 | 7 | 99 | 17 | 10 | 4 | **161** |
| Intesa SanPaolo (It) | 105 | 5 | 39 | 46 | 36 | 1 | **232** |
| UniCredit (It) | 25 | 7 | 34 (of which 2 mergers) | 51 | 23 | 3 | **143** |
| Deutsche Bank (DE) | 250 | 9 | 85 (of which 1 merger) | 42 | 39 | 3 | **428** |
| Commerzbank (DE) | 31 | 0 | 10 | 7 | 6 | 2 | **56** |
| **Total** | **1,008** | **56** | **596** | **282** | **197** | **34** | **2,173** |

*Source*: Own processing of Zephyr Database.

If we now proceed to examine the deal types for each banking group from 2000 to 2008, Table 5.2 shows a combination of consolidation modes for all groups. Although this indicates a tendency to exploit the full range of deal types available, from 100 per cent acquisitions to minority and majority stakes, two deal types were particularly significant:

- minority stakes, a deal type used inevitably in countries with legal restrictions still in force that are only now opening up to international competition. This is the case in the emerging countries of the Middle and Far East, where many of the 15 banking groups completed a significant number of deals, as indicated below. On several occasions minority stakes were acquired in emerging countries, since this type of deal lends itself to gradual market penetration, and allows stable relationships to be established as a prelude to closer and more complex forms of integration and consolidation;
- 100 per cent acquisitions, a deal type used on more than one occasion in mega-mergers, principally domestic or international sector mergers. As the data indicate, the majority of the banking groups pursuing strategic external growth through large-scale operations opted for 100 per cent acquisitions. However, important M&As were also completed with other, less frequently-used deal types used, such as majority stakes or acquisition of a remaining per cent.

In future, when the banks have recovered from the difficulties of the recent crisis, the widespread recourse to minority stakes and 100 per cent acquisitions seen in the period 2000–8 seems likely to decrease. In the aftermath of the crisis, external growth policies are likely to be oriented principally towards strategic alliances and cooperation projects in specific business sectors or types of country.

## 5.4   Cross-border and cross-sector activities

Proceeding to a more detailed analysis of specific aspects, Tables 5.3 and 5.4 contain data on types of growth activity from 2000 to 2008.

Table 5.3 shows domestic and cross-border (intra- or extra-EU) deals by the banking groups, while Table 5.4 displays sector and cross-sector deals for

*Table 5.3*   Domestic vs cross-border M&As (2000–8)

| Groups (Country) | Domestic M&A | Cross-border intra-EU M&A | Cross-border extra-EU M&A |
|---|---|---|---|
| BBVA (ES) | 23 | 11 | 37 |
| Banco Santander (ES) | 23 | 34 | 41 |
| BNP Paribas (FR) | 31 | 58 | 40 |
| Société Générale (FR) | 25 | 29 | 37 |
| Crédit Agricole (FR) | 27 | 33 | 15 |
| HSBC (UK) | 20 | 27 | 42 |
| RBS (UK) | 47 | 16 | 12 |

(*Continued*)

*Table 5.3* *(Continued)*

| Groups (Country) | Domestic M&A | Cross-border intra-EU M&A | Cross-border extra-EU M&A |
|---|---|---|---|
| Barclays (UK) | 207 | 34 | 22 |
| Crédit Suisse (CH) | 22 | 0 | 70 |
| UBS (CH) | 21 | 0 | 149 |
| ING (NL) | 33 | 69 | 59 |
| Intesa SanPaolo (It) | 168 | 29 | 35 |
| UniCredit (It) | 55 | 65 | 23 |
| Deutsche Bank (DE) | 55 | 246 | 127 |
| Commerzbank (DE) | 15 | 24 | 17 |
| **Total** | **772** | **675** | **726** |

*Source*: Own processing of Zephyr Database.

*Table 5.4*  Sector vs cross-sector M&As (2000–8)

| Groups (Country) | Sector M&A | Cross-sector M&A |
|---|---|---|
| BBVA (ES) | 48 | 23 |
| Banco Santander (ES) | 62 | 36 |
| BNP Paribas (FR) | 64 | 65 |
| Société Générale (FR) | 33 | 58 |
| Crédit Agricole (FR) | 35 | 40 |
| HSBC (UK) | 45 | 44 |
| RBS (UK) | 9 | 66 |
| Barclays (UK) | 34 | 229 |
| Crédit Suisse (CH) | 21 | 71 |
| UBS (CH) | 44 | 126 |
| ING (NL) | 29 | 132 |
| Intesa SanPaolo (It) | 151 | 81 |
| UniCredit (It) | 92 | 51 |
| Deutsche Bank (DE) | 88 | 340 |
| Commerzbank (DE) | 30 | 26 |
| **Total** | **785** | **1,388** |

*Source*: Own processing of Zephyr Database.

each bank. Combined analysis of the tables makes it possible to capture, at individual and aggregate level, the geographical and business expansion strategies pursued by the banking groups. Further information on industry classification and country of target is contained in subsequent tables for a more complete and accurate vision of M&A types used.

Table 5.3 illustrates how at an aggregate level, the banks pursued geographical expansion principally through cross-border operations, and only to a lesser extent through domestic operations during the time horizon. This reflects the maturity of domestic markets and the limited growth opportunities associated with maturity. More than half of the 2,173 M&As performed by the 15 banking groups from 2000 to 2008 were cross-border deals (1,401), compared to only 772 domestic deals. The 1,401 cross-border M&As were fairly evenly distributed between intra-EU deals involving banks from different EU countries (675) and the slightly higher number of extra-EU deals involving EU and non-EU groups (726). Bank intermediaries based in Europe, attracted by promising growth prospects and less stringent regulations on bank ownership structure, directed their attention towards Rest of Europe, North America, Latin America or Asia Pacific. This aspect will be explored in detail later.

Growth objectives were pursued across national borders, and in particular beyond the EU (cross-border extra-EU deals) by several banking groups with a significant international dimension, including BBVA, Banco Santander, Société Générale, Crédit Suisse, UBS and HSBC. Similarly, ING, Deutsche Bank, BNP Paribas, UniCredit, Crédit Agricole and Commerzbank showed a clear preference for cross-border deals over domestic deals, despite concluding more cross-border intra-EU M&As than extra-EU M&As.

Three banks were an exception to the general trend. In the period 2000–8 RBS, Barclays and Intesa SanPaolo pursued a geographical strategy diametrically opposed to that of the other banks in the study. In particular, they sought growth through domestic rather than cross-border deals, focussing principally on the home market. All three completed a higher number of domestic M&As than cross-border M&As; this focus on the domestic market was not however incompatible with a widespread international presence (Barclays) or significant cross-border acquisitions (see the disastrous RBS takeover of ABN AMRO).

The domestic and cross-border deals indicated in Table 5.3 relate to total M&As on banking (sector) and non-banking (cross-sector) targets. Table 5.4 provides information on the number of sector and cross-sector deals completed by the 15 banks from 2000 to 2008, though there is no breakdown of domestic and cross-border (intra- and extra-EU) activities. Further details of these aspects are shown in later tables.

From Table 5.4 it emerges that the majority of banking groups sought to diversify through cross-sector rather than sector deals. More than half of the 2,173 M&As carried out by the banks during the time horizon involved non-banking targets (1,388). M&As on banks (sector) totalled 785.

Growth strategies in non-banking sectors were pursued, to varying degrees, by several banks: Société Générale, RBS, Barclays, Crédit Suisse, UBS, ING and Deutsche Bank. On the other hand, the M&A activities of BNP Paribas, Crédit Agricole, HSBC and Commerzbank were more evenly balanced between sector and cross-sector deals. Finally, the growth strategies of BBVA, Banco Santander, Intesa SanPaolo and UniCredit focused principally on banking targets, evidence of a preference for more traditional types of business. For the latter banks the number of sector M&As was significantly higher than cross-sector deals, in contrast with the general tendency at an aggregate level.

Table 5.5 provides more detailed information on domestic M&As by the banks in the study, and in particular the distribution of deals between sector and cross-sector.

*Table 5.5*   Domestic sector and cross-sector M&As (2000–8)

| Groups (Country) | Banks | Insurance | Asset Management & Wealth Management | Investment Services | Consumer Finance | Specialty Finance | Other |
|---|---|---|---|---|---|---|---|
| BBVA (ES) | 11 | 7 | – | 1 | – | – | 4 |
| Banco Santander (ES) | 9 | 6 | – | 3 | – | 1 | 4 |
| BNP Paribas (FR) | 12 | 5 | – | 3 | 4 | 1 | 6 |
| Société Générale (FR) | 7 | – | 4 | – | – | – | 14 |
| Crédit Agricole (FR) | 4 | 9 | 1 | 2 | – | – | 11 |
| HSBC (UK) | 2 | – | – | 4 | 1 | 2 | 11 |
| RBS (UK) | 1 | 5 | 2 | 4 | 1 | 1 | 33 |
| Barclays (UK) | 18 | 59 | 14 | 6 | 20 | 1 | 89 |
| Crédit Suisse (CH) | 4 | 3 | 3 | – | – | – | 12 |
| UBS (CH) | 5 | 1 | 1 | – | – | – | 14 |
| ING (NL) | 3 | 6 | 1 | 4 | – | – | 19 |
| Intesa SanPaolo (It) | 106 | 11 | 4 | 15 | 2 | – | 30 |
| UniCredit (It) | 26 | 5 | – | 12 | 5 | 1 | 6 |
| Deutsche Bank (DE) | 7 | 9 | 3 | 4 | 3 | – | 29 |
| Commerzbank (DE) | 5 | – | 1 | – | 2 | – | 7 |
| Total | 220 | 126 | 34 | 58 | 38 | 7 | 289 |

*Source*: Own processing of Zephyr Database.

Data from the Zephyr database on the industry classification of targets made it possible to divide domestic deals into two groups:

1   M&As on bank targets (sector M&As);
2   M&As on non-banking targets (cross-sector M&As). To facilitate analysis and provide a more precise and complete picture of alternative targets, the six main non-bank activities that attracted the interest of the majority of the banking groups were identified as: (1) Insurance; (2) Asset Management & Wealth Management, including Non-equity Investment Instruments; (3) Investment Services; (4) Consumer Finance, including also Consumer Services and Mortgage Finance; (5) Speciality Finance; (6) Other, comprising activities not included in the previous categories, such as for example Real Estate and Information Technology.

From analysis of Table 5.5 it emerges that, as seen above, at an aggregate level domestic deals were principally cross-sector. More than half of the M&As undertaken by the 15 banks during this period (772) involved non-banking (552) rather than banking targets (220).

A preference for domestic consolidation through cross-sector rather than sector deals was by all the banks in the study to a greater or lesser extent, and was particularly strong in the case of two British banks, Barclays and RBS, the German Deutsche Bank and the Dutch ING conglomerate. As the data in Table 5.5 indicate, the business strategies implemented within national borders by these four banks had a significant impact on the aggregate number of domestic cross-sector M&As during the time horizon. Other banks in the study clearly favoured non-banking targets in their domestic M&A activities, including Société Générale, Crédit Agricole, HSBC, Crédit Suisse and UBS. For groups such as BBVA, Banco Santander, BNP Paribas, UniCredit and Commerzbank, the difference between the number of cross-sector and sector deals was insignificant.

The behaviour of one bank was entirely different. Intesa SanPaolo chose not only to focus on the domestic market but also showed a clear preference for banking targets: of the 168 M&As concluded within national borders, 106 were sector deals while only 62 were cross-sector deals.

Thanks to detailed information in Table 5.5 on the various non-banking targets acquired by the banking groups in the study, it was possible to identify which sectors were the focus of domestic cross-sector M&As during this period.

In particular, it can be seen from Table 5.5 that the 552 domestic cross-sector deals principally involved targets operating in the sectors Other (289) and Insurance (126), followed at a distance by Investment Services (58); Consumer Finance (38) and Asset Management & Wealth Management (34). A very limited number of domestic cross-sector M&As were seen on Specialty Finance targets (7).

Such behaviour was typical of a number of banking groups, particularly Barclays, which, as is shown by Table 5.5, had the highest level of diversification on the domestic market, despite the centrality of Other and Insurance. Table 5.5 reveals also that Barclays' high level of diversification into non-banking sectors had a significant impact on aggregate data.

However, Barclays was not the only bank in the study to adopt a strategy of broad diversification on the domestic market over the period under review. Other banks – BNP Paribas, RBS, Deutsche Bank, Intesa SanPaolo and UniCredit – pursued targets in a wide range of non-banking sectors, showing varying degrees of preference for Insurance and Other. The two Italian banks were typified by frequent domestic M&As, some on targets in Investment Services.

The domestic growth strategies of the remaining banking groups focussed almost exclusively on targets in Insurance and/or Other sectors. A very limited number of transactions involved Investment Services (BBVA, Banco Santander, Crédit Agricole, HSBC and ING); Asset Management & Wealth Management (Société Générale, Crédit Suisse and UBS); or Consumer Finance (Commerzbank).

Table 5.6 presents data on cross-border intra-EU M&As in the period 2000–8.

For each of the 15 banks in the study, the following information on targets is specified:

1  Country of origin (Western Europe or Eastern Europe);
2  Industry classification, with a distinction between banking (cross-border intra-EU sector) and non-banking deals (cross-border, intra-EU cross-sector). The non-banking sectors are those highlighted in Table 5.5 (Insurance; Asset Management & Wealth Management; Investment Services; Consumer Finance; Specialty Finance and Other).

From the analysis of Table 5.6, it can be seen that at an aggregate level the cross-border intra-EU deals concluded by the banking groups in the study were principally cross-sector. More than half of the 675 consolidation operations involved non-banking targets (407); the remainder were banking targets (268).

Only a small minority of banks in the study conducted more cross-border intra-EU cross-sector M&As than sector M&As. Nevertheless, these cross-sector transactions had a significant impact on aggregate data.

In particular, Table 5.6 reveals three different types of behavioural approach to cross-border intra-UE sector and cross-sector M&As:

1  banks with a marked propensity for non-banking targets, such as Deutsche Bank, ING, Société Générale and Barclays. Of these four, the German Deutsche Bank and the Dutch ING stand out for their strategic orientation towards cross-sector M&As;

*Table 5.6*  Cross-border intra-EU sector and cross-sector M&As (2000–8)

| Groups (Country) | Banks | | Insurance | | Asset Management & Wealth Management | | Investment Services | | Consumer Finance | | Specialty Finance | | Other | |
| --- | --- | --- | --- | --- | --- | --- | --- | --- | --- | --- | --- | --- | --- | --- |
| | WE | EE | WE | EE | WE | EE | WE | EE | WE | EE | WE | EE | WE | EE |
| BBVA (ES) | 6 | – | 1 | – | 1 | – | – | – | 3 | – | – | – | – | – |
| Banco Santander (ES) | 23 | 3 | 2 | – | – | – | – | – | 4 | – | – | – | 2 | – |
| BNP Paribas (FR) | 25 | 4 | 5 | – | – | – | 11 | – | 2 | 2 | 2 | – | 6 | 1 |
| Société Générale (FR) | 7 | 3 | 1 | – | 4 | – | – | – | – | – | – | – | 14 | – |
| Crédit Agricole (FR) | 19 | 2 | 6 | – | – | – | 3 | – | – | – | – | – | 3 | – |
| HSBC (UK) | 12 | 5 | – | – | 5 | – | 1 | – | – | 1 | 1 | – | 2 | – |
| RBS (UK) | 5 | 1 | 2 | – | – | – | 1 | – | 1 | – | 1 | – | 5 | – |
| Barclays (UK) | 9 | – | 4 | – | 2 | – | 5 | – | 1 | – | – | – | 13 | – |
| Crédit Suisse (CH) | – | – | – | – | – | – | – | – | – | – | – | – | – | – |
| UBS (CH) | – | – | – | – | – | – | – | – | – | – | – | – | – | – |
| ING (NL) | 13 | 4 | 3 | 1 | 2 | 2 | 5 | – | 3 | – | – | 3 | 30 | 3 |
| Intesa SanPaolo (It) | 9 | 12 | – | – | – | – | 3 | – | – | – | – | 1 | 4 | – |
| UniCredit (It) | 18 | 28 | 1 | 1 | – | – | 5 | – | 1 | 1 | 3 | 4 | 2 | 1 |
| Deutsche Bank (DE) | 31 | 17 | 33 | 3 | 11 | 1 | 29 | 2 | 2 | – | 1 | – | 108 | 8 |
| Commerzbank (DE) | 85 | 4 | 3 | – | 3 | – | 4 | – | – | – | – | – | 2 | – |
| **Total** | **185** | **83** | **61** | **5** | **28** | **3** | **67** | **2** | **17** | **4** | **8** | **8** | **191** | **13** |

*Source*: Own processing of Zephyr Database.

2  banks with a distinct preference banking targets, such as Banco Santander, Crédit Agricole, HSBC, Intesa SanPaolo and UniCredit;
3  banks with an even balance of sector and cross-sector cross-border intra-EU M&As, such as BBVA, BNP Paribas, RBS and Commerzbank.

The two Swiss banks (Crédit Suisse and UBS) are absent from Table 5.6 given that cross-border M&As are defined as transactions involving one EU operator and one non-EU operator.

The detailed data on country and industry classification of targets shown in Table 5.6 made it possible to specify:

- for cross-border intra-EU sector M&As, the geographical area in which the banks in the study concentrated the highest number of deals (Western Europe or Eastern Europe);
- for cross-border intra-EU cross-sector M&As, the geographical area (Western or Eastern Europe) and the sector (Insurance; Asset Management & Wealth Management; Investment Services; Consumer Finance; Specialty Finance and Other).

In terms of cross-border intra-EU sector M&As, at aggregate level more than half of the 268 external growth operations pursued by the banking groups (185) related to banking targets headquartered in Western Europe, while only 85 involved banks based in Eastern Europe. This preference for M&As on banks in Western rather than Eastern Europe was common to all the banks in the study to a greater or lesser extent, with two exceptions: the Italian banks Intesa SanPaolo and UniCredit, both of which showed a keen interest in the Eastern European banking market. Conversely, BBVA and Barclays did not complete a single acquisition in Eastern Europe, all their targets being based in Western Europe.

In terms of cross-sector intra-EU cross-border deals, at an aggregate level it can be seen that the 407 transactions completed by banks in the study principally concerned targets in Western Europe (372). Of these, 191 deals related to targets in Other, followed at some distance by Investment Services (67) and Insurance (61). There were considerably fewer acquisitions of targets headquartered in Western Europe operating in Asset Management & Wealth Management (28), Consumer Finance (17) or Specialty Finance (7).

Only 35 cross-sector intra-EU cross-border M&As were completed on targets in Eastern Europe. These deals involved companies in the sectors Other (13) and Speciality Finance (8), followed by Insurance (5); Consumer Finance (4); Asset Management & Wealth Management (3) and finally Investment Services (2).

Aggregate results on strategic choices at a geographical and business level relating to cross-border intra-EU cross-sector deals do not necessarily reflect the behaviour of all the banking groups in the study. Specifically, in the case of cross-border intra-EU cross-sector M&As by individual banking groups, it can be seen that:

1  only a limited number of banks actually conformed to behaviour at an aggregate level, in both geographical and business terms, by focussing on targets in Western Europe in Other, Investment Services and Insurance, and targets in Eastern Europe in Other and Speciality Finance. Examples of such banks are Deutsche Bank, ING, BNP Paribas and UniCredit;

2  a significant number of banking groups preferred cross-sector cross-border intra-EU deals involving targets in Western Europe. These included BBVA, Banco Santander, Société Générale, Crédit Agricole, RBS, Barclays, and Commerzbank. HSBC and Intesa SanPaolo completed only one deal on an Eastern European target from 2000 to 2008. The preferred business sectors of these banks were diversified and included Other, Insurance, Investment Services, Asset Management & Wealth Management and Consumer Finance.

## 5.5   Geographical diversification

Finally, in order to capture the more innovative and complex aspects of M&A activities, it is useful to take a closer look at international transactions (extra-EU). The two following tables (Tables 5.7 and 5.8) provide information on cross-border extra-EU deals by the banking groups in the study between 2000 and 2008.

In particular, Table 5.7 highlights the geographical areas in which growth operations were concentrated: Europe, North America, Latin America, Africa and Asia Pacific. For a correct interpretation of results, note that for all except the two Swiss groups (Crédit Suisse and UBS), Europe refers to all non-EU European countries, whereas for Crédit Suisse and UBS, Europe includes all European countries.

Table 5.8 focuses on the industry classification of cross-border extra-EU targets, distinguishing between acquisitions of banking (cross-border extra-EU sector deals) and non-banking targets (cross-border extra-EU cross-sector deals). The non-banking business sectors are those identified in Tables 5.5 and 5.6.

Combined analysis of the two tables is required to capture at aggregate and at individual level the geographical diversification of M&A strategies during the time horizon.

From Table 5.7 it becomes evident that at an aggregate level, the banks in the study tended to pursue cross-border extra-EU growth strategies principally in Europe (264), although a significant number of deals were concluded also in Asia Pacific (195), Latin America (122) and North America (115). The number of M&As involving targets based in Africa (just 30) was significantly lower.

*Table 5.7*   Geographic and territorial diversification of cross-border extra-EU M&As (2000–8)

| Groups (Country) | Europe | North America | Latin America | Africa | Asia - Pacific |
|---|---|---|---|---|---|
| BBVA (ES) | 1 | 5 | 24 | 2 | 5 |
| BSCH (ES) | 1 | 11 | 25 | 1 | 3 |
| BNP Paribas (FR) | 11 | 13 | 2 | 2 | 12 |
| Société Générale (FR) | 16 | 8 | 4 | 5 | 4 |
| Crédit Agricole (FR) | 2 | 1 | 3 | 4 | 5 |
| HSBC (UK) | 1 | 5 | 17 | 2 | 17 |
| RBS (UK) | 2 | 5 | – | – | 5 |
| Barclays (UK) | 3 | 4 | 5 | 4 | 6 |
| Crédit Suisse (CH) | 46 | 10 | 2 | 2 | 10 |
| UBS (CH) | 112 | 13 | 2 | 1 | 21 |
| ING (NL) | 5 | 13 | 17 | – | 24 |
| Intesa SanPaolo (It) | 14 | 4 | 11 | 1 | 5 |
| UniCredit (It) | 21 | 1 | – | – | 1 |
| Deutsche Bank (DE) | 24 | 19 | 8 | 2 | 74 |
| Commerzbank (DE) | 5 | 3 | 2 | 4 | 3 |
| Total | 264 | 115 | 122 | 30 | 195 |

*Source*: Own processing of Zephyr Database.

Detailed examination of Table 5.7 based on an analysis of international expansion policies pursued by each bank during the study period reveals that:

- the majority of the European banking groups oriented cross-border extra-EU growth strategies towards the geographical areas listed above, with a strong focus on specific areas, showing a marked propensity for international diversification. This was true of BBVA, Banco Santander, BNP Paribas, Société Générale, HSBC, Barclays, Crédit Suisse, UBS, ING, Deutsche Bank and Commerzbank;
- a minority of banks in the study had a small yet growing international presence. For certain banks, this was justified by their strategic focus on the domestic market (Intesa SanPaolo and RBS), while for others the thrust was towards intra-EU rather than extra-EU expansion (Crédit Agricole and UniCredit). Intesa SanPaolo, RBS, Crédit Agricole and

*Table 5.8*  Cross-border extra-EU sector and cross-sector M&As (2000–8)

| Groups (Country) | Banks | Insurance | Asset Management & Wealth Management | Investment Services | Consumer Finance | Specialty Finance | Other |
|---|---|---|---|---|---|---|---|
| BBVA (ES) | 31 | 2 | 3 | – | 1 | – | – |
| Banco Santander (ES) | 29 | 4 | 1 | 3 | 1 | 1 | 2 |
| BNP Paribas (FR) | 24 | 1 | 6 | 2 | 1 | 2 | 4 |
| Société Générale (FR) | 20 | 2 | 3 | – | 2 | – | 10 |
| Crédit Agricole (FR) | 10 | – | 1 | 2 | – | – | 2 |
| HSBC (UK) | 26 | 2 | 5 | 3 | 2 | – | 4 |
| RBS (UK) | 2 | 1 | – | 2 | 2 | 1 | 4 |
| Barclays (UK) | 7 | 4 | – | 2 | 2 | – | 7 |
| Crédit Suisse (CH) | 19 | 20 | 8 | 12 | 2 | – | 9 |
| UBS (CH) | 43 | 28 | 6 | 35 | – | – | 37 |
| ING (NL) | 9 | 26 | 4 | 1 | – | 2 | 17 |
| Intesa SanPaolo (It) | 29 | 1 | 1 | 2 | – | – | 2 |
| UniCredit (It) | 20 | – | 1 | 1 | – | – | 1 |
| Deutsche Bank (DE) | 33 | 10 | 11 | 12 | 5 | – | 56 |
| Commerzbank (DE) | 14 | – | 2 | – | – | – | 1 |
| **Total** | **316** | **101** | **52** | **77** | **18** | **6** | **156** |

*Source*: Own processing of Zephyr Database.

UniCredit were characterised by a moderate level of international diversification.

The banking groups with a strong international dimension did not necessarily pursue M&As in the same geographical areas. In fact, Table 5.7 shows that:

- the two Spanish banks BBVA and Banco Santander showed a clear propensity to invest in the Central and South American markets during the time horizon, with important recent developments in the US, and in the case of BBVA, also in China;
- the French bank BNP Paribas and the two German banks Deutsche Bank and Commerzbank all had a well-established presence in the US and a strong, though recent interest in the emerging markets of Eastern Europe, Asia and the Middle East;
- the French bank Société Générale focused principally on non-EU Eastern European countries, and only recently stepped up the pace of expansion in Africa and the emerging market countries in Asia and South America;
- the British bank HSBC and the Dutch bank ING were typified by a well-established presence in several countries, particularly in the Far East and the Americas. Both banks were strongly oriented also towards expansion in emerging-market countries, particularly in Asia, and further development of the Latin American market;
- the British bank Barclays, despite firm roots in the domestic market, was characterised by geographical and territorial diversification, and a distinctive presence on the African market;
- the two Swiss banks, Crédit Suisse and UBS, were characterised by a widespread presence in Europe (Italy, Germany, France and the United Kingdom) as well as their preference for the US and the principal emerging-market countries of the Asia Pacific region.

A final detail worthy of note was the limited international diversification of several banking groups in the study. In fact, RBS, Intesa SanPaolo, UniCredit and Crédit Agricole showed a clear preference for growth though domestic or cross-border intra-EU deals. In particular, it can be seen from Table 5.7 that:

- RBS had firm roots in the domestic market, and a very limited international presence, principally on the US market and only more recently in the emerging countries of Asia;
- the Italian banking group Intesa SanPaolo was still suffering the negative effects of it strong geographical focus on the domestic market, and consequently, its limited diversification, almost exclusively in Eastern Europe;

- the Italian UniCredit Group stood out above all for its remarkable diversification at a European level, the result of a clear preference for intra-EU deals over extra-EU deals, coupled with a clear strategic orientation towards emerging markets in Eastern Europe;
- the French group Crédit Agricole, having concentrated on intra-EU rather than extra-EU cross-border deals, was distinguished by its significant presence on the European market. At an international level, the group had a relevant presence only in Africa.

Using the information on industry classification contained in Table 5.8, it was possible to highlight the extra-EU distribution of sector and cross-sector deals, and for cross-sector deals, the business areas in which the banking groups pursued growth strategies between 2000 and 2008.

Table 5.8 indicates that at an aggregate level the cross-border extra-EU deals by the banks in the study were principally cross-sector. More than half of the total deals during the time horizon (726) involved non-banking targets (410), compared to the relatively smaller number of banking targets (316). Although such behaviour was typical of only a minority of banking groups in the study, this minority had a significant impact on aggregate results.

In particular, further analysis of Table 5.8 makes it possible to divide the banks into two groups according to the strategies pursued:

1 on the one hand, banks that showed a clear preference for acquisition of non-banking targets, such as Deutsche Bank, ING, UBS, Crédit Suisse, Barclays and RBS. Of the six, four in particular stand out: the German Deutsche Bank, the Dutch ING and the two Swiss banks, Crédit Suisse and UBS;
2 on the other hand, banks that opted prevalently for banking targets, such as BBVA, Banco Santander, BNP Paribas, Société Générale, Crédit Agricole, HSBC, Intesa SanPaolo, UniCredit and Commerzbank. Of these nine, the two Spanish groups BBVA and Banco Santander, the two Italian groups Intesa SanPaolo and UniCredit and the German bank all showed a clear preference for banking targets.

In terms of business activity, two sectors attracted the majority of cross-border extra-EU deals. More than half of international cross-sector transactions (410) involved targets operating in Other (156) and Insurance (101), well ahead of Investment Services (77) and Asset Management & Wealth Management (52). A very limited number of cross-border extra-EU deals involved targets in Consumer Finance (18) and Speciality Finance (6).

Aggregate results on the types of international business strategies pursued by the banks in the study were representative of groups with a greater propensity towards the acquisition of non-banking targets (Deutsche Bank,

ING, UBS, Crédit Suisse, Barclays and RBS). The high degree of business diversification of Deutsche Bank, ING, Crédit Suisse and UBS had a significant impact on aggregate data, despite the evident centrality of Other, Insurance, Investment Services and Asset Management & Wealth Management.

## 5.6  Conclusions

The study showed that during the period 2000–8 consolidations played a fundamental role in the growth of the 15 banking groups, particularly operations across national borders. Through their M&A activities the banks were able to diversify strategic objectives in terms of business activities and/or geographical location, albeit to a varying extent.

During the time horizon, a common feature was the brisk pace of acquisitions and the wide range of deal types and purposes, though all the banking groups demonstrated a clear preference for minority stakes and 100 per cent acquisitions.

Certain differences emerged in strategic set-ups, in terms of geographical locations and business sector, reflecting the diverse origins and histories of the groups. Groups with a strong international dimension contrasted with a minority of institutions firmly rooted in the domestic market; some banks were clearly oriented towards cross-sector M&As within and across national borders, whilst others showed a clear preference for domestic and cross-border sector deals.

Recently, the pursuit of external growth strategies by the major European banking groups has been affected by the subprime mortgage crisis. Data analysis highlighted how M&A behaviour during the 2007–8 crisis was by no means uniform, probably because not all the 15 banking groups were affected to the same extent.

At an aggregate level, however, despite the recent turmoil, the banking groups in the study continued to pursue M&A activities. A number of deals were facilitated by the crisis; some were highly selective, with a relatively low unit value (acquisitions by UBS and ING), whereas others were mega-deals (the acquisition of Fortis by BNP Paribas, Dresdner by Commerzbank and the Lloyds–HBOS merger).

From a long-term perspective, it is very unlikely that the major European banking groups will be able to maintain the same growth and the same dynamism. In particular, the ability of the banks in the study to continue expansion at least in part through acquisitions of large banking or finance groups in the EU or beyond appears to depend ultimately on their exposure to the subprime crisis. It is too soon to gauge with accuracy the permanent impact of the financial crisis on external growth strategies. However, three developments are plausible: (1) the worst-hit banking groups (including RBS, UBS, Crédit Suisse, ING and to a certain extent Commerzbank and UniCredit), some renowned for past mega-mergers, are unlikely to continue to play a leading role on the European merger scene, other than in domestic consolidation operations imposed by public authorities; (2) groups less affected by the crisis (at present BBVA, Banco Santander, BNP Paribas, HSBC, Intesa SanPaolo) will enjoy greater opportunities for large-scale expansion; (3) in general, the banks seem destined to focus on selective growth in specific geographical areas or business sectors, or on rationalisation operations.

# 6
# Financial Crisis and Ownership of Global Banks

*Roberto Bottiglia and Andrea Paltrinieri*

## 6.1   Introduction

The aim of this chapter is to analyse the shareholder structure of the major European and American banking groups, with particular emphasis on the period surrounding the subprime mortgage crisis and the subsequent recapitalisation initiatives undertaken by Sovereign Wealth Funds (SWFs) and national governments.

SWFs are financial investment vehicles owned by sovereign states that hold, manage and administer public funds, specifically current-account surpluses generated by exports of raw materials and energy (International Monetary Fund (IMF), 2008). By exploiting increases in raw material prices or strong export capabilities, these entities have accumulated substantial liquidity to invest in financial instruments (Balding, 2008), including equity participations in major international banks.

Equity investments in banks by SWFs are destined to modify significantly the flow of liquidity available to intermediaries and to the global financial system. This is the picture beginning to emerge from the currently scarce literature in this field (Kern, 2007; Moshirian, 2008); the massive recapitalisation programmes implemented by national governments in response to the crisis will have similarly far-reaching implications.

The purpose of this study was to assess the shareholder structure of major banks in the principal nations in the light of equity acquisitions by SWFs and government recapitalisation measures.

The choice of observation period (June–December 2008) was motivated by the fact that the impact of most private and state recapitalisation operations was substantially marginal until mid-June, and affected only a restricted number of banking groups in the study.

The study analysed the 44 most important global banking groups in terms of capitalisation (at 30 June 2008) and total assets (end of 2007). Twenty-three groups are based in Europe, 18 in the United States and Canada, and three in Japan. One smaller bank, Standard Chartered, was also included following the massive recapitalisation of the group by SWFs.

The source of data at 30 June 2008 was Bankscope, a database that provides detailed information on:

- controlling/strategic holdings vs float;
- type of shareholders, for example bank, employees/managers, financial company, foundation/research, industrial company, insurance company, mutual and pension fund, private equity firms, self-owned shares, individuals and families and state-public authority;
- country of origin of shareholders.

With use, three limitations of the database became apparent: (1) the exact percentage of shares held by the various investor types sometimes conflicted with data in the public domain; (2) certain ambiguities related to the classification of investor types. For example, the state-public authority category included both government shareholdings and SWF shareholdings; in the same way, the importance of the foundation/research category varied from one country to the next; (3) in some cases the nationality of certain shareholder categories, such as individuals and families, and self-owned shares, was missing.

Because of the different meanings of the various investor types, it was decided to re-group the data as follows:

- the categories insurance company, mutual and pension fund, and private equity firms were reaggregated into asset managers;
- the categories employees/managers, and individuals and families were considered a residual category (others).

One further reaggregation of data was performed with respect to geographical area, in view of the numerous different countries of origin of shareholders. The resulting areas were Europe, North America, Middle East, Far East and Oceania.

In the few cases of missing information on shareholders' country of origin, shareholdings were excluded from the total.

In order to analyse bank recapitalisations by SWFs, data were retrieved from a variety of sources: newspaper articles, press releases from the various banking groups, papers on SWFs, documents and publications from banking associations, central banks and authorities. Capital injections from SWFs were included in private recapitalisations for two reasons. Although SWFs are state investment vehicles: (1) their country of origin differed from the home country of the banks in the study; (2) SWF intervention was not designed to rescue financial institutions but rather to maximise yields in exactly the same way as any other institutional investor.

Government recapitalisation measures were reconstructed through aggregation of data from US and UK Treasury websites, from a Mediobanca document of 24 October 2008 (Mediobanca, 2008) from a Clifford Chance document of 7 November 2008 (Clifford Change, 2008) and from press releases issued by the banking groups.

## 6.2   Shareholder typology

A first aspect that deserves consideration is the share of capital owned by institutional investors (controlling/strategic holdings) in relation to free float, defined as the total value of equity held by small private shareholders. Table 6.1 shows for individual banks the percentage ratio of controlling/strategic holdings to free float on the market.

*Table 6.1*   Controlling/strategic holdings vs float (June 2008)

| Bank | Controlling/strategic holding (%) | Float (%) |
| --- | --- | --- |
| Fortis | 49.52 | 50.48 |
| Dexia | 92.84 | 7.16 |
| KBC | 68.76 | 31.24 |
| Royal Bank of Canada | 50.63 | 49.37 |
| Toronto Dominion Bank | 64.92 | 35.08 |
| Danske Bank | 81.58 | 18.42 |
| BNP Paribas | 67.92 | 32.08 |
| Crédit Agricole | 72.68 | 27.32 |
| Société Générale | 69.75 | 30.25 |
| Deutsche Bank | 50.60 | 49.40 |
| Commerzbank | 66.25 | 33.75 |
| UniCredit | 59.24 | 40.76 |
| Intesa SanPaolo | 73.07 | 26.93 |
| MPS | 97.45 | 2.55 |
| Mitsubishi UFJ | 34.88 | 65.12 |
| Mizhuo | 33.91 | 66.09 |
| Sumitomo Mitsui | 44.80 | 55.20 |
| ING Group | 78.40 | 21.60 |
| Banco Santander | 59.40 | 40.60 |
| BBVA | 46.41 | 53.59 |
| Nordea Bank | 78.51 | 21.49 |
| UBS | 53.81 | 46.19 |
| Crédit Suisse | 62.63 | 37.37 |
| Royal Bank of Scotland | 70.64 | 29.36 |

(*Continued*)

*Table 6.1   (Continued)*

| Bank | Controlling/strategic holding (%) | Float (%) |
| --- | --- | --- |
| Barclays | 77.58 | 22.42 |
| HSBC | 54.08 | 45.92 |
| HBOS | 80.39 | 19.61 |
| Lloyds TSB | 65.98 | 34.02 |
| Citigroup | 63.21 | 36.79 |
| Bank of America | 52.15 | 47.85 |
| JP Morgan | 68.32 | 31.68 |
| Goldman Sachs | 71.67 | 28.33 |
| Morgan Stanley | 66.92 | 33.08 |
| Merrill Lynch | 73.53 | 26.47 |
| Wachovia | 50.74 | 49.26 |
| Lehman Brothers | 58.16 | 41.84 |
| Wells Fargo | 66.14 | 33.86 |
| Washington Mutual | 73.40 | 26.60 |
| US Bancorp | 53.35 | 46.65 |
| New York Mellon | 69.78 | 30.22 |
| SunTrust Banks | 56.12 | 43.88 |
| National City Corporation | 54.19 | 45.81 |
| American Express | 74.43 | 25.57 |
| BB&T Corporation | 30.21 | 69.79 |

*Source*: Own processing of Bankscope Database.

For the majority of banks the float was between 25 per cent and 50 per cent, with certain exceptions:

- the float of the three Japanese banks was significantly higher than 50 per cent (66 per cent in the case of Mizhuo), indicating a progressive alignment with public company models even in contexts traditionally dominated by an insider system (control by a nucleus of shareholders);
- the public company model of governance seems to be confirmed by the relatively high free float of the Spanish and Swiss banks in relation to the British banks in the study (with the exception of a 46 per cent free float for HSBC); in the banking sector the Anglo-Saxon model of public company is evidently applied also (and perhaps even more so) in other geographical areas;
- from a comparison of British and North American banks, a public company structure was apparent in the American and Canadian banks. Take, for example, the free float of Bank of America (48 per cent), Wachovia

(49 per cent) and Royal Bank of Canada (49 per cent), compared to HBOS (20 per cent) and Barclays (22 per cent);

- the low free float of Italian banks, particularly Intesa SanPaolo and MPS, was explained by the relative weight of foundations vis-à-vis other shareholders. ('Foundations' in the Italian banking system are grant-making foundations that result from the former public banks. They are shareholders of the major banking groups);
- among the French banks the case of Crédit Agricole is worthy of note: the low free float reflected the presence of a financial holding company that centralised the shareholdings of a number of regional cooperative banks (the so-called *Caisses Régionales*), and that had a controlling stake in excess of 50 per cent as a result;
- the very low free float of Danske Bank, Nordea and Dexia was due on the one hand to a substantial government shareholding, and on the other to the numerous banks among shareholders.

Table 6.2 highlights for individual banks the shareholder types with controlling/strategic holdings: note how the banks' shareholders were for the most part financial institutions. Indeed, 20 banking groups reported banks as the shareholder type with the highest aggregate shareholding, while 19 declared as their main shareholders asset management organisations, such

*Table 6.2*  Shareholder structure (controlling/strategic holdings); % on total share capital (June 2008)

| Bank | Bank (%) | Financial company (%) | Foundation/ Research Institute (%) | Industrial company (%) | Asset manager (%) | State, Public Authority (%) | Other (%) |
|---|---|---|---|---|---|---|---|
| Fortis | 29.62 | 2.80 | 3.00 | 0.72 | 6.50 | 6.27 | 0.61 |
| Dexia | 55.14 | 0.97 | | 2.69 | 16.61 | 12.83 | 4.60 |
| KBC | 7.26 | 46.04 | 4.66 | 3.80 | 2.62 | 0.56 | 3.82 |
| Royal Bank of Canada | 26.62 | 8.18 | | 0.12 | 11.01 | 0.30 | 4.40 |
| Toronto Dominion Bank | 31.88 | 9.70 | | | 16.98 | 0.73 | 5.63 |
| Danske Bank | 13.67 | 0.92 | 11.81 | 20.54 | 27.79 | 5.57 | 1.28 |
| BNP Paribas | 18.42 | 2.75 | | 4.49 | 27.75 | 2.20 | 12.81 |
| Crédit Agricole | 4.59 | 55.81 | | 0.82 | 10.73 | 0.73 | |
| Société Générale | 13.82 | 4.48 | 1.64 | 12.30 | 17.21 | 3.04 | 17.26 |

*(Continued)*

*Table 6.2*    (*Continued*)

| Bank | Bank (%) | Financial company (%) | Foundation/ Research Institute (%) | Industrial company (%) | Asset manager (%) | State, Public Authority (%) | Other (%) |
|---|---|---|---|---|---|---|---|
| Deutsche Bank | 25.45 | 4.38 | | 2.14 | 13.03 | 0.59 | 5.01 |
| Commerz-bank | 22.26 | 7.64 | | 1.16 | 33.32 | 1.34 | 0.53 |
| UniCredit | 15.97 | 2.60 | 11.82 | 1.03 | 26.22 | 1.23 | 0.37 |
| Intesa SanPaolo | 14.33 | 4.68 | 26.85 | 6.88 | 13.50 | 0.94 | 5.89 |
| MPS | 17.57 | 7.30 | 55.49 | 3.78 | 8.97 | 0.38 | 3.96 |
| Mitsubishi UFJ | 17.27 | 1.04 | | 3.74 | 11.90 | 0.64 | 0.29 |
| Mizhuo | 18.48 | 3.12 | | 0.12 | 11.39 | 0.80 | |
| Sumitomo Mitsui | 26.77 | 2.50 | | 0.57 | 14.01 | 0.95 | |
| ING Group | 35.09 | 7.35 | 0.12 | 1.43 | 25.05 | 1.23 | 8.13 |
| Banco Santander | 15.81 | 4.09 | | 3.90 | 29.61 | 0.96 | 5.03 |
| BBVA | 13.05 | 7.65 | | 11.49 | 6.99 | 1.43 | 5.80 |
| Nordea Bank | 24.49 | 0.86 | 0.50 | 2.22 | 24.05 | 24.98 | 1.41 |
| UBS | 22.36 | 1.55 | | 1.13 | 20.32 | 0.73 | 7.72 |
| Crédit Suisse | 10.71 | 2.74 | | 2.40 | 22.84 | 11.74 | 12.20 |
| Royal Bank of Scotland | 28.01 | 4.98 | | 1.29 | 35.44 | 1.56 | 0.65 |
| Barclays | 31.14 | 2.95 | | 4.44 | 31.53 | 1.66 | 5.86 |
| HSBC | 23.58 | 5.68 | | 0.78 | 22.16 | 1.04 | 0.84 |
| HBOS | 19.77 | 3.62 | | 2.01 | 53.34 | 0.72 | 0.93 |
| Lloyds TSB | 28.32 | 4.02 | | 0.99 | 31.35 | 1.25 | 1.04 |
| Citigroup | 23.49 | 4.49 | | 1.13 | 23.47 | 6.55 | 4.08 |
| Bank of America | 20.05 | 5.67 | | 0.95 | 22.51 | 1.18 | 1.79 |
| JP Morgan | 26.88 | 7.79 | | 6.70 | 25.49 | 1.01 | 0.45 |
| Goldman Sachs | 24.11 | 7.25 | | 6.24 | 23.60 | 1.37 | 9.10 |
| Morgan Stanley | 40.40 | 7.28 | | 1.28 | 16.31 | 1.52 | 0.13 |
| Merrill Lynch | 29.35 | 3.02 | | 1.01 | 22.18 | 17.97 | |

(*Continued*)

*Table 6.2   (Continued)*

| Bank | Bank (%) | Financial company (%) | Foundation/ Research Institute (%) | Industrial company (%) | Asset manager (%) | State, Public Authority (%) | Other (%) |
|---|---|---|---|---|---|---|---|
| Wachovia | 18.22 | 3.59 | | 1.45 | 24.19 | 1.36 | 1.93 |
| Lehman Brothers | 23.57 | 11.12 | | 1.58 | 20.59 | 1.19 | 0.11 |
| Wells Fargo | 23.84 | 4.06 | | 2.89 | 32.89 | 1.60 | 0.86 |
| Washington Mutual | 21.62 | 2.08 | 0.28 | 0.34 | 48.03 | 1.05 | |
| US Bancorp | 22.65 | 5.77 | | 0.83 | 20.64 | 1.43 | 2.03 |
| New York Mellon | 28.17 | 8.96 | | 0.98 | 28.88 | 1.43 | 1.36 |
| SunTrust Banks | 24.86 | 2.80 | | 2.81 | 21.48 | 1.17 | 3.00 |
| National City Corporation | 19.77 | 2.30 | | 0.70 | 27.51 | 0.84 | 3.07 |
| American Express | 24.32 | 5.88 | | 1.69 | 40.89 | 1.65 | |
| BB&T Corporation | 15.88 | 1.76 | | 0.52 | 11.32 | 0.87 | 1.62 |

*Source*: Own processing of Bankscope Database.

as insurance companies, mutual and pension funds and private equity funds.

This tendency was particularly marked among British and American banks. Foundations, industrial companies and state/public authorities had very limited shareholdings compared to shareholders from the financial sector (banks, financial companies and asset managers). This was seen in several other contexts (German, French, Swiss, Belgian and Dutch banks) where, however, there were significant differences between stakes held by banks and by other financial intermediaries (financial companies and asset managers). In certain cases, significant concentration of capital in the hands of single banks or intermediaries was evident. Consider the following examples:

- the principal shareholders of HSBC were banks, with an aggregate stake of 23.58 per cent. In particular, Deutsche Bank had a 5 per cent stake and Barclays a 3 per cent stake; asset managers held an aggregate stake of 22.16 per cent, around 10 per cent of which was held by Legal & General, an insurance and investment company;

- the dominant shareholders of both TD Bank and Royal Bank of Canada were banks, with 31.88 per cent and 26.62 per cent stakes respectively. Furthermore, TD Bank had a 9 per cent cross-shareholding in Royal Bank of Canada, while the principal shareholder of the latter was TD Bank, with a 7 per cent stake;
- the principal shareholders of JP Morgan and Goldman Sachs were banks, with 26.88 per cent and 24.11 per cent stakes respectively, closely followed by asset managers with 25.49 per cent and 23.60 per cent respectively. Among the shareholders of JP Morgan and Goldman Sachs were Barclays and State Street (with stakes of 4.5 per cent and 3.5 per cent respectively). AXA and Capital Group stood out among asset managers for their respective stakes of around 3.5 per cent and 2.5 per cent in the two companies;
- a similar situation applied to Citigroup, in which banks held a 23.49 per cent stake. Barclays and State Street were both significant shareholders, followed by asset managers with 23.47 per cent (of which around 7 per cent held by Capital Group alone).

Citigroup was the bank involved in the first round of recapitalisation by SWFs in June 2008, with the acquisition of a 4.9 per cent stake by the Abu Dhabi Investment Authority to rebuild the group's capital ratio eroded by the crisis. The other American bank recapitalised by SWFs before Summer 2008 was Merrill Lynch, in which Temasek of Singapore acquired a 14 per cent stake.

In Japan also, the financial sector held the highest percentage of bank capital. Banks had an 18 per cent stake in Mitsubishi and Mizhuo; Japan Trustee Services Bank, State Street, Chase Manhattan Bank and Barclays had an aggregate shareholding of around 10 per cent in both banks. Japan Trustee Services Bank's stake in excess of 10 per cent in Sumitomo influenced the 26.77 per cent aggregate shareholding held by banks.

In a European context, several interesting situations deserve analysis:

- the strong presence of foundations among the shareholders of Intesa SanPaolo and Monte dei Paschi di Siena. Foundations held a 26.85 per cent stake in Intesa SanPaolo (Compagnia di San Paolo alone had an 8 per cent stake); the Monte dei Paschi di Siena Foundation had an absolute majority (55.49 per cent) in the corresponding bank. UniCredit was an entirely different case: the significant shareholdings of foundations (approximately 12 per cent) were much lower than the aggregate 26.22 per cent stake held by asset managers or the 20.28 per cent stake held by insurance companies such as Munich Re and Allianz;
- in Germany, prior to the acquisition of Dresdner Bank, the shareholder structure of Commerzbank resembled that of UniCredit: asset managers held a 33.32 per cent stake; in particular, insurance companies had a relevant shareholding (around 23 per cent, of which 8 per cent held by Generali alone). In Deutsche Bank, banks were significant shareholders

with a 24.45 per cent stake; among the banks, Barclays, Crédit Suisse and UBS had an aggregate shareholding of around 15 per cent. These three banks were also shareholders of Commerzbank, though with lesser stakes;

- in France, apart from Crédit Agricole, asset managers held a significant interest in BNP Paribas (27.75 per cent) and Société Générale (17.21 per cent). Insurance companies, in particular AXA with a stake of around 15 per cent, were the major shareholders of BNP Paribas; insurance companies also held a 14 per cent stake in Société Générale, although in this case individual shareholdings were fragmented;
- in Spain, asset managers were significant shareholders of Banco Santander, with a 29.61 per cent stake; Chase Nominees alone held 10.5 per cent. The principal shareholders of BBVA on the other hand were banks, with an aggregate shareholding of 13.05 per cent;
- in Switzerland, banks and asset managers, particularly mutual funds, were among the principal shareholders of both UBS and Crédit Suisse. In particular, a substantial shareholder of Crédit Suisse is the Olayan Group, a SWF from Saudi Arabia that held a 7 per cent stake.

In overall terms, the analysis highlights how, at least until the onset of the crisis, the shareholder structure of the major banking groups was relatively homogenous, characterised by a widespread predominance of institutional investors and in many cases a significant concentration of large but minority stakes held by the banks. With a few notable exceptions, this type of shareholder structure was undoubtedly indicative of a public company model of corporate governance.

## 6.3 Geographical origin of shareholders

Moving on to a more detailed level of analysis, Table 6.3 highlights for each bank the country of origin of controlling/strategic holdings, reaggregated by geographical area.

Note how all the banks, with the exception of UBS, had relative majority shareholders from the geographical area in which they were based.

*Table 6.3* Shareholders by geographical area (controlling/strategic holdings); % on total share capital (June 2008)

| Bank | Europe (%) | America (%) | Asia (ME) (%) | Asia (FE) (%) | Oceania (%) |
|---|---|---|---|---|---|
| Fortis | 35.07 | 8.85 | | 4.99 | |
| Dexia | 86.72 | 1.39 | | 0.13 | |
| KBC | 61.56 | 3.11 | | | |
| Royal Bank of Canada | 8.54 | 39.66 | | 0.12 | |

*(Continued)*

*Table 6.3*  (*Continued*)

| Bank | Europe (%) | America (%) | Asia (ME) (%) | Asia (FE) (%) | Oceania (%) |
|---|---|---|---|---|---|
| Toronto Dominion Bank | 7.18 | 52.29 | | | |
| Danske Bank | 75.88 | 5.15 | | 0.52 | |
| BNP Paribas | 46.56 | 8.55 | | | |
| Crédit Agricole | 64.51 | 1.91 | | | |
| Société Générale | 42.41 | 5.81 | | 4.27 | |
| Deutsche Bank | 40.22 | 3.44 | | | |
| Commerzbank | 51.36 | 14.36 | | | |
| UniCredit | 47.00 | 12.52 | | | |
| Intesa SanPaolo | 61.53 | 5.65 | | | |
| MPS | 84.01 | 9.48 | | | |
| Mitsubishi UFJ | 5.18 | 6.91 | | 16.59 | |
| Mizhuo | 5.13 | 4.50 | | 22.26 | |
| Sumitomo Mitsui | 12.34 | 8.07 | | 18.52 | |
| ING Group | 49.78 | 20.30 | | | |
| Banco Santander | 36.63 | 16.45 | | | |
| BBVA | 31.47 | 9.19 | | | |
| Nordea Bank | 71.12 | 2.43 | 0.13 | 0.12 | |
| UBS | 21.16 | 24.13 | | 0.80 | |
| Crédit Suisse | 33.90 | 13.00 | 6.88 | | |
| Royal Bank of Scotland | 49.95 | 19.94 | 0.31 | 0.97 | 0.11 |
| Barclays | 54.70 | 12.48 | 0.25 | 1.15 | |
| HSBC | 40.62 | 12.39 | 0.12 | 0.11 | |
| HBOS | 64.48 | 13.74 | 0.28 | 0.84 | 0.12 |
| Lloyds TSB | 42.46 | 22.29 | 0.53 | 0.65 | |
| Citigroup | 15.69 | 39.50 | 4.90 | | |
| Bank of America | 11.29 | 39.07 | | | |
| JP Morgan | 21.08 | 46.79 | | | |
| Goldman Sachs | 12.33 | 44.92 | | 0.12 | 5.20 |
| Morgan Stanley | 20.46 | 46.33 | | | |
| Merrill Lynch | 14.39 | 42.09 | | 17.05 | |
| Wachovia | 8.95 | 39.86 | | | |
| Lehman Brothers | 15.19 | 41.81 | | 1.05 | 0.14 |
| Wells Fargo | 11.15 | 54.19 | | | |
| Washington Mutual | 17.87 | 55.53 | | | |

(*Continued*)

*Table 6.3*   *(Continued)*

| Bank | Europe (%) | America (%) | Asia (ME) (%) | Asia (FE) (%) | Oceania (%) |
|---|---|---|---|---|---|
| US Bancorp | 8.17 | 42.82 | | 0.33 | |
| New York Mellon | 15.37 | 52.94 | | 0.11 | |
| SunTrust Banks | 11.85 | 41.27 | | | |
| National City Corporation | 9.24 | 41.88 | | | |
| American Express | 10.06 | 64.37 | | | |
| BB&T Corporation | 6.56 | 24.19 | | | |

*Source*: Own processing of Bankscope Database.

Upon closer analysis, it can be seen that in only five cases (Fortis, Deutsche Bank, UniCredit, Banco Santander and Crédit Suisse) were the relative majority shareholders not from the same country of origin as the bank itself. A number of special cases deserve attention:

- in the case of the Belgian and Dutch banks, European shareholders held a very high proportion of total controlling/strategic holdings. This proportion was particularly high for Dexia and KBC, and more evenly balanced in relation to other areas for ING and Fortis; considered individually, however, no single country of origin accounted for more than a minority shareholding;
- in the case of the French banks, European investors accounted for between 80 per cent and 97 per cent of total equity interests held by institutional investors, leaving marginal shareholdings for investors from the other geographical areas;
- the same situation applied to the German banks: European investors accounted for up to 92 per cent of total controlling/strategic holdings in the case of Deutsche Bank;
- similarly in the case of the Italian banks, European shareholders accounted for between 80 per cent and 95 per cent of equity held by the institutional investor block. UniCredit differed from Intesa SanPaolo and MPS – both of which had a majority of Italian shareholders – in so far as German shareholders held the highest stake (16.76 per cent of total share capital);
- although the Spanish banks had a higher number of American shareholders than other banks in the study, European investors nevertheless held significant stakes: 77 per cent of controlling/strategic holdings in BBVA and 69 per cent of strategic/controlling holdings in Banco Santander. The latter bank also had a significant concentration of British shareholders (12.24 per cent of share capital);
- the Swiss banks showed the greatest signs of American influence: the principal shareholders of UBS were of American origin (52 per cent of

total controlling/strategic holdings), while Crédit Suisse had a slightly higher number of investors from Europe (63 per cent);

- European institutional investors accounted for between 70 per cent and 85 per cent of total controlling/strategic holdings in British banks; the majority of shareholders were from Great Britain itself. For example, at the time of the study British shareholders held a 35.76 per cent stake in Royal Bank of Scotland and a 38.66 per cent stake in Barclays, much higher levels than those seen in other contexts;
- of the Japanese banks, note how the shareholders of Sumitomo Mitsui were evenly distributed among the Far East, the Americas and Europe (47 per cent, 21 per cent and 32 per cent of controlling/strategic holdings respectively); on the other hand the major shareholders of Mitsubishi and Mizhuo were from the Far East (58 per cent and 70 per cent respectively);
- the principal shareholders of US banks were from the same geographical area, with stakes ranging from 65 per cent to 90 per cent of controlling/strategic holdings. This was even more true for the Canadian banks (Royal Bank of Canada 82 per cent and Toronto Dominion Bank 88 per cent respectively) and for the small or specialised US intermediaries (National City 82 per cent and American Express 86 per cent). The only US bank that differed in this respect was Merrill Lynch: US shareholders accounted for 57 per cent of controlling/strategic shareholdings, while shareholders from the Far East held 23 per cent, principally due to the presence of Temasek SWF.

The data reveal that even institutional investors showed home bias, in other words a tendency to invest in the domestic market. There are a number of reasons for this phenomenon: a better understanding of the regulatory framework in the home country; the desire to avoid exchange rate and country risk; greater familiarity with the operating environment, business strategies and expected profitability of the bank in question (overconfidence). To some extent, the home bias may also have reflected the sedimentation of past situations and the institutional importance of the major banking groups.

The tables analysed so far underline the substantially traditional and consolidated shareholder structure of the major banking groups prior to the onset of the crisis. Most groups were characterised by diffuse shareholdings, a priority role played by intermediaries/institutional investors, and a clear majority of investors from the same geographical area and often from the same country of origin.

## 6.4   Equity investments by SWFs

Between July and September 2008, at the onset of the crisis, the financial position of the banks in the study deteriorated considerably in terms of stock market capitalisation (often more than 50 per cent lower than the start of

2008), profitability and capital adequacy: in some instances the Tier 1 capital ratio fell below 6 per cent, in others it remained marginally above.

In this situation, the shortage of liquidity in the system demanded recapitalisation initiatives from both private (non-governmental financial institutions) and public sources (government recapitalisation schemes).

Examples of recapitalisation by non-governmental financial institutions included the acquisition by Berkshire Hathaway of $5 billion in Goldman Sachs preference shares and the massive investment ($9 billion) by Mitsubishi UFJ in Morgan Stanley convertible preferred stock; upon conversion, this stock would give the Japanese bank a 21 per cent stake in the New York investment bank. Capital injections by SWFs also belong to this category of interventions.

Table 6.4 highlights, among their various assets, SWFs' holdings in the banks in the study at the end of December 2008; with the exception of Abu Dhabi Investment Authority's stake in Citigroup and Ping an Insurance's

*Table 6.4*  SWF holdings in major international banks; % on total share capital (December 2008)

| SWF \ Bank | For (%) | DB (%) | Unic (%) | UBS (%) | CS (%) | Bar (%) | HSBC (%) | St.Ch. (%) | Citi (%) | Morg (%) | Merr (%) | Wach (%) |
|---|---|---|---|---|---|---|---|---|---|---|---|---|
| Abu Dhabi IA (UAE) | | | | | | 16.30 | | | 4.90 | | | |
| Dubai Int Financial (UAE) | | 2.20 | | | | | 3.00 | | | | | |
| China Dev Bank (CN) | | | | | | 3.10 | | | | | | |
| China Inv Corporation (CN) | | | | | | | | | | 9.90 | | |
| Ping an Insur (CN) | 4.99 | | | | | | | | | | | |
| Korea Inv Corp (KR) | | | | | | | | | | | 7.40 | |
| Kuwait IA (KW) | | | | | | | 0.12 | | 6.00 | | 4.80 | |
| Libyan IA (LY) | | | 4.90 | | | | | | | | | |
| Govt Pension Fund (NO) | | | | | | | | | | | | 2.47 |

*(Continued)*

*Table 6.4   (Continued)*

| SWF \ Bank | For (%) | DB (%) | Unic (%) | UBS (%) | CS (%) | Bar (%) | HSBC (%) | St.Ch. (%) | Citi (%) | Morg (%) | Merr (%) | Wach (%) |
|---|---|---|---|---|---|---|---|---|---|---|---|---|
| Challenger (QA) | | | | | | 2.80 | | | | | | |
| Qatar IA (QA) | | | | | 8.87 | 12.70 | | | | | | |
| Olayan (SA) | | | | | 6.88 | | | | | | | |
| Saudi Arabia Ma (SaA) | | | | 2.00 | | | | | | | | |
| GIC (SG) | | | | 10.00 | | | | 18.79 | 3.70 | | | |
| Temasek Holdings (SG) | | | | | | 3.00 | | 19.03 | | | 13.70 | |
| TOTAL | 4.99 | 2.20 | 4.90 | 12.00 | 15.75 | 37.90 | 3.12 | 37.82 | 14.60 | 9.90 | 25.90 | 2.47 |

*Source*: Various.

stake in Fortis, the capital injections were made during the subprime mortgage crisis.

From the table it can be seen that SWFs established by the State of Singapore were those most actively engaged in recapitalisation activities:

- the Government of Singapore Investment Corporation (GIC), with assets under management of $330 billion, injected $9.7 billion into UBS, acquiring a 10 per cent stake, and $6.8 billion into Citigroup, increasing its stake to 3.70 per cent;
- Temasek, with assets under management of $134 billion, injected more than $2 billion into Barclays, bringing its total stake up to 3 per cent; in addition, the SWF held a 19.03 per cent stake in Standard Chartered and a 13.70 per cent stake in Merrill Lynch. Following the acquisition of Merrill Lynch by Bank of America, Temasek held a 3.8 per cent stake in Bank of America. Given that Temasek was the principal shareholder of Merrill Lynch and Standard Chartered, the State of Singapore effectively had a controlling stake in Standard Chartered, thanks to an additional strategic holding (18.79 per cent) though GIC.

The SWFs of Qatar were also actively engaged in recapitalisation operations: if the 12.7 per cent equity interest in Barclays and the 2.80 per cent equity interest in Challenger held by the Qatar Investment Authority are aggregated, this state was the second-largest shareholder of the British banking group, the largest being another SWF from the same area, the Abu Dhabi Investment Authority. The Qatar Investment Authority is a SWF set up to invest oil revenues with assets under management of $60 billion; Challenger is an investment vehicle guided by the president of Qatar Holding and controlled by Qatar's royal family. The SWF has acquired, through a series of capital injections, an 8.87 per cent stake in Crédit Suisse.

The United Arab Emirates also took an active part in recapitalisation operations. In addition to the above-mentioned Abu Dhabi Investment Authority (the commodity SWF with the highest assets under management of $875 billion) that acquired a 4.9 per cent stake in Citigroup with a capital injection of $7.5 billion, and a 16.3 per cent interest in Barclays acquired in a series of tranches, another SWF in the Emirates, Dubai International Financial, acquired a 2.20 per cent stake in Deutsche Bank and a 3 per cent stake in HSBC.

Through the commodity SWF Libyan Investment Authority with assets under management of $50 billion, Libya acquired a 4.9 per cent stake in UniCredit; in a second operation to boost its stake the SWF acquired UniCredit convertible bonds which upon conversion would make Libyan Investment Authority the leading shareholder with a stake of 7 per cent.

Another interesting case is the commodity SWF Kuwait Investment Authority, with assets under management of $264 billion, which acquired a 6 per cent stake in Citigroup and a 4.8 per cent stake in Merrill Lynch.

Data analysis reveals that many of the banking groups in the study had a very traditional shareholder structure until June; however, by December 2008 overseas institutional investors had become their principal shareholders, giving rise to a number of striking situations. In particular:

- Standard Chartered was substantially controlled by two SWFs from Singapore that held a combined 38 per cent stake;
- prior to its acquisition by Bank of America, the principal shareholders of Merrill Lynch were three SWFs with a combined stake in the region of 25 per cent;
- among the shareholders of Barclays were four SWFs with a combined stake of around 15 per cent;
- SWF had stakes in the two Swiss banks in the study, Crédit Suisse (15.75 per cent) and UBS (12 per cent).

SWFs acquired various types of securities, all of which, however, were convertible into ordinary shares with a potentially significant impact on corporate governance. At the time of the study, despite heavy losses on investments, the SWFs had nevertheless acted as passive investors, neither intervening in issues of corporate governance or strategic planning, nor demanding board representation.

## 6.5   Government recapitalisation schemes

The second type of support offered to financial institutions during the study period consisted of government recapitalisation schemes within a wider programme of measures designed to alleviate the impact of the crisis. These included government guarantees of deposits, government guarantees of bank bonds, swaps of illiquid with liquid assets and more generally the injection of liquidity into the financial system.

Table 6.5 focuses on government recapitalisation measures directed towards individual banks, with details of the type of intervention, the financial instruments deployed and the total amount of recapitalisation.

Table 6.5 illustrates the remarkable diversity of government recapitalisation schemes: the more coherent organisation of measures in America, Britain and France contrasted with other European countries in which

*Table 6.5*   Banks recapitalized by governments (2008–February 2009)

| Bank Recapitalized | Instruments | Amount |
| --- | --- | --- |
| Fortis | Belgium and Netherlands common shares; Luxembourg mandatory convertible loan | €28 billion[1] |
| Dexia | Belgium new shares; France new shares; Luxembourg convertible bonds | €6.4 billion |
| KBC | Tier1 debt securities | €7 billion |
| BNP Paribas | Tier1 subordinated securities | €5.1 billion |
| Crédit Agricole | Tier1 subordinated securities | €3 billion |
| Société Générale | Tier1 subordinated securities | €1.7 billion[2] |
| UniCredit | Tier1 debt securities | €4 billion |
| Intesa SanPaolo | Tier1 debt securities | €4 billion |
| MPS | Tier1 debt securities | €4 billion |
| Commerzbank | Quasi equity state | €18.2 billion |
| ING Group | Core Tier1 securities | €10 billion |
| UBS | Mandatory convertible notes | CHF6 billion |
| Royal Bank of Scotland | Preference shares | £45.5 billion[3] |
| HBOS | Preference shares | £11.5 billion |
| Lloyds TSB | Preference shares | £5.5 billion |
| Citigroup | Senior preferred shares (SPS Tier1); warrants | $45 billion[4] |
| Bank of America | Senior preferred shares (SPS Tier1); warrants | $45 billion[4] |

(*Continued*)

*Table 6.5   (Continued)*

| Bank Recapitalized | Instruments | Amount |
| --- | --- | --- |
| JP Morgan | Senior preferred shares (SPS Tier1); warrants | $25 billion |
| Goldman Sachs | Senior preferred shares (SPS Tier1); warrants | $10 billion |
| Morgan Stanley | Senior preferred shares (SPS Tier1); warrants | $10 billion |
| Merrill Lynch | Senior preferred shares (SPS Tier1); warrants | $10 billion |
| Wells Fargo | Senior preferred shares (SPS Tier1); warrants | $25 billion |
| US Bancorp | Senior preferred shares (SPS Tier1); warrants | $6.599 billion |
| New York Mellon | Senior preferred shares (SPS Tier1); warrants | $3 billion |
| SunTrust Banks | Senior preferred shares (SPS Tier1); warrants | $4.85 billion |
| BB&T Corporation | Senior preferred shares (SPS Tier1); warrants | $3.134 billion |

*Notes*:
1. Total funds invested by the governments of B, NL and L to bail out the group.
2. The group announced its acceptance of a further capital infusion of an equal amount from the government.
3. The government recapitalised the group twice (injecting £20 billion and £25.5 billion); subsequently, the government converted its preference shares into ordinary shares, thereby raising its stake to 90 per cent of equity capital.
4. In view of the exceptional nature of the crisis, these two banks requested a further capital injection of $20 billion from the US government, exceeding the cap imposed by the Capital Purchase Program.

*Source*: Various.

intervention was differentiated in relation to the characteristics of individual banks. In Japan, no government recapitalisation of banks had been seen at the time of the study.

The most important government recapitalisation plan in quantitative terms was the US Capital Purchase Program announced in October 2008 as part of the $700 billion Troubled Asset Relief Program, under which the US Treasury pledged to acquire $250 billion of senior preferred stocks and warrants from stricken financial institutions. All banks were eligible to benefit from the program, to an extent ranging from a minimum of 1 per cent to a maximum of 3 per cent of Risk Weighting Assets (RWA), with a cap of $25 billion. Table 6.5 shows capital infusions to major banks that applied for relief: Citigroup, JP Morgan and Wells Fargo received the maximum amount, New York Mellon and BB&T just over $3 billion. Citigroup and

Bank of America subsequently received a second infusion of capital for an equivalent amount; in the case of Citigroup, the gravity of the situation induced the US government to convert part of its preferred shares into ordinary shares, in what was effectively a partial nationalisation.

Senior preferred stocks qualified as Tier 1 capital and ranked senior to common stock and other preferred shares. Other details of the programme included:

- an annual dividend of 5 per cent for the first 5 years, increased to 9 per cent after year 5 (the step-up clause);
- non-voting shares, except in the event of non-payment of dividends for six consecutive years, in which case the US Treasury would be entitled to elect two board directors.

Furthermore, the US Treasury had the right to purchase warrants up to 15 per cent of the value of senior preferred shares held; and to exercise the warrants at any time in the 10 years following purchase.

The second most important plan was the recapitalisation scheme proposed by the UK government on 13 October 2008 that made £50 billion available to the nation's banks. Among the eligible banks were HBOS, Lloyds TSB, Royal Bank of Scotland, HSBC and Barclays. Only the first three accepted government aid for a total of £37 billion; HSBC, with Tier 1 capital of 8.8 per cent following recapitalisation by institutional investors, was not willing to participate in the Treasury initiative at the time of the study. Similarly, Barclays, having received a massive capital injection from SWFs, and with a Tier 1 capital ratio considered adequate, had not applied for government aid.

The UK government plan envisaged the purchase of ordinary shares and preference shares eligible as core Tier 1 capital, and resulted in:

- the underwriting of £15 billion of new ordinary shares and the purchase of £5 billion of preference shares in Royal Bank of Scotland;
- the purchase of £8.5 billion of ordinary shares and £3 billion of preference shares in HBOS;
- the purchase of £4.5 billion of ordinary shares and £1 billion of preference shares in Lloyds TSB.

The preference shares paid an annual dividend of 12 per cent for the first five years, and after year five a dividend based on the three-month LIBOR with a 7 per cent spread. HM Treasury was entitled to appoint two independent directors to the board of Lloyds TSB and HBOS, and three to the board of Royal Bank of Scotland in relation to the higher level of investment. In the event of the non-payment of dividends, the Treasury would acquire voting rights in certain circumstances; limits were also imposed on executive remuneration. In view of the gravity of Royal Bank of Scotland's situation, the government announced the conversion of its preference shares into ordinary shares, thereby increasing its shareholding in the bank to 70 per cent. Following the second tranche of recapitalisation in February 2009, the Treasury's stake rose to 95 per cent, although the goverment declared the intention to impose a 75 per cent cap on its voting rights. The Treasury also became a majority shareholder in the new Lloyds Banking Group plc, following the decision to convert preference shares into ordinary shares.

In the European area, the plan proposed by the French government allocated €10.5 billion for the recapitalisation of six leading banks through the acquisition of Tier 1 subordinated securities: Crédit Agricole received a capital injection of €3 billion, BNP Paribas €2.55 billion, Société Générale €1.7 billion. The hybrid securities did not entitle the French government to voting rights. A second round of financing operations for a total of €10.5 billion was announced in January 2009: BNP Paribas was due to issue preference shares for a total value of €5.1 billion to the French government, in exchange for the previous debt of €2.55 billion. Société Générale announced its willingness to receive a second tranche of public funds equivalent to the amount received in the first round of the plan.

Among the other recapitalisation schemes, we can cite the Swiss government's plan accepted by UBS (but not Crédit Suisse at the time of the study) for the establishment of a special investment vehicle in conjunction with the Swiss Federal Bank to purchase illiquid assets, particularly collateralised debt obligations; the Swiss government also pledged to cover UBS's losses and to inject new capital. A total of CHF6 billion were injected in the form of mandatory convertible notes that had to be converted into ordinary shares within thirty months of issue. The Swiss Confederation was entitled to an annual dividend of 12.50 per cent, and after conversion would hold a 9.3 per cent stake in UBS.

The Dutch government's rescue plan allocated €20 billion to recapitalise the nation's banks. ING participated in the scheme and issued €10 billion of Tier 1 securities underwritten by the government with a dividend structure as follows: an annual dividend equal to the higher of 8.5 per cent and 110 per cent of the dividend paid on ordinary shares in 2008, 120 per cent in 2009 and 125 per cent in subsequent years, only in the event of the actual payment of dividends. Tier 1 securities did not give the Dutch government any voting rights, but entitled it to appoint two members of the supervisory board responsible for approving new share issues or buy-backs in excess of 25 per cent of funds made available by the government. A second substantial round of government support to ING came in the form of guarantees on its structured portfolio.

The rescue plan proposed by the German government included €80 billion to recapitalise the banking system through the Financial Markets Stabilisation Fund (SoFFin), of which €8.2 billion were injected into

Commerzbank in the form of a quasi-equity stake or 'silent participation' eligible as core Tier 1, thus bringing the bank's Tier 1 capital ratio to 11.2 per cent. A 9 per cent annual dividend was due and no voting rights accrued to the German government. In January 2009, SoFFin injected a further €10 billion into Commerzbank principally through an additional silent participation. After this second round of intervention, the German government's stake in Commerzbank stood at 25 per cent.

Rather than announcing a general recapitalisation plan for financial institutions, the Belgian government offered ad hoc support to KBC by injecting €3.5 billion in the form of non-transferable, non-voting core Tier 1 capital debt securities, thereby raising KBC's Tier 1 capital ratio to 10.7 per cent. The Belgian government will receive an annual dividend equivalent to the higher of 8.5 per cent and 105 per cent of the expected dividend on ordinary shares in 2008, 110 per cent in 2009, and 115 per cent in subsequent years, only in the event of actual payment of dividends on ordinary shares. A second recapitalisation of KBC was provided by the government of the Flemish Community with a €2 billion injection in the form of non-voting shares eligible as core Tier 1; the new shareholder will receive interest at an annual rate of 8.5 per cent and will infuse a further €1.5 billion in the next five years.

The Danish government initially took steps only to guarantee deposits; however, at a later stage (February 2009) it announced a recapitalisation plan that Danske Bank opted to participate in, receiving a capital injection of $4.48 billion. The details of the operation had not been disclosed at the time of study.

One of the last countries to announce a state recapitalisation scheme was Italy. Most of the major banking groups applied for and received support in the form of Tier 1 debt securities subscribed to by the government.

Finally, three governments took concerted action to support the Dexia and Fortis banking groups (Chapter 9):

- the French and Belgian governments each injected  3 billion into Dexia by underwriting new shares, while the government of Luxembourg underwrote  400 million in convertible bonds. Added to previous intervention, this gave the French and Belgian governments respective shareholdings of 23.3 per cent and 11.5 per cent in Dexia;
- the governments of the Netherlands, Belgium and Luxembourg nationalised Fortis in a coordinated operation conducted in a number of stages, recapitalising the group to the tune of over €28 billion; this was followed by the sale of the Fortis group's Belgian banking operations to BNP Paribas. Regardless of the outcome of the latter operation, at the centre of a fierce legal battle at the time of writing, the total nationalisation of the Dutch branch of Fortis remains valid, and includes the stake in the domestic operations of ABN AMRO acquired through a previous takeover.

## 6.6   Conclusions

When the tables are viewed together, it becomes apparent that in the period June–December 2008 a significant change took place in the shareholder structure of many of the major banking groups at a global level: at the start of the period, the main shareholders were banks and asset managers (insurance companies, investment and pension funds), many based in the same country as the banks themselves.

After a relatively brief period of exposure to the crisis, and following substantial losses and consequent capital erosion, SWFs and national governments shouldered the burden of recapitalisation. In the majority of cases, the scale of the operations brought about major changes in shareholder structure.

At the end of 2008, with the exception of the Japanese banks, the main shareholders of the majority banks in the study had become the respective national governments (and in some cases foreign governments), in addition to a small group of SWFs with strong geopolitical overtones.

While government purchases of bank equity constituted a watershed (often a sea change) in relation to previous policy directions, the strong presence of SWFs in the equity capital of European and American banks raised a number of problematic issues. In political and institutional terms, the interests of some of the SWFs' home countries (the United Arab Emirates, Kuwait, Saudi Arabia and Libya) were at odds with those of the banks' home countries, particularly in terms of oil prices; in almost every case, the political systems were entirely different; and at least one of the home countries, China, was a major competitor of the European and American economies. Furthermore, the SWFs typically lacked transparency, as revealed by the most widely used indicator, the Linaburg–Maduell index, based on information provided to the public on shareholdings, results, governance and ethical standards. The fact that the SWFs involved in recapitalising the major banks did not rank highly is indicative of their inadequate transparency. Such opacity is partly due to the absence of a mandatory international code of conduct, other than voluntary acceptance of the Santiago principles on transparency, corporate governance, risk management, investment policies and objectives (IWG, 2008).

The acquisition by SWFs of shareholdings in what is effectively a strategic sector, though perhaps not in the sense commonly applied to other sectors, would become a critical issue if the SWFs opted to play an active role as investors. In fact, at the time of the study these investment vehicles continued to respect their neutral role despite facing heavy losses, and did not demand changes in corporate strategy or board representation (with the sole exception of the Libyan Investment Authority's stake in UniCredit). However, difficulties could arise if SWFs were to interfere in the management of the banking groups.

It is more difficult to assess whether SWFs will continue to sustain the capital base of the major banking groups, particularly in view of the combined effects of massive losses in share values, falling oil prices, and SWFs' neutral stance towards corporate governance, all factors that make it hard to envisage other justifications for their continued financial support. Collectively, these factors may undermine the creation of new liquidity to inject into the banking system, or may even give rise to divestments that would invariably have a negative impact on the greatly diminished market value of the banking groups.

The overall sensation is that in the immediate and more distant future, financial support from SWFs will accompany the significant measures undertaken in Europe and America by national governments, from whom further and decisive action can reasonably expected.

In the medium and longer term, a few considerations can be made in terms of the relationship between SWFs and M&A activities: a recent study by the European Central Bank (ECB, 2008a, p. 67) demonstrated that a greater presence of overseas institutional investors among bank shareholders fosters cross-border M&As, due to the breakdown of information barriers between different regulatory frameworks.

In the light of ECB analysis, it would be reasonable to suppose that a higher level of SWF investments in the capital of banks could revive M&A activity.

Finally, although perhaps obvious, we should be aware that the substantial changes in the shareholder structure of the major banking groups will have a fundamental impact on corporate governance, the full implications of which it only be possible to perceive and evaluate in the coming years.

# 7
# Bank Size, Consolidation and Operational Risk

*Veronica De Crescenzo and Flavio Pichler*

## 7.1 Introduction

With the accord entitled *International Convergence of Capital Measurement and Capital Standards*, issued by the Basel Committee on Banking Supervision in June 2006 (Basel II) and transposed into EU and member states legislation by Directives 2006/48/EC and 2006/49/EC, operational risk in the banking sector came to be defined and regulated for the first time. In particular, operational risk was no longer considered a residual risk with respect to credit and market risk, but was defined explicitly as the risk of 'loss resulting from inadequate or failed internal processes, people and systems or from external events'.

These four categories of operational risk thus captured a wide range of risk factors. Those relating to internal processes included model risk, transaction risk, security risk, settlement error, inadequate formalisation of internal procedures, shortcomings in internal control systems and errors in the definition and assignment of roles and responsibilities (microstructure design). Among the risk factors relating to people were errors deriving from incompetence, negligence or lack of experience, mobbing, fraud, collusion or other criminal activities, breaches of laws, international regulations, company regulations and ethical standards. The risk factors deriving from internal systems, principally of a technical nature, concerned IT and technology systems, as well as public utility providers: in other words the limited availability, inefficiency, malfunctioning or breakdown of hardware, software, telecommunications and information providers. Finally, external risk factors included political, fiscal and legislative risks, intentionally fraudulent acts, external non-fulfilment of obligations, political and military events, and natural disasters.

Defined in this way, operational risk includes legal risk, but excludes strategic and reputational risk. Hence operational risk, originating from various shortcomings in operational mechanisms (including internal control systems) and organisational structures, mismanagement of human resources, and external events, emerges as a pure risk typical of corporate activity.

Management of operational risk consists principally in mitigation and/or transfer rather than optimisation of the trade-off between expected return and risk, as in the case of financial risk.

Operational risk is mainly related to the strategic choices, operating methods and organisational characteristics of each bank. Differences in the breadth and uniformity of activities, organisational models and operational processes tend to have an impact on the configuration and dimension of operational risk across banks. Obviously, the evolution of operational risk depends not only on microeconomic and bank-specific factors, but also on systematic macroeconomic factors, such as the general outlook in the banking sector and in the economy, as well as social and cultural factors. In the light of the above considerations, it would be reasonable to assume that banks operating on a large scale, often with a significant degree of sectoral and geographical diversification and a very complex organisational structure, would incur higher operational losses than small banks, at least in relative terms, and that in qualitative terms, the large banks would display a percentage composition of operational losses closer to the sector average.

It can also be presumed that the type of growth, whether internal or external, will have an impact on the qualitative and quantitative composition of operational losses; in particular, external growth may be a source of greater operational risk, above all in the immediate post-merger period, in view of the need to complete the merger process as swiftly as possible. Consider, for example, issues relating to the integration or replacement of ICT systems, the modification/standardisation of processes and products, the introduction of new procedures, human resource management (redundancies, reallocations, re-qualifications, etc.), customer disservices, and the probable decrease in the effectiveness of controls.

Finally, it should also be noted that the merger process, as it unfolds, might itself constitute an additional source of operational losses.

The purpose of this chapter is to investigate the relationship between bank size and the qualitative and quantitative composition of operational risk.

The chapter deals firstly with the definition and classification of operational risk, and the identification of dimensional variables relevant to the investigation of this relationship. Subsequently, the results of the most important data collections on operational losses conducted at an international level are presented and the critical aspects of data collection are discussed.

The second part of the chapter tests empirically the hypothesis of a positive relationship between bank size and the scope and composition of operational risk by examining two M&A case studies, UniCredit-HVB and Intesa SanPaolo.

## 7.2   Operational risk, bank size and growth

The belief that operational risk is linked to the firm size is confirmed by the Basel Committee's decision to use gross income as the reference aggregate for calculating capital requirements under the Basic Indicator (BIA) and Standardised Approaches (SA). Under SA, the different operational risk weighting of the individual business lines (Corporate Finance, Trading & Sales, Retail Banking, Commercial Banking, Payment & Settlement, Agency Services, Asset Management, Retail Brokerage) is reflected in the different coefficients used for the calculation of capital adequacy.

The importance of the relation between operational risk and consolidation also emerges clearly from analysis of the motivations typically cited to justify the introduction of specific supervisory regulations for operational risk. Among the factors that have polarised attention on operational risk are the globalisation of financial markets and financial innovation; M&A activities and the formation of corporate groups diversified by sector and geographical area; technological innovation; the growth and spread of e-banking and e-commerce; and the rise in the outsourcing of processes.

Nevertheless, it would be reasonable to suppose that larger banks will have organisational structures and operational mechanisms better suited to the identification, assessment and management (for example: prevention, mitigation, and transfer) of operational risk, a stronger control culture, and more sophisticated risk management and internal audit procedures (Basel Committee on Banking Supervision, 2003a). Presumably, larger banks will also have a higher level of process automation and make more extensive use of ICT, on the one hand a source of operational risk deriving from internal systems, on the other hand an effective prevention tool against other types of operational losses (due to human error, for example).

Moreover, it can be assumed that growth in operational risk – at least on a certain scale – is typically non-linear with respect to bank size.

These considerations provide a starting point for this chapter, that sets out to evaluate the dynamics of operational risk in consolidation processes, and to identify potential qualitative and quantitative changes in operational risk following consolidation vis-à-vis the risk configuration of the individual banks prior to the merger.

In order to assess with greater accuracy the impact of consolidation processes on operational risk, it is helpful to use the Basel Committee's classification of loss event types (Table 7.1).

Table 7.1 attempts to identify the size variables that make it possible to analyse the potential link between operational risk and bank size. Size is generally measured in terms of total assets, gross income and the number of employees.

The relationship between firm size and operational losses has not yet received adequate treatment in the literature. The aspects that deserve further

*Table 7.1*  Classification of loss event types and size variables

| Event type | Size variable |
| --- | --- |
| Internal Fraud | Number of employees |
| External Fraud | Number of branches and geographical distribution; Number of tied agents; Number of on-line accounts |
| Employment Practices and Workplace Safety (*Employment*) | Number of employees |
| Clients, Product & Business Practices (*Product Distribution*) | Number of employees; Number of branches; Number of tied agents; Number of clients; Deposits; Assets under management |
| Damage to Physical Assets (*Physical Assets*) | Physical assets |
| Business Disruption and System Failures (*IT Systems*) | Physical and intangible assets (net of goodwill) |
| Execution, Delivery & Process Management (*Processes*) | Number of clients; Number of transactions; Number of employees; Number of suppliers; Number of outsourcing contracts; Size of internal audit function |

*Source*: Own processing of Basel Committee on Banking Supervision (2006), Annex IX, pp. 305–7.

investigation concern two distinct phenomena: the existence of a link, and its relevance, on the one hand, and the type of size variable that best describes this link on the other. In relation to the first aspect, one study has challenged the existence of a strong link between operational risk and firm size (Shi et al., 2000), claiming that only a very small proportion of operational losses are actually related to size variables. Though not particularly significant, the study also pointed to a non-linear relationship. The motivations put forward to explain the link between firm size and operational risk concern management competence and quality of internal control procedures, both assumed superior in large firms.

The second aspect that deserves special consideration is the type of size variable used to measure bank size. The study cited above employed three typical size variables: total assets, revenue and number of employees. The variable most strongly correlated with loss size was revenue.

Two further studies that set out to identify size variables and to evaluate their relationship to operational risk are the loss data collected exercises conducted in 2005 by the Federal Reserve System (FRS, 2005, pp. 14–18), and in 2007 by the Japanese Financial Services Agency (FSeA) in conjunction with the Bank of Japan (BOJ, 2007, pp. 12–13). Both studies selected as a proxy for bank size total assets (like the previous study), gross income (in the line with the supervisory standards of SA) and the Tier 1 capital requirement.

As Table 7.1 highlights, this chapter attempts to identify a broader set of variables as a proxy for size that makes it possible to relate more accurately the type of loss event with the best explanatory variable. The chosen size variables are number of employees, number and geographical distribution of branches, number of online accounts, number of tied agents, number of suppliers and outsourcing contracts, total physical and intangible assets, deposits and assets under management, and human resources dedicated to the internal control function.

In particular, among the factors crucial to an understanding of the link between operational risk and size variables are bank distribution structures (specifically the territorial distribution of branches) and alternative distribution channels (the inexorable rise of the Internet and tied agents). Indeed, it has been seen that the use of tied agents may encourage very aggressive sales policies, with consequent repercussions on the operational loss category Clients, Product & Business Practices (Prosperetti, 2008, pp. 10–15). It also seems legitimate to suppose that incentive schemes for distribution personnel and top management responsible for the corporate budget function may encourage unscrupulous behaviour on the borderline of regulations designed to protect depositors and investors.

The choice of this set of size variables was justified by the relevance to the present chapter of the link between operational risk and bank size. Dimensional growth, often achieved by creating huge banking groups diversified across sectors and geographical areas, poses organisational problems (relating also to distribution systems), and complicates the design of emergency plans in the event of breakdowns in operational and IT systems.

It is also essential to remember that the success of M&As depends on the integration of distinct company cultures and managerial styles, as well as operational, risk management and ICT systems: the latter is a lengthy process, and there is a high probability of malfunctions and errors.

Returning to the four risk categories – procedures, human resources, systems and external events – it can be said that both organisational structures and related processes, and human resources are widely implicated in M&A processes.

Within the context of the integration of ICT systems, an inevitable part of any merger, it is important to underline the importance of the choice of migration strategy: the decision to implement a 'roll out'(involving groups of branches or functions simultaneously) or a 'big bang' (involving all branches or all functions simultaneously) may have a significant impact on operational risk.

External growth therefore appears to increase the risks associated with organisational and control aspects in particular.

The operational risk consequences of M&As are particularly evident in the case of cross-border M&As. In operations of this type, several aspects are especially problematic: on the one hand, linguistic and cultural barriers may exacerbate human resource management issues; on the other hand, the more complex territorial distribution may heighten problems of organisation and control. Finally, legislative differences between countries may be a further source of operational risk for banks operating at a transnational level.

## 7.3  Operational loss data collection

Before examining the impact of M&As on operational risk through two case studies, it is useful to consider the results of the main operational loss data collection exercises conducted at an international level to gain an overview of areas that are critical to operational risk management. This will provide a benchmark for subsequent analysis of the composition of such risk in a number of banks involved in mergers.

The loss data collection exercises compared below are those conducted by the Federal Reserve System in 2005 and by the Financial Services Agency in conjunction with the Bank of Japan in 2007, in addition to an exercise conducted in 2003 by the Basel Committee on Banking Supervision (BCBS, 2003b). A new loss data collection using 2008 data by the Basel Committee on Banking Supervision was forthcoming at the time of writing.

Comparison of the results of the studies makes it possible to identify the most critical event types in terms of frequency and severity of operational losses. However, it is important to note the diversity of sample banks: the BCBS (2003b) survey was based on a set of banks based in G10 countries; on the other hand, the FRS (2005) survey was restricted to banks operating on the US market; the FSeA survey conducted in conjunction with BOJ (2007) included only Japanese banks.

In terms of loss event type and frequency (Table 7.2), the results of the BCBS survey highlight how the principal causes are, on the one hand, fraudulent acts committed by outsiders (External Fraud: 43 per cent of loss events) and failures in internal processes on the other, due to ineffective communication, or failure to define or assign roles and responsibilities (Processes: 35 per cent of cases).

Note the concentration of losses by event type. Indeed, 94 per cent of losses relate to four event types: firstly, External Fraud and Processes; secondly, issues relating to health and safety legislation (Employment: 8.6 per cent) and negligence or incompetence in the fulfilment of obligations towards clients (Product Distribution: around 7 per cent).

This risk configuration is largely confirmed by the two other loss data collection exercises, both of which report a significant number of loss events due to External Fraud (39 per cent and 36.5 per cent respectively for the FRS 2005 survey and the FSeA 2007 survey) and failures in internal processes (Processes: 35.3 per cent and 38.6 per cent respectively for 2005 and 2007). The surveys also confirm the high concentration of losses (90–95 per cent)

*Table 7.2* Number of losses and amount of losses by event type

| Event Type | BCBS – 2003 | FRS – 2005 | FSeA & BOJ – 2007 | BCBS – 2003 | FRS – 2005 | FSeA & BOJ – 2007 |
|---|---|---|---|---|---|---|
| | Number of losses – % of total | | | Amount of losses – % of total | | |
| Internal Fraud | 3.34 | 3.40 | 1.80 | 7.30 | 0.90 | 2.90 |
| External Fraud | 42.82 | 39.00 | 36.50 | 15.67 | 5.10 | 8.30 |
| Employment | 8.61 | 7.60 | 1.50 | 6.82 | 1.70 | 1.00 |
| Product Distribution | 7.24 | 9.20 | 8.80 | 13.27 | 79.80 | 24.80 |
| Physical Assets | 1.41 | 0.70 | 1.90 | 24.50 | 1.40 | 4.50 |
| IT Systems | 1.16 | 0.70 | 10.90 | 2.76 | 0.80 | 3.90 |
| Processes | 35.42 | 35.30 | 38.60 | 29.68 | 9.60 | 54.60 |
| Other | – | 4.10 | – | – | 0.70 | – |

*Source*: Own processing of Basel Committee on Banking Supervision (2003b), pp. 6–7; Federal Reserve System (2005), pp. 28–9 and Financial Service Agency, Bank of Japan (2007), pp. 8–9.

in four or five categories of event type: External Fraud, Processes, Product Distribution, Employment and IT Systems.

With reference to loss severity (Table 7.2), the BCBS data confirm that the most important loss event type in relative terms is failures in internal process management (Processes: around 30 per cent of overall operational losses). Other particularly critical areas include External Fraud (around 16 per cent) and negligence or incompetence in the fulfilment of obligations towards clients (Product Distribution: 13 per cent).

The last two data collections present analogies in terms of event types associated with serious losses (External Fraud, Product Distribution, Processes), but differ significantly in terms of the relative importance of single loss event types. While the FRS exercise conducted in 2005 highlights an absolute predominance of Product Distribution (around 80 per cent of losses), in the 2007 FSeA exercise Processes is the single most important event type (54.6 per cent).

The loss data collection exercises underline the uniformity of risk areas in terms of frequency and severity of losses. However, the distribution of loss events is more even in terms of frequency than in terms of severity; in the latter case, there are significant differences in the relative importance of the different loss event types.

In this context, it is essential to remember that these data collections, based on aggregate data, not only offer a limited picture of the unique risk profile of each bank, but in some cases are also somewhat outdated. Over the years, there have been remarkable improvements in loss data collection by banks.

## 7.4   Critique of data collection methods

Any approach to the quantification, assessment and composition of operational risk should consider the many doubts and problems inherent in data collection that can invalidate analyses based on historical data.

The first problem concerns the limitations implicit in the definition and hence the quantification of risk. The Basel Committee's definition of operational risk has been criticised for taking into account only causal factors, and for the possible overlaps between causal factors, as well as the imperfect distinction between cause, event and effect of the loss (damage to Physical Assets may be interpreted both as an event and an effect) (Basel Committee on Banking Supervision – The Joint Forum, 2003, p. 9).

Although a definition of operational loss based on causal factors is extremely useful, particularly for identifying critical areas in organisational structures and possible remedies, a further aspect that could be evaluated is the impact of operational losses, particularly on the cost side of the income statement (Write-downs, Loss of Recourse, Restitutions, Legal Liability, Regulatory and Compliance, Loss of or Damage to Assets).

In outlining the critical aspects relating to the definition and quantification of operational risk, it is essential to remember that there may be overlaps between this type of risk and market and credit risk.

An appropriate definition of operational risk thus provides a starting point from which to identify a correct approach to the quantification of risk and to adequate loss data collection.

Indeed, the identification of an appropriate method for the measurement of operational risk is a much-debated issue, especially for small banks that may lack the resources and skills required to put in place an internal model for the measurement of operational losses.

The complexities of implementing internal models for the measurement of operational risk include not only the availability of adequate resources and skills, but also the availability of historical data sets on operational losses. One particularly critical aspect is the unwillingness of banks to disclose information on operational risk, and above all on Internal and External Fraud.

In terms of the availability of reliable data on operational losses, of particular relevance here is the opinion of a study that points to a link between the quality of data and the realisation of M&As (Wahlstrom, 2006, p. 508). Banks undergoing consolidation tend to be deprived of a stable organisational structure, and this has an adverse impact on the effective operational loss data collection.

Loss data collection is fundamental for the management of operational risk, and in strategic terms is as important as the definition of operational risk itself. Indeed, good loss data collection is relevant to the determination of expected and unexpected losses, and the treatment of catastrophic events.

However, even with an adequate definition of operational risk, the use of loss data from company accounts is potentially restrictive given the extent of the phenomenon. A further objection is that the use of historical data to calculate capital requirements is punitive since internal controls are refined and upgraded on the basis of past experience (Power, 2003, p. 10). Finally, it is well known that future trends of operational losses, particularly peak values, cannot be inferred with certainty from historical data.

Although it is beyond the scope of this chapter to provide a thorough investigation of the specificities of loss data collection and data quality, the doubts and concerns surrounding this issue should be taken into account when using this kind of data.

The remainder of the chapter is concerned with the analysis of operational losses using internal loss data collections from two banks involved in M&A processes.

## 7.5   Case studies: UniCredit Group and Intesa SanPaolo

The case studies examine two mergers: UniCredit-HVB and Intesa SanPaolo. This choice was justified by the importance of these operations on the M&A landscape in Italy, and by the opportunity they provide to analyse the implicit differences between cross-border and domestic mergers.

The time horizons of the two case studies are different and reflect the time of completion of the mergers: 1 January 2006 for UniCredit Group and 1 January 2007 for Intesa SanPaolo. In both cases, data from the first two post-merger years was analysed.

For UniCredit Group, the time horizon spanned from 2005 to 2007: for 2005, data were analysed separately for UniCredit and HVB. For Intesa SanPaolo, the data set covered the period from 2005 to 2008: for the two years 2005 and 2006, Intesa and SanPaolo were analysed separately.

Table 7.3 shows total assets of the banks involved in the two mergers. The data gives an indication of the size of banks.

*Table 7.3*   Total assets of UniCredit Group and Intesa SanPaolo (billions of euros)

| Year | UniCredit Group | | | Intesa SanPaolo | | |
|---|---|---|---|---|---|---|
| | HVB | UniCredit | Merger | Intesa | SanPaolo | Merger |
| 2005 | 493.5 | 304.5 | | 273.5 | 263.3 | |
| 2006 | | | 823.3 | 291.8 | 288.6 | |
| 2007 | | | 1,021.8 | | | 572.9 |
| 2008 | | | | | | 633.8* |

*Note*: *Data at 30 September 2008.
*Source*: own processing of UniCredit Group and Intesa SanPaolo Annual Reports.

The initial dataset included daily losses classified by event type and business line. Figures refer to date of occurrence. In terms of the severity of loss events, note that in both cases data was provided on a scale, with 100,000 representing the maximum loss during the time horizon and the remaining losses proportional to this value. Although this solution safeguards the confidentiality of data, the fact that losses are not expressed in euros prevents comparison of results between case studies. Nevertheless, data on frequency of occurrence is comparable.

Before evaluating results, note that in the process of data elaboration a number of working hypotheses were introduced to ensure uniform treatment of loss data across the two case studies.

For the UniCredit Group, it is important to highlight the solution adopted for operational losses in Central and Eastern Europe (CEE) in 2005. Since data related to the area in which the loss event occurred, it was necessary to relate the losses for that year to either UniCredit or HVB. It was decided to allocate loss events in proportion to the total assets of each bank, and then to attribute the single events on a random basis.

In the case of Intesa SanPaolo, it is essential to underline that some losses were labelled 'post merger' since they were recorded after completion of the merger, but were dated prior to 1 January 2007. Therefore, for the period 2005–6 loss events were reallocated to the separate banks (Intesa and SanPaolo) in relation to the frequency of occurrence of loss events during the year, and the loss amounts attributed to one or other bank on a random basis.

In the first instance, analysis consisted of an evaluation of the relative composition of operational losses in terms of severity and frequency; the aim was to capture any similarities or differences in loss composition before and after the merger operation.

Note firstly the asymmetric distribution of activities among Strategic Business Units (SBUs) for both UniCredit and HVB prior to the merger. UniCredit focussed prevalently on Retail, Private and Asset Management, while HVB was clearly oriented towards Corporate and Investment banking. Conversely, the Intesa and SanPaolo portfolio of activities was more evenly distributed among SBUs.

The percentage composition of loss severity for UniCredit (Figure 7.1) in 2005, the year prior to the merger, reveals significant differences between the two banks. In fact, HVB's losses were concentrated in Processes (around 55 per cent), while UniCredit was more exposed in Product Distribution (40 per cent). Another difference between the two banks can be seen in the Internal Fraud category, which is significantly higher in percentage terms for UniCredit than HVB, while values are very similar in the case of External Fraud.

In the first two post-merger years, analysis of the percentage weight of the severity of loss events highlights two opposing tendencies: an increase in the relative weight of Product Distribution (around 52 per cent) and a decrease in Processes (23 per cent on average in the two years).

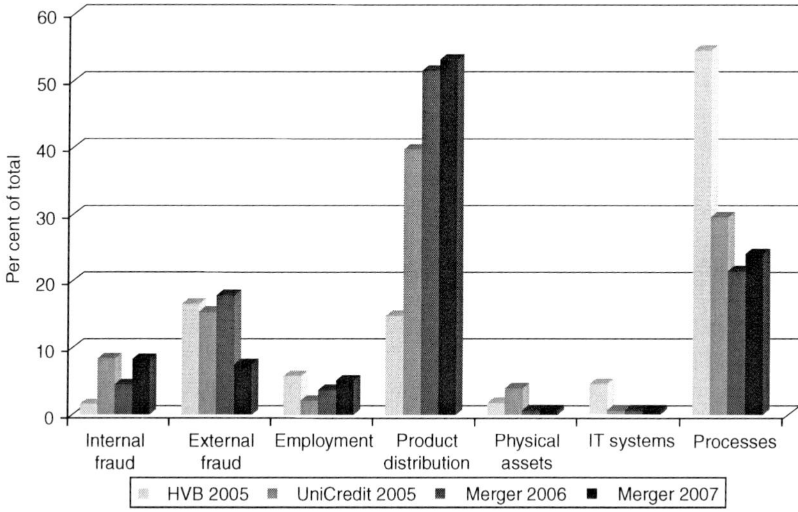


*Figure 7.1*   Total amount of losses by event type for UniCredit Group
*Source*: Own processing of UniCredit Group internal data.

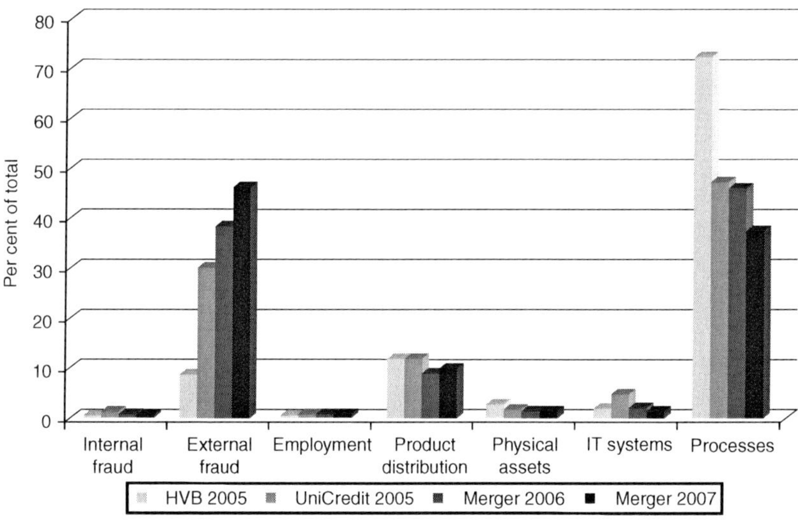


*Figure 7.2*   Number of losses by event type for UniCredit Group
*Source*: Own processing of UniCredit Group internal data.

Overall, the post-merger severity of operational losses appears to reflect UniCredit pre-merger values. A striking decrease in External Fraud in 2007 can also be highlighted.

As Figure 7.2 shows, percentage data on frequency of loss events prior to the merger confirm the greater risk exposure of HVB compared to UniCredit in Processes (74 per cent against 48 per cent), while values are similar for Product Distribution (12 per cent). Note the much higher relative risk exposure of UniCredit in relation to HVB in External Fraud.

In the two years following the merger, the only event type that decreased in relative weight, mirroring data on loss severity, was Processes (47 per cent in 2006 and 38 per cent in 2007). Other aspects worthy of note include the substantial stability of Product Distribution and the considerable increase, above all in 2007, in External Fraud (that peaked at 47 per cent in 2007).

In the case of Intesa SanPaolo, during the pre-merger period and especially in 2005, it can be seen from Figure 7.3 that the severity of losses was very similar for the two banks. In particular, losses were concentrated in Product Distribution and Processes (75–80 per cent of total loss events). Data for 2006 point to an increase in the relative weight of Internal Fraud for both banks, and changes in the relative composition of loss events for SanPaolo in the form of a significant decrease in Product Distribution (down to 48 per cent) and a corresponding increase in Processes (up to 17 per cent).

In the post-merger period, two contrasting tendencies emerge in the percentage composition of loss events. These are particularly evident in 2008: the marked decline in the relative weight of Product Distribution (20 per cent in 2008) and the considerable increase in the relative weight of

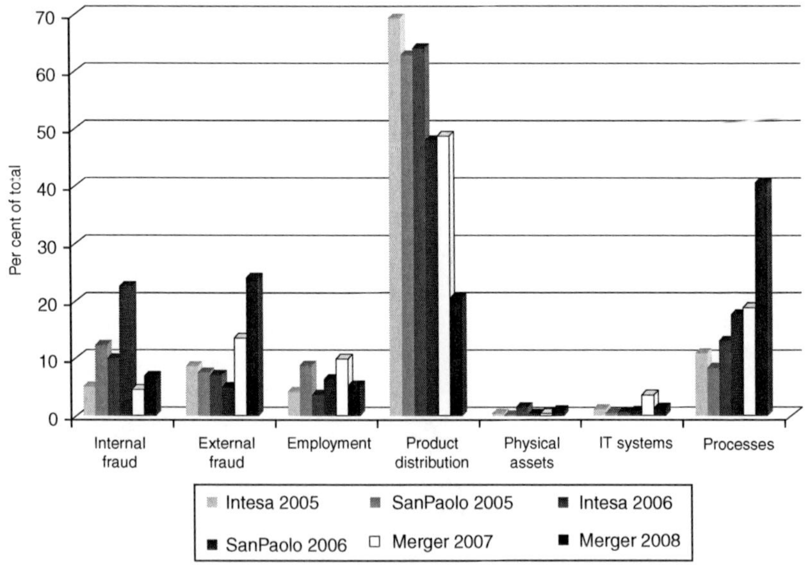


*Figure 7.3* Total amount of losses by event type for Intesa SanPaolo
*Source*: Own processing of Intesa SanPaolo internal data.

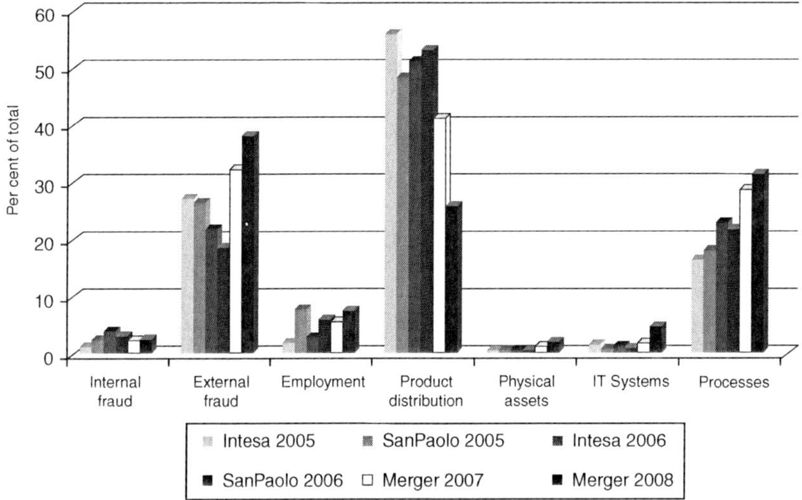


*Figure 7.4*   Number of losses by event type for Intesa SanPaolo
*Source*: Own processing of Intesa SanPaolo internal data.

Processes (41 per cent), a total reversal of the UniCredit Group trend. The significant increase in the percentage of External Fraud and the decrease in Internal Fraud can also be observed.

In terms of the frequency of loss events, the percentage composition for the two banks prior to the merger (Figure 7.4) was essentially the same. The event types Product Distribution (in excess of 50 per cent), External Fraud (24 per cent) and Processes (around 15 per cent) were particularly critical.

The evolution in the percentage composition of loss event frequency in the post-merger period brings us to the same conclusions as those on loss severity: there was a significant decrease in the percentage weight of Product Distribution (23 per cent), above all in 2008, and, conversely, an increase in the percentage weight of Processes (28 per cent) and External Fraud (34 per cent), the latter being the only event type that presented analogies to the UniCredit Group.

As well as changes in the percentage composition of operational losses, in order to capture possible links between operational risk and company size, it was decided to assess the absolute and relative severity of operational losses in the two cases. For loss severity, the sum of the scale values of annual losses was related to a variable representing bank size.

In order to identify a size variable suited to all event types, and in line with the other studies examined above, in the first stage of analysis the severity of single loss events was related to total bank assets expressed in billions of euros (see Tables 7.4 and 7.6).

Conversely, in the second stage it was decided to use size variables differentiated both in relation to the type of loss event, on the basis of the links described above and summarised in Table 7.1, and also in relation to the availability of public data. The chosen size variables (from those indicated in Tables 7.5 and 7.7) were the following:

- Total employees for Internal Fraud and Employment;
- Number of branches for External Fraud;
- Deposits and assets under management for Product Distribution;
- Physical assets for Physical Assets;
- Physical and intangible assets for IT Systems;
- Total assets for Processes.

For the purposes of data elaboration, accounting data at 31 December of each year was used with the exception of the year 2008 for Intesa SanPaolo, when it was necessary to use data at 30 September 2008.

In the case of UniCredit Group it was impossible to obtain data on assets under management: together with deposits, this variable was replaced by total assets.

For UniCredit Group, note the marked asymmetry in the severity of operational losses for the two banks in the pre-merger period. The loss events recorded by UniCredit were three times higher, and less frequent than those reported by HVB. In absolute terms, following the merger a significant increase in the severity and frequency of operational losses was seen compared to the sum of the pre-merger values for the two banks.

In relative terms, prior to the merger UniCredit recorded operational losses to total assets (Table 7.4) almost five times higher than HVB. The total assets of the HVB were 1.6 times higher than those of UniCredit. This result might appear to exclude any direct link between bank size and severity of operational losses.

In the post-merger period, operational losses to total assets were significantly higher than HVB's pre-merger values, but marginally lower than pre-merger values for UniCredit. This is explained by the trends in operational losses and total assets in the post-merger period compared to pre-merger figures for the two banks. On the one hand, the post-merger operational losses in absolute terms increased considerably in 2006, particularly when compared to HVB losses (+625 per cent compared to +142 per cent pre-merger for UniCredit); on the other hand, the post-merger value of total assets shows a less than proportional increase in relation to HVB losses (+67 per cent) and a more than proportional increase compared to UniCredit (+170 per cent).

Moving on to a more detailed analysis of the relative severity of loss event types, Tables 7.4 and 7.5 highlight an increase in the severity of losses in the categories Employment and Product Distribution in the post-merger

*Table 7.4*   Loss amount in relation to total assets for UniCredit Group

| Event Type | 2005 | | 2006 | 2007 |
| --- | --- | --- | --- | --- |
| | **HVB** | **UniCredit** | **Merger** | **Merger** |
| Internal Fraud | 2.452 | 62.133 | 29.230 | 57.306 |
| External Fraud | 25.097 | 112.411 | 117.158 | 52.282 |
| Employment | 8.724 | 15.706 | 23.854 | 35.247 |
| Product Distribution | 22.267 | 292.310 | 337.726 | 363.156 |
| Physical Assets | 2.845 | 29.445 | 3.422 | 4.755 |
| IT Systems | 7.066 | 4.587 | 5.186 | 4.156 |
| Processes | 82.738 | 217.008 | 139.522 | 165.173 |
| *Total* | *151.189* | *733.600* | *656.099* | *682.074* |

*Source*: Own processing of UniCredit Group internal data.

period. In terms of operational loss events deriving from human resource management, an increase in relative severity, both to total assets and to employee, is indicative of the problems of integration and reorganisation of functions. These factors can be particularly relevant in cross-border consolidation.

The relative severity of Internal Fraud and Processes is in line with overall results, with a post-merger value somewhere between the equivalent values for the two separate banks in 2005 (with the exception of relative severity per employee in 2007 for Internal Fraud), and higher in 2007 than in 2006.

Results are entirely different in External Fraud and IT Systems. The relative severity, to total assets and per branch, of External Fraud losses increased in 2006 compared to pre-merger values for the two banks, and then levelled out at a much lower value in 2007. Loss events relating to IT Systems decreased in relative severity (contrary to the experience of Intesa SanPaolo examined below); this decrease was particularly remarkable in the light of the ratio of Physical Assets to total assets, and 2007 values compared to 2006.

*Table 7.5*   Loss amount in relation to bank size for UniCredit Group

| Event Type | 2005 | | 2006 | 2007 |
| --- | --- | --- | --- | --- |
| | **HVB** | **UniCredit** | **Merger** | **Merger** |
| Internal Fraud | 0.020 | 0.265 | 0.175 | 0.345 |
| External Fraud | 5.376 | 7.015 | 13.111 | 5.499 |
| Employment | 0.070 | 0.067 | 0.143 | 0.212 |
| Product Distribution | 22.267 | 292.310 | 337.726 | 363.156 |
| Physical Assets | 431.127 | 2,121.743 | 326.985 | 336.539 |
| IT Systems | 876.659 | 303.590 | 194.513 | 108.078 |
| Processes | 82.738 | 217.008 | 139.522 | 165.173 |

*Source*: Own processing of UniCredit Group internal data.

In the case of Intesa SanPaolo, no significant differences between the two banks in terms of severity or frequency of loss events are evident in the pre-merger period, although Intesa recorded higher operational losses than SanPaolo (+20 per cent in 2005 and +26 per cent in 2006), despite the fact that Intesa's total assets were only 4 per cent higher than those of SanPaolo. Similarly, loss event frequency was higher for Intesa than for SanPaolo in the same period.

One aspect worthy of note is the absolute values for loss severity and frequency, which declined sharply in the post-merger period in relation to both Intesa pre-merger values and aggregate pre-merger values. In other words, despite an almost twofold increase in the post-merger total assets of Intesa SanPaolo, the frequency and severity of post-merger operational losses fell in absolute terms; this in turn produced a marked decline in relative terms as well. These results suggest that in this case the merger did not result in an increase in loss frequency or severity, although the organisational complexity of the new banking group was presumably greater.

As the case study demonstrates, even the sudden increases in size typically seen in external growth do not necessarily result in an increase in operational risk. It is possible that decreases in risk are the result of external and exogenous factors, more efficient systems of internal control, in other words more efficient operational risk management tools (prevention and mitigation) and optimal management of the merger process and the post-merger critical issues.

The severity of single event types can be analysed in detail using data in Tables 7.6 and 7.7. In the post-merger period, there is evidence of a progressive reduction in the relative severity of Internal Fraud and Product Distribution. A slightly different trend is seen in Processes: in this case,

*Table 7.6*   Loss amount in relation to total asses for Intesa SanPaolo

| Event Type | 2005 | | 2006 | | 2007 | 2008 |
|---|---|---|---|---|---|---|
| | Intesa | SanPaolo | Intesa | SanPaolo | Merger | Merger |
| Internal Fraud | 101.251 | 201.753 | 174.654 | 309.444 | 42.488 | 30.273 |
| External Fraud | 165.692 | 124.520 | 124.841 | 71.629 | 115.171 | 104.368 |
| Employment | 85.122 | 142.943 | 64.150 | 88.960 | 84.084 | 24.752 |
| Product Distribution | 1,336.850 | 1,053.546 | 1,116.075 | 674.920 | 419.082 | 89.972 |
| Physical Assets | 6.388 | 2.539 | 28.068 | 4.465 | 2.765 | 5.363 |
| IT Systems | 23.792 | 3.633 | 11.653 | 5.075 | 31.976 | 7.832 |
| Processes | 207.762 | 137.490 | 225.397 | 242.163 | 159.140 | 180.888 |
| *Total* | *1,926.857* | *1,666.426* | *1,744.837* | *1,396.657* | *854.705* | *443.449* |

*Source*: Own processing of Intesa SanPaolo internal data.

*Table 7.7*   Loss amount in relation to bank size for Intesa SanPaolo

| Event Type | 2005 | | 2006 | | 2007 | 2008 |
| --- | --- | --- | --- | --- | --- | --- |
| | Intesa | SanPaolo | Intesa | SanPaolo | Merger | Merger |
| Internal Fraud | 0.456 | 1.255 | 0.899 | 1.783 | 0.253 | 0.170 |
| External Fraud | 11.416 | 9.910 | 9.171 | 5.585 | 8.926 | 7.805 |
| Employment | 0.383 | 0.889 | 0.330 | 0.513 | 0.501 | 0.139 |
| Product Distribution | 769.211 | 648.840 | 646.662 | 412.275 | 232.722 | 53.945 |
| Physical Assets | 597.567 | 307.072 | 2,796.990 | 436.623 | 305.188 | 582.080 |
| IT Systems | 1,520.579 | 300.320 | 789.062 | 278.603 | 592.750 | 142.768 |
| Processes | 207.762 | 137.490 | 225.397 | 242.163 | 159.140 | 180.888 |

*Source*: Own processing of Intesa SanPaolo internal data.

relative severity decreased in 2007, but then began to increase again in 2008, though growth was less than proportional to size.

The relative values for External Fraud to total assets and per branch decreased in 2008 in relation to 2007, and settled at an intermediate level between the peak values of Intesa and the lower values of SanPaolo in the two years prior to the merger. These results seem to confirm the doubts concerning a direct link between size and operational risk, and may be due to the geographical distribution of the branches of the two banks and to crime rate differentials.

Of particular interest is the trend in relative severity in the Employment and IT Systems event type categories. In both cases, an increase in the first year after the merger was followed by a significant decrease in 2008.

As concerns the case of Employment in particular, this trend confirms that merger processes may give rise to problems of reorganisation of tasks and functions, a potential source of operational risk that tends however to diminish over time.

A similar trend in loss events relating to IT Systems, both to total assets and to physical and intangible assets, provides further evidence that the merger integration process may have a significant impact on operational losses due to substitution of IT platforms rather than the larger size of the newly formed group.

## 7.6   Conclusions

The aim of the present chapter was to understand the possible links between growth, bank size and operational risk, and to examine the dynamics of operational risk during consolidation by seeking to identify changes in the quality and quantity of operational risk in the newly merged group compared to pre-merger operational loss events recorded by the individual banks.

In terms of quality of risk, opposing trends in two different classes of risk, Product Distribution and Processes, traditionally considered the most critical for operational risk management, emerged very clearly from the case studies. In percentage terms, in the post-merger period UniCredit Group recorded an increase in loss events in Product Distribution and a decrease in Processes. Results for Intesa SanPaolo were the exact opposite.

Subsequently, the hypothesis of a possible link between bank size and the magnitude of operational risk was evaluated – the same hypothesis underlying the Basic Indicator and Standard Approaches for the calculation of capital requirements to cover expected and unexpected losses. In other words, an attempt was made to verify whether there is a relation – not necessarily a linear relation – between bank size and operational loss severity and frequency. The conclusions must take into account certain limitations of the historical data set used in the studies, in particular the limited time horizon and a number of exceptional events that had an abnormal impact on certain types of loss contained in the data set.

With these limitations in mind, it is not possible to identify a strong link between the size of a bank and its operational risk, as demonstrated by HVB and UniCredit pre-merger data, and analysis of Intesa SanPaolo's operational losses in relation to the two banks prior to the merger. Furthermore, the process of external growth itself does not necessarily imply an increase in operational risk in absolute or relative terms, as demonstrated by Intesa SanPaolo (and in contrast to UniCredit Group).

The only feature common to both case studies was an increase in operational losses in Employment.

What also emerged – and was confirmed by operational risk managers – is that increases in operational losses depend on factors not necessarily related to the process of external growth.

Leaving these considerations aside, it should be remembered that from a methodological standpoint two case studies are not sufficient to confirm or refute the existence of a link between bank size and operational risk.

If these findings are true, it may be that variables other than size contribute to, or have an impact on, operational risk. A more thorough understanding of the factors governing the dynamics of operational losses, particularly in the context of external growth, may therefore constitute an interesting direction for future research.

# 8
# The Supervision of European Insurance Groups

*Alberto Dreassi and Stefano Miani*

## 8.1  Introduction

The regulation of cross-border and cross-sector financial activities is currently facing several issues and challenges, most of which are the result of the lack of a thorough cross-national harmonisation of business and supervisory practices. The European legislator is expending substantial energy on its forthcoming Solvency 2 framework which, despite its scheduled implementation in 2012, is still struggling to achieve a standard approach for the financial requirements, supervisory review process and market conduct of European insurers and reinsurers.

Recent events linked to the financial turmoil, and originating mainly in liquidity issues in the subprime mortgage business but extending rapidly to all economic sectors, are underlining the importance of innovative and more active supervision and regulation. Liquidity and credit risks have brought about significant threats to the banking sector, but the impact on the insurance industry is, at this stage, still limited. This is attributable mainly to existing differences in the two core activities, with insurers investing in more secure and long-term assets, subject to relatively stable cash outflows and featured by the inversion of the operating cycle. However, crisis has also emerged in this sector: severely affected by liquidity shortages after a rating downgrade and the resulting need for collateral, the American International Group (AIG) (the world's largest insurer by asset value) is meeting its obligations only through a rescue plan launched by the Federal Reserve Bank, after shareholders' value depleted almost completely in only a few weeks. The need for intervention to avoid bankruptcy was manifested several times during the financial crisis: currently, after the initial bailout of September 2008, in at least other two major circumstances modifications and integrations to the original plan were issued (October and November). This global group, nonetheless, is also active outside the insurance business (for instance, mortgages, the leasing of aircrafts and real estate), raising doubts about the true capability of markets and supervisors to assess properly the risk profile of cross-border and cross-sector financial and industrial conglomerates. More recently, the group reported a loss for the fourth quarter of 2008 that was greater than $60 billion (the largest in history for a single group) and called for further financial support from the US government (totalling more than $180 billion). This example is far from being over at this time, and led to greater public attention being given to the issue of corporate and regulatory/supervisory responsibility of the global economy.

In this chapter, following a brief description of insurance groups in Europe (section 8.2), we examine the limited literature on this topic, providing a detailed discussion on the development of proper principles and rules for the supervision and regulation of cross-border and cross-sector financial groups, with particular reference to insurance activities, which are less internationalised than banks but show greater potential for further consolidation (section 8.3).

We then analyse the overarching and still evolving contribution of the International Association of Insurance Supervisors (section 8.4), as a benchmark for the following comparison of the current European approach to insurance groups supervision (section 8.5), as opposed to the current stage of development achieved by the forthcoming Solvency 2 project (section 8.6).

We find that, despite the size of the cross-border insurance business, many challenges are still faced by regulators and supervisors.

Some issues arise from the differences in supervision applied to European groups acting outside the European Union, and alien insurers willing to do business in the Common Market. The shift towards a risk-based approach of supervision, together with the right of passporting granted by European regulation, poses significant issues to supervisors and undertakings, given that a greater level of discretionality and coordination is required and that authorities have different experience in this field.

Moreover, the introduction of the group support regime to recognise capitals' fungibility casts some questions on the potential increase of contagion and systemic risks across entities, given that no consensus has yet emerged on diversification benefits.

In section 8.7 we finally provide some policy remarks in the light of the improvements that need to be achieved in European regulation, to mark a new step in supervision of insurance groups and, therefore, financial conglomerates.

## 8.2  Overview of European insurance groups

Since the 1990s global financial sectors have been experiencing a period of increased convergence and consolidation. In particular, in the European Union, insurance companies were substantially influenced by liberalisation and deregulation, which culminated with the Third Generation Insurance

Directives, leading to increased competition and lower prices (Swiss Re, 2000). The main purpose and effects of that provision were to create and promote a single internal market for financial services, at that time subject to several regulatory restrictions and institutional barriers across member states. Afterwards, the introduction of a single currency in 1999 pushed this unprecedented evolution even further, resulting in a wave of cross-border mergers and acquisitions, not only within the same financial sector but also across sectors (banks, insurance companies, pension funds and investment firms), as described by the Comité Européen des Assurances (CEA, 2008a).

This phenomenon was even stronger in the insurance sector itself: between 1990 and 2003, 30 per cent of all deals involved cross-border entities, more than double the rate for banks (Focarelli and Pozzolo, 2008). As a result of this consolidation, most international insurers adopted the legal and governance model of groups to run their business.

The process itself is continuing to involve the insurance sector, and further efforts have been spent by the European Union in harmonising the regulation and supervision of insurance groups: the Insurance Groups Directive came into force in 1998, whereas the Helsinki Protocol was issued in 2000.

Currently, a new impulse to mergers and acquisitions is expected as a consequence of the forthcoming European solvency framework (Solvency 2): despite the fact that its contents are still under discussion, it is reasonable to expect further improvements and more accurate approaches to regulation and supervision of insurance groups.

As at June 2008, the Helsinki Protocol list updated by the Committee of European Insurance and Occupational Pensions Supervisors (CEIOPS) lists 112 European groups with cross-border activities, with the largest 20 accounting for approximately 50 per cent of the total volume of premiums in Europe and 27 already part of a financial conglomerate. Among others (small and medium-sized), almost half are licensed in two countries, whereas the others are present in more (up to nine) EU/EEA members.

It is interesting to underline how many groups are active in specific European regions, such as Belgium–Netherlands–Luxembourg or Scandinavia. Moreover, despite the fact that only some of them act as global players, many have subsidiaries or head offices in the USA, while their presence in other non-EU countries is relevant in individual groups for specific reasons: as will be discussed in the next section, close links exist between cross-border consolidation and 'social' features of insurance markets (among others, language, culture and local regulation – as taxes and social security systems), and not only with reference to their size and profitability.

In 2006, the 20 largest insurance groups in the EU accounted for almost 50 per cent of total internal gross direct premiums written, but at the same time they collected almost 30 per cent of their turnover outside Europe, principally in North America (15 per cent) and the Asia-Pacific region (9 per cent) (CEA, 2008a).

Given the size and importance of this phenomenon, it is quite reasonable to expect that running an international insurance business through groups provides competitive advantages when compared to individual entities. Nonetheless, affiliation to groups provides both opportunities (such as access to sources of capital, expertise, brand, and so on) and threats: contagion risks, regulatory arbitrage, failure in conducting effective supervision are just the most cited.

It should be noted that a significant degree of heterogeneity encompasses all groups, each of which could represent a specific case study: nonetheless, regulation and supervision have to cope with the challenge of providing a harmonised framework and a level playing field to enhance the protection of customers in the single market.

## 8.3   Literature review on cross-border insurance groups

A wide literature is available on internationalisation in the banking sector: readers should refer to previous chapters for a complete review. At the same time, only recently has this field of research focused specifically on the insurance sector.

Mergers and acquisitions, in general, aim to increase value for shareholders through the achievement of synergies between entities (Berger et al., 1999): economies of scale and scope, product or geographical diversification are also the most recurrent factors for insurance companies (Cummins et al., 1999; Amel et al., 2004; Group of Ten, 2001). But this process can be explained by other reasons: an increase in market power to reduce competition, defensive acquisitions but also agency issues between shareholders and managers (Floreani and Rigamonti, 2001). The evidence relating to the efficiency gains of mergers and acquisitions is controversial, underlining the existence of potential diseconomies of scale and other issues of integration (Group of Ten, 2001; Cummins and Weiss, 2004), as well as the debated presence of value discounts in diversified mergers and acquisitions (Berger and Ofek, 1995; Van Lelyveld and Knot, 2008). The risk level of groups could be higher or lower than individual entities, depending on reputational and contagion effects as opposed to diversification gains (Gruson, 2004; Darlap and Mayr, 2006; Laeven and Levine, 2007). Other studies, however, underline that cross-border mergers and acquisitions are value-neutral for acquirers but value-creating for targets (Cummins and Weiss, 2004).

Another field of research focused on the drivers of intra-industry trade in the insurance sector. The Organisation for Economic Co-operation and Development (OECD, 1999) provided a comprehensive identification and analysis of conditions and obstacles to the establishment of branches or agencies of foreign insurers, such as specific regulatory requirements. Furthermore, tax issues have an impact on cross-border business (McGowan and Carr, 2000). Despite these obstacles, international insurance companies are able to increase the volume of insurance services, providing product differentiation and consumer welfare (Li et al., 2003).

The pace of these phenomena is not constant across time. In the period 1994–9, for instance, European mergers and acquisitions accounted for more than half of the total acquired life premiums, with one-third attributable to cross-border operations. Five years later these shares had decreased to almost one-third and 16 per cent, respectively (Swiss Re, 2000).

The path followed by entities in establishing cross-border operations is influenced by market structure (competitive markets are preferred), the presence of trade barriers, the strength of demand for insurance, profitability and 'follow the client' considerations (Ma and Pope, 2003). At the same time, location-specific factors (human capital, cultural affinity, geographical proximity) are also significant drivers for internationalisation (Outreville, 2008), as well as internal and external governance (Boubakri et al., 2006).

Integration is strategic for insurance companies as well as banks, but the former are less likely to be affected by taxation and demography and more likely to expand towards countries with lower stock market capitalisation, higher 'market contestability' and G10 countries, at the same time experiencing lower entry barriers (Focarelli and Pozzolo, 2008). However, despite the achieved level of integration and internationalisation, insurance remains a local business (Schoenmaker et al., 2007).

All of these considerations discussed above have important influences on regulatory and supervisory issues (Van den Berghe et al., 1999; Group of Ten, 2001).

Consolidation itself might threaten financial stability, as the least efficient firms increase their risk in order to achieve greater expected returns: even diversification gains show mixed evidence, whereas riskier portfolios or increased operational and managerial issues might arise. Moreover, a more integrated environment might increase systemic risks and their transmission to the real economy. Increased complexities could reduce market discipline, when not balanced by increased transparency, but also improve capital markets. Regarding competition, consolidation might increase the market power of some entities, leading to greater prices and lower volume than in a competitive environment (Group of Ten, 2001).

Among the main conclusions achieved, crisis prevention and management should be improved, especially through a more effective risk-based supervision (Group of Ten, 2001): double gearing of capital, excessive leverage, intra-group transactions, convergence across sectors/countries and contagion risks are the main challenges (see, among others, Joint Forum, 1999a).

## 8.4   International supervisory principles: the IAIS

The path to international convergence on insurance supervision has been greatly influenced by the work of the International Association of Insurance Supervisors (IAIS).

Several principles and standards deal with insurance groups. The main reference for IAIS contributions is represented by the Insurance Core Principle 17, which calls for group-wide supervision, complementary to solo supervision: affiliation to a group is capable of altering risk profiles, financial positions, the role of management and business strategies (IAIS, 2003). Therefore, group-wide supervision should encompass financial requirements as well as the structure of management, fit and proper testing and legal issues, assessing that proper information systems are in place to support this activity. At the same time, group-wide supervision calls for proper cooperation and coordination among supervisors (IAIS, 2000): powers, responsibilities and mutual recognition of supervisory frameworks are essential.

Group supervision should at least involve governance, capital adequacy, the double gearing of capital, intra-group transactions, internal controls and risk management, reinsurance and risk concentration. But this should follow a specific identification of each group's borders: through particular control structures regulatory limitations could be exploited to avoid the construction of a comprehensive picture of the group. For example, a parent company can provide a loan to a non-regulated subsidiary, that could afterwards downstream this capital to an insurance subsidiary: if the non-regulated entity falls outside group-wide supervision, it is possible to generate the double gearing of capital. Finally, coordination of supervisors across countries and sectors involves appropriate protocols on the exchange of prudential information and on protection of confidentiality and secrecy of collected data.

These principles have been further detailed (IAIS, 1999, 2002b), especially on the prerequisites of supervisory coordination, such as the information needs of home and host supervisors, their exchange and confidentiality.

More recently, group-wide supervision emerged as a specific topic (IAIS, 2008a), involving areas such as capital adequacy and assessment methodologies (aggregation, consolidation and legal entity methods), governance, risk management, supervision and supervisory approach. Moreover, this was complemented by guidance on the identification of a group-wide supervisor, the definition of its responsibilities and functions, its powers and authorities and the coordination activity with other supervisors (IAIS, 2008b).

No further guidance is currently provided on specific issues, such as group solvency assessment (a specific contribution is expected in 2009).

Supervision at the group level is required if risk profiles of individual entities might be influenced by this affiliation, especially when intra-group transactions or the double gearing of capital for solvency purposes are involved (IAIS, 2002a). This activity should aim at achieving a full picture of the group, involving financial requirements, corporate governance and market conduct, to identify if and when an issue for the protection of customers might arise. Despite these considerations, the IAIS underlines that group-wide supervision is among the least developed of its core principles (IAIS, 2008a).

Such conclusions call for the intervention of a group supervisor that is granted powers and responsibilities to promote the coordination and cooperation of supervision at the solo level. However, this task is far from being simple as long as a global standard on insurance supervision is not in place: overlaps and deficiencies might arise whenever cooperation and exchange of information across supervisors show some imperfections. Therefore, supervision at the solo level can not be replaced by group-wide supervision.

These overarching principles are not able to provide more insights on issues such as the opportunistic behaviour of national supervisors, for example in case of a financial crisis, that could lead to supervisory actions aiming at protecting domestic branches compared to foreign parent companies or other subsidiaries. Without illustrating such contributions in greater detail, as a general remark we note that only recently European regulation showed greater convergence towards this international supervisory benchmark, as discussed in the following two sections.

## 8.5   The current European insurance groups supervision

### Origins and the three insurance directives

The accomplishment of a single market has been included in European projects since the Treaty establishing the European Community, signed in Rome in 1957. Its Article 52 requires a gradual approach that encompasses, as a first stage, the abolition of restrictions to the freedom of establishment of agencies, branches and subsidiaries across Member States, whereas Article 59 involves the freedom to provide services and Article 73b (replaced) deals with the freedom of movement of capital.

The process involved the following phases:

- with the two First Directives (1973 and 1979), the establishment of branches was free but still subject to control by the host country;
- with the two Second Directives (1988 and 1990), the freedom to provide services was introduced, but private business (as opposed to company business) and small risks (as opposed to large risks) still fell under the host country control.

Only with the Third Directives (1992), in particular, insurance companies were granted the right to obtain only a single license to carry on insurance activities in the common market, implying also free accessibility to foreign products for European customers.

The main achievements of this regulation can be summarised as follows:

- establishment of branches in other European countries requires only the fulfilment of home country requirements;
- insurance products can be sold without prior approval of host country supervisor, but companies are still subject to transparency requirements;
- liberalisation of innovative forms of capital and finance (such as derivatives and hybrid/subordinated loans).

To balance the interests of European customers, harmonised financial and solvency requirements were established at the EU level, in fact introducing a framework later called Solvency 0, to distinguish it from its recent update (Solvency 1: Directives 2002/12/EC and 2002/13/EC).

This new relationship between home and host country supervisors could lead to conflicts of interest, as far as the goal of policyholders' protection is seen in a nationalistic way: therefore, the need of coordination of supervisory action could be seen as essential. Nonetheless, differences in terms of law, taxation, regulation and business practices still exist, potentially reducing the benefits of a single market for European customers. Moreover, the introduction of a clause allowing each supervisor to refuse access to foreign companies and products to protect the 'public interest', given the lack of a specific declination of such principle, could lead to discretionality and discrimination in promoting the common market.

### The Insurance Groups Directive

The adoption of the Insurance Groups Directive (IGD) (98/78/EC) in late 1998 marked another step towards the improvement of the supervision of cross-country insurance groups. A comprehensive picture of the financial situation of an insurance company cannot avoid its group relationships, since these are able to bring about significant changes to its solvency and risk profile.

The Directive should be seen as an improvement for the assessment of individual companies and, consequently, the protection of national policyholders for each supervisory authority. For the first time the European regulator is giving consideration to the potential effects of group participation for individual companies, in both directions: the availability or multiple gearing of financial resources as well as the aggravation or amelioration of the overall risk profile. Moreover, without consistent rules encompassing both individual companies and groups there could be room for regulatory arbitrage or other distortion to a desirable level playing field across entities, with potential adverse consequences to the stability of financial markets. The IGD introduces a supplementary level of supervision on insurance groups, leading to the so-called 'solo-plus' approach: intervention at the entity level is not replaced, but strengthened through the provision of rules concerning intra-group transactions and an adjusted solvency requirement. The latter, in particular, involves alternative methodologies for the calculation of the solvency margin, considering the effects of double-gearing and intra-group creation of capital.

The shift in the scope of insurance supervision, however, does not involve the group level itself as a stand-alone objective, but rather considering the effects of the overall participating environment on the individual insurance company. It is notable, too, that this supplementary supervision suffers from the same pitfalls of the solo solvency margin, namely the lack of risk sensitivity of the overall requirement and the absence of a comprehensive assessment of risk management, internal controls and corporate governance of supervised entities.

Finally, the IGD represents a first milestone on the information needs, the identification of responsible authorities and their cooperation and coordination for the supplementary supervision of insurance groups: in this regard, principles on access to relevant data and collaboration between supervisors were established for the first time, although with little details. Nonetheless, this represents an initial approach to an effective supervision of groups, but lacks consistent methodologies and powers to assess, among others, risks of contagion across entities specific to each insurance group (CEIOPS, 2005c).

The IGD is going to be repealed by the Solvency 2 framework Directive.

## The Helsinki Protocol

Two years later, this picture was further clarified through the agreement of member states on the so-called Helsinki Protocol, aimed at harmonising cooperation between supervisory authorities on cross-border insurance groups: complex entities, often part of international financial conglomerates, present several issues to their supervision, and therefore need coordination and convergence in practices of several authorities. As a general remark, this is a dynamic activity, whereas borders of insurance groups and conglomerates change over time and might develop across sectors or even outside the European Economic Area.

The formation of a Co-ordination Committee represents a first step to promote supervisory cooperation, involving all interested parties to identify the dimensions and risk profile of each group and the relevant relationships between individual entities. This activity leads to a clearer understanding of leading supervisors and consequent information gathering, exchanging, confidentiality and dissemination needs. All this activity should be carried out on an ongoing basis, under the lead of an appointed lead supervisors and the greater participation of one or more key coordinators.

This supplementary supervision should encompass the group's environment and operations both ongoing and in emergency situations, especially regarding intra-group loans, commitments and off-balance sheet items, investments, reinsurance operations, sharing of costs and the solvency margin. These principles recognise and further develop the Joint Forum's contributions, taking into account the need of convergence across countries and financial sectors (Joint Forum, 1999b and 1999c).

Despite these efforts, however, it is recognised that a significant degree of heterogeneity still affects international regulatory and supervisory practices. For instance, the Italian law grants to the insurance supervisor the right to be informed in advance about some categories of intra-group transactions, providing also the power to forbid operations that could jeopardise the groups' solvency. Nonetheless, the Financial Conglomerates Directive (FCD) (2002/87/EC) shows profiles of inconsistency with the insurance supplementary supervision established in the IGD: examples involve a more comprehensive approach to internal control and risk management and eligible elements of capital. A detailed revision process of the FCD is currently involving several EU bodies, and is expected to achieve its final results in early 2009.

## Other recent regulatory measures

The update of the solvency margin developed in 2002 brought only some minor changes applicable to insurance groups and financial conglomerates, namely newly established parameters and thresholds for calculations and an increased recognition of innovative sources of capital as available funds.

In the same year, however, Directive 2002/83/EC recast the contents of previous directives into a comprehensive document for life insurance products. Here it is worth noting the presence of references to the general good principle, already established in previous directives, allowing single European countries to introduce restrictive legislation to protect the 'general good' of the country, therefore limiting the potential for harmonisation: in some cases, national insurance sectors have been subject to penalties, constraints or conditions regarding the conduct of business of foreign entities within their borders.

More recently, in the effort of promoting an increasing degree of international convergence of supervisory practices, the Commitee of European Insurance and Occupational Pensions Supervisors (CEIOPS) issued a document on Coordination Committees (2005a), followed by guidelines for lead supervisors (2006) and about information exchange (2007a). Despite these contributions, however, supervision of cross-border activities still represents a case-by-case activity, with diverging practices in managing detailed situations, potential conflicts of interest between supervisors (especially in crisis management) and reluctancy in sharing information if confidentiality protocols are not fully agreed.

Moreover, outside the EEA European regulation and rules on coordination across supervisors do not apply, therefore originating the need to build convergence in practices towards third countries: when dealing with global players, supervisors might lack the knowledge about other regulatory systems or practices and proper tools for their intervention. In particular, conflicts of interest and information exchange issues could arise more relevantly. In this regard, the main tool adopted is represented by bilateral memorandum of understanding, as those achieved with the USA and Switzerland.

Another field of recent improvement is represented by the convergence of market and supervisory reporting. Given the global nature of financial entities and affinities or differences in their risk-taking activities, this goal is welcomed but particularly complex: at this stage, no suitable balance has been attained between recognition of specificities and consistent treatment of similarities across financial products and sectors. In this area, CEIOPS is collecting contributions from market participants in order to develop EU-wide reporting formats as planned by the ECOFIN Lamfalussy Roadmap. The benefits of such an achievement would be a greater level-playing field across countries and sectors, enhanced disclosure, avoidance of regulatory arbitrage and reduction of costs for both entities and supervisors (CEIOPS, 2007b).

## Lessons learnt from the recent financial crisis

In mid-2007 a severe credit crunch, which had its origins in the mortgage lending sector, hit the USA and spread rapidly across the industrialised countries. This in turn generated a liquidity crisis that deepened substantially, extending to the whole financial sector, and eventually also having a damaging impact on real economies.

The substantial level of insolvencies had an impact on the banking sector and on entities involved in the securitisation of mortgages, and also affected insurance companies. Remarkable regulatory and strategical mistakes are now considered to be the source of this deep and quick inversion of the economic cycle, namely a high leverage of financial firms, an artificially low cost of raising capital and a high degree of unsupervised participation and contractual links between undertakings across countries and sectors.

The overall impact on insurers, however, is now apparently limited, if we exclude credit and suretyship insurance, which are naturally closely connected with the economic cycle. Typical insurance operations themselves give rise to negligible liquidity risks, compared to the overall financial sector; however, as the AIG case suggested, when a departure from insurance core activities is registered, the liquidity and credit crisis might impact with severe consequences. Being part of a global financial conglomerate, and involving also activities such as mortgage lending, exposed the company to contagion risks that materialised in September 2008 and resulted in a bailout by the Federal Reserve.

At the same time, insurers represent a major share of world's financial and real estate investments, and the fall in their values, the flight-to-liquidity and the rise of credit spreads connected to the crises significantly impacted the asset side of their balance sheets. However, their exposure to liquidity risks is lower when compared to other players on financial markets, given the particular nature of their liabilities, linked to events outside the direct influence of financial turmoil.

The existence of financial groups and financial conglomerates and the resulting connections between individual entities within their borders can have a strong influence on their operations and, through contagion, leveraging or double-gearing effects, reduce the strengths and opportunities linked with typical insurance operations. Moreover, several groups extend their activities also across national borders, resulting in challenges and issues for regulation, especially towards the achievement of greater international and cross-sector convergence on prudential supervision.

Finally, as the main outcomes of the recent financial crisis came to the attention of supervisors and policy makers, evidence emerged on the limited knowledge on where riskier assets played their negative influence and how securitisation and structured financial products could rapidly spread the contagion across countries and sectors. This represents, again, an issue for regulators and supervisors, but underlines the need for global transparency, enhanced disclosure and accountability of financial operations, towards international authorities, customers and financial markets: some argue that the limited impact is due to limited transparency of insurers' accounts, the lack of a really common international method to measure solvency requirements and the limitations in scope of International Financial Reporting Standards to date (Lannoo, 2008).

## 8.6   Solvency 2 and supervision of insurance groups

Initiatives to promote a new European framework for insurance solvency supervision date back to at least the 1990s (European Commission, 1999), when some general objectives of the project were first outlined. Since then, the discussions have expanded and deepened, as reflected in a huge number of documents and contributions. It is not the aim of this section to provide further details on these documents: refer to the European Union and CEIOPS websites for further details.

The project itself has been subject to several changes and is now facing its final stage of discussion before full implementation, expected in 2012.

Since its inception, integration processes during the 1990s suggested a greater attention towards groups and cross-sector or cross-border issues. In 2005 we find the first conclusion on this subject (CEIOPS, 2005b):

- consistency and compatibility across sectors and countries reduces the scope for regulatory arbitrage, but through recognition of specialities and not dogmatic application of identical rules;
- diversification benefits should be recognised only at the group level: feasibility and issues on transferability of capital within groups are topics that should be subject to further research;

- contagion risks should be subject to specific quantification and qualification within each undertaking;
- cross-sectoral issues result also in unregulated entities belonging to a group, giving rise to additional contagion, leveraging and double-gearing risks;
- coordination across national authorities is crucial to achieve the scope of group prudential supervision;
- there is explicit need to reformulate the IGD.

More recently, a proposed framework directive was issued by the European Commission (2007b). Several articles involve supervision of insurance and reinsurance undertakings in a group (arts 219–77). In this section we mention those more relevant for the purpose of describing the main challenges of cross-border and cross-sector supervision.

With respect to Solvency 1, the new framework establishes an economic approach for group supervision, that involves a more consolidated view compared to the previous supplementary supervision. The rationale is consistent with other risk-based principles, but results in new issues such as the recognition of diversification benefits and contagion risks, as well as the need for greater cooperation and coordination across supervisors. At the same time advantages consist, among others, in recognition of transferability of capital and its real allocation within groups.

The mechanisms adopted to achieve such goals are mainly represented by the group support regime and the College of Supervisors.

Through the group support regime, the parent undertaking voluntarily issues a legally binding commitment to transfer own funds to its subsidiaries whereas there is a breach in its solvency requirements (namely, the difference between the solvency and the minimum capital requirements), subject to specific conditions and to supervisory approval, but regardless of national borders within the EU. Capital could be raised in this way also from other subsidiaries, if all conditions for eligibility are met.

The group support represents a substantial move towards the development of a more risk-based and integrated financial supervision. Currently, group supervision has a supplementary role if compared to solo supervision; through this new approach, the two are mutually dependent and achieve the same level of importance. Through group support, groups can more easily manage internal capital across countries, avoiding the regulatory costs associated with solo supervision with limited economic perspectives on intra-group transactions. It also represents a consistent recognition of groups' strategies, together with diversification benefits within solvency requirements.

However, group support also presents some unsolved issues.

On one side, diversification and capital transferability within groups might prove to enhance contagion and reputational risks, rather than minimising their effects. The transfer could also be subject to national regulatory restrictions, corporate law restrictions (especially in the case of winding up the business), taxation issues, or non-regulatory consequences, such as towards third parties or considering rating agencies' capital requirements.

On the other side, group support implies a solution to some political issues within the EU. According to the group support regime, host countries shall waive some of their supervisory influence on the subsidiaries of foreign groups, at least in relation to controls on capital adequacy. The leading role in group supervision shall be covered by a group supervisor, usually located in each group's home country: despite cooperation and coordination rules, the powers and responsibilities of the group supervisor are greater. Historically, several countries proved to be reluctant to move in such directions. However, under the group support regime host countries will have the power to call for this transfer of high-quality own funds in case of a breach of solvency control levels.

At the same time, the new dimension of the group's regulation and supervision suggested that coordination–cooperation committees would have proved insufficient to fulfil all of their duties. Colleges of supervisors, led by the group supervisor, would have been the tool to achieve those goals. Moreover, the new requirements implied even a greater attribution of powers and responsibilities to group supervisors than in the previous framework.

Controversies surrounded the discussions and consensus around these particular two issues, leading to the postponing of voting within the European Council of Ministers on several occasions and eventually leading the Presidency to give up group support and return to the previous principles of cross-border supervision (CEA, 2008b). This decision could be seen as a huge step back for Solvency 2 and cross-border insurance supervision as well, a major and still unsolved delay in the path to its final implementation.

## 8.7 Conclusions

The regulation of cross-border and cross-sector groups emerged only recently as a supplementary field of the supervision of financial entities. Moreover, its current development is rapidly achieving a new stage of full integration within the scope of entities' supervision, consistent with effective changes experienced by worldwide markets.

Developments in this area are proved to move gradually aim to convergence and to a uniform assessment of consolidated risk profiles, despite not equal, at the same time underlining the importance of prudential rules also at solo level.

In this discussion we supported the consideration on the significant achievements that the process is showing; however, it could be said that regulatory and supervisory action proved to have developed more slowly than the true picture shown by financial markets, where consolidation and conglomerisation processes have been recorded for several years. Only recently, as a result of the materialisation of one of the most severe financial crises in recent decades, the weaknesses and risks of this approach have become evident and subjected to a closer analysis.

One of the main reasons behind this outcome is represented by limited capability of national policy makers and regulators to properly, consistently and efficiently deal with cross-border and cross-sector issues, given the difficulties in harmonising experiences, history and practices that have been consolidating through time in different countries. However, attention to this challenge is greater than before: international bodies have achieved knowledge, authority and resources to actively play their role.

The recent financial turmoil, which emerged in the banking sector and then diffused throughout the overall financial sector and the real economy, demonstrates how contagion and systemic risks have been underestimated. Insurance companies, deemed to be less prone to these risks, still hold most of their assets in listed and unlisted securities, loans and real estate, whereas liabilities are often uncorrelated with economic cycles (except, for instance, credit and suretyship business lines). Together with the conglomerisation of insurance business, this exposes these companies to contagion and systemic risks that are similar to those experienced by banks, although probably with a limited time delay before it fully materialises, despite the lack of a risk of 'run' as in the banking sector.

Within the European Union, the financial crisis materialised at a time when the process of establishing the new regulatory framework is facing its final and most debated phase: Solvency 2 is now asked to bridge the gap between regulation and business operations. This is a significant leap for which national supervisors and, probably, also companies, might not prove to be ready in the short term. As attested by recent controversies relating to the group support regime and the role of group supervisors, even a compromise solution is yet to be found.

# 9
# Cross-Border Groups: Supervision after the Crisis

*Simonetta Cotterli and Elisabetta Gualandri*

## 9.1   Introduction

The financial crisis which began in 2007 has dramatically laid bare the limits and shortcomings of the current financial regulatory system and supervisory controls both at the national level (although there are often considerable differences between the various contexts) and internationally. The situation is, if possible, even more critical with regard to cross-border and cross-sector operators. There had been warnings for some time (see, for example, Vella, 2002) of the risk that the financial system that had emerged from the consolidation and internationalisation process of the past decade would not be capable of dealing adequately with any faults which might occur within it. But as is demonstrated by the history of financial crises, and is confirmed by the current situation, unfortunately regulators tend to respond to market failures rather than preventing them in the first place.

The European Union is a special case, where the problem is more complex due to two main structural factors. Firstly, the EU may have common financial regulation based on its directives, but there are still wide variations with regard to the implementation of this legislation within the individual member states. Moreover, there are no EU regulations for dealing with crises affecting individual companies or groups. Secondly, supervision is still performed on the principle of home country control, with systems which differ from state to state, where agencies operate with different powers, procedures and styles.

The asymmetries outlined above are even more noticeable in the case of cross-border and cross-sector financial groups, the development of which has been one of the most significant phenomena in the European financial industry of the past decade. For these groups, the multiplicity of regulators and supervisors implies high compliance costs, operating difficulties with regard to group risk management, and an increase in forum shopping in search of more relaxed legal and regulatory frameworks. The limitations of the current regulatory and control structure were dramatically revealed in the Autumn of 2008, when two of the EU's largest cross-border and cross-sector groups, Fortis and Dexia, found themselves in financial difficulties. The rescue measures taken led to a reversal of the process of financial integration, as the groups were broken up and renationalised in a trend towards retrenchment within national borders.

The scale and depth of the current crisis have provided a powerful stimulus for the debate on regulation and controls, in order to strengthen financial systems (Financial Stability Forum, 2009; Draghi, 2008). There are now a large number of proposals for modifying the supervisory framework, including both suggestions for the establishment of global supervision, and less ambitious models focusing on supervision for Europe only.

This survey aims to identify the asymmetries between the development of banking and financial groups at the pan-European level and that of the regulation of and controls over these groups, and highlight the main failures. A critical analysis will then be made of the proposals for an EU-wide control and supervisory framework now being considered, which are based mainly on the de Larosière Report. The analysis will centre on the three means available for safeguarding stability and protecting the financial markets: the provision of rules, the performance of controls on operations and players, and crisis prevention and management.

## 9.2   The development of EU cross-border groups

During the past decade, thanks to the single currency, there has been a considerable acceleration in the consolidation and integration of the European Union's banking system. The ongoing concentration of the market can clearly be seen in the reduction in the number of banks and the growth of several groups through both domestic and cross-border M&A operations. The number of such operations taking place peaked at 140 in 2000 and remained constantly above 100 until 2008. The value of operations fell from the 100 billion in 2000 to 25 billion in 2002, before commencing a period of constant growth. It exceeded the 2002 value in both 2006 and 2007, before reaching almost 150 billion in 2008, with the acquisition of ABN Amro by the European consortium of Royal Bank of Scotland, Fortis and Santander, which actually took place after the crisis had begun (European Central Bank, 2009, Tables 1 and 2).

Although most consolidation was at the national level, a significant proportion of M&A operations, in numerical terms but above all by value of the transactions involved, were cross-border deals within the EU. This led to strong acceleration in the process of market integration, demonstrated by the operations of 45 cross-border groups, which in 2008 accounted for more than two-thirds of business in the EU banking sector. Moreover, in a large number of states more than 50 per cent of the domestic market is in the hands of the branches and subsidiaries of the banks of other member states (Saccomanni, 2009).

A European Central Bank (ECB) survey (2008b, Box 2) reveals the search for higher profits in new markets as the key driver of European banks' cross-border growth: faced with limited growth potential in their home countries, banks have set out to access host states with higher potential, mainly the new-entry states of Eastern Europe. Response to the expansion and internationalisation strategies, and chosen locations, of customer firms emerges as another important factor, while the search for economies of scale and scope appears to be less significant.

In response to the dynamism of the market forces driving towards the growing integration of the EU banking sector, efforts to provide a regulatory framework led to the launch of the Financial Services Action Plan 1999–2005 (FSAP). In addition, the Comitology process, or Lamfalussy method, aimed on the one hand to make the regulatory process faster and more effective, and on the other to ensure more uniform subsequent implementation of directives at the national level.

However, regulatory asymmetries persist, which have arisen from two main aspects: first and foremost, the directives allow national governments options and discretionality when it comes to implementation. What's more, this process is based on the principle of minimal harmonisation, and leaves room for 'gold plating', or the addition of extra requirements at the national level (Saccomanni, 2009). The situation is without a doubt even more critical with regard to the supervisory function, which continues to be conducted at the national level, on the principle of home country control. The individual countries have different regulatory frameworks, adopting the twin peaks model, with responsibility allocated depending on the purpose of the supervision (stability, fairness and transparency), the institutional model, which assigns responsibility for supervision to specific agencies depending on the sector of the industry concerned (banking, securities and insurance), and, finally, the single regulator model, in which all types of control over the entire financial sector are combined. Thus, within the EU there are a plethora of national supervisors, with different powers and aims, working with different methods and approaches.

In Europe, the fragmentation of the regulatory framework and, above all, of controls has particularly detrimental implications for cross-border groups. The need to comply with national regulatory systems which vary in some aspects, and conform to different supervisory frameworks, leads, above all, to a general increase in compliance costs; there is also the danger of competitive inequality amongst groups, and between the cross-border groups and the banks working at the national level; and last but not least, this situation may lead to a reduction in operating efficiency and the failure to achieve economies of scale and scope. Centralised risk management becomes problematical, with regard to both the transfer of assets between different parts of the group operating in different countries, and compliance with capital adequacy requirements (UniCredit Group, 2009; Zadra, 2009). It must also be remembered that liquidity regimes vary from country to country: this not only poses problems of competitive inequality and difficulties in centralised liquidity management but also, as occurred during the crisis, the inability to transfer surplus liquidity from one country to another state where a shortfall is being experienced.

Not only does this situation have negative implications for financial intermediaries; it also has high costs for the national supervisory authorities, in terms of coordination between the authorities of the various states within which the group operates. Furthermore, the cooperation between authorities is limited, especially when it comes to the sharing of sensitive information, as was clearly seen in Autumn 2008. Finally, this situation leaves scope for forum shopping, as intermediaries look for the most beneficial locations in terms of regulation and controls.

The creation of the Colleges of Supervisors (CoS), which bring together the national supervisors and to which the cross-border groups look for guidance, was a first step in reducing the costs and inefficiencies described above. The first task facing the CoS bodies, which initially were not established for all groups and had no effective powers, was to approve the IRB methods proposed for the fulfilment of capital adequacy obligations.

All the inadequacy of this fragmented system, and the problems arising from the lack of a common crisis management framework, were revealed at the height of the crisis in 2008, which culminated in the cross-border disintegration of Fortis and Dexia, a genuine reversal of the financial integration process.

## 9.3   The crisis and EU cross-border groups

In September 2008, the liquidity crisis triggered by the Lehman Brothers crash exploded into a solvency crisis affecting the whole system. The monetary authorities' interventions, increasingly coordinated at the international level, used conventional and unconventional measures to restore the markets' liquidity, while national governments on the one hand reinforced their guarantees for deposits and on the other launched rescue packages, involving recapitalisations and nationalisations, intended to restore banks' capital resources and public trust.

The most sophisticated intermediaries, those most active in credit risk transfer techniques, and groups operating at the cross-border level, were especially hard hit by the crisis. In many cases, including some of the most dramatic crashes, banks' difficulties arose from bad strategic planning, ineffective governance systems, poor management, the presence of perverse incentives, and genuine fraud. Cross-border groups face more complex categories of risks, and in many cases this was not countered by the development of a suitable risk management system. Their high degree of dependence on the interbank markets meant they were more exposed to the liquidity crisis, which rapidly degenerated into a solvency crisis. In view of the conglomerates' size, implications of a systemic nature gradually became inevitable.

Cross-border groups' shares suffered greater collapses in their value than those of banks operating at the national level. This appears to indicate that the market realised that the regulatory framework was not suited to the problems posed by operators, and was also aware of inadequacies in the cross-border collaboration between the supervisory authorities, and limits in information sharing (UniCredit, 2009).

The crisis dramatically highlighted the limitations of regulation and controls when faced with the development of financial innovation and the new banking practices based on the Originate-to-Distribute (OTD) model (Gualandri et al., 2009). The gap was especially obvious in the case of European cross-border groups, especially with regard to the problem of the fragmentation of supervision, and the lack of a single supervisor and a single procedure for dealing with cross-border crises. Within the EU, a country by country approach was thus adopted, both for verifying the condition of the various banking systems and in terms of measures taken to resolve crises. The only two mechanisms established in this area, not even legally recognised by the various member states, did not make any contribution to resolving the crisis. Firstly, the Memorandum of Understanding (MoU) on cross-border financial stability, signed on 1 June 2008, was of no help in managing the crisis; it is laden with guidelines and good intentions, but has no legal value. Secondly, the part played by the CoS bodies proved to be ineffective, if not non-existent, because these bodies were not institutionalised, they were only in operation for a few groups, and in any case their area of observation was restricted and further reduced by the absence of genuine information sharing in major areas.

The whole dramatic emergency was initially managed at the national level: not only did the various member states introduce their rescue packages piecemeal, bank by bank, but in the case of cross-border groups, bank crises were managed without rescue plans which considered these groups in their entirety. Furthermore, the dimensions of some banking groups proved to be much too large in relation to the financial resources their countries of origin were able to muster to stage a rescue (they were 'too large to save'). Intervention was thus fragmented, undertaken by individual governments and the relevant national authorities of the group's main members, from a perspective limited only to the part of the group which 'belonged' to the individual state. An approach of this kind inevitably fails to bear in mind the possible detrimental effects the individual national rescue operations may have at the cross-border level, and it may therefore have increased the cost of the rescue plans for society as a whole (UniCredit, 2009).

The rescues of Dexia and, above all, Fortis groups, which were not only cross-border but also cross-sector, are emblematic in this respect. The crises affecting the two groups had different underlying causes (Box 9.1), but there was the common need, due to the two conglomerates' size and the absence of European regulations, to find a solution involving the combined intervention of the governments and authorities of the main states in which they operated, with a substantial renationalisation of the two conglomerates (cross-border disintegration) as well as the transfer of assets. In the case of Fortis, the Benelux governments intervened with an initial payment of 11.2 billion on 28 September 2008. In the case of Dexia, it was France, Belgium and Luxembourg which intervened, on 29 September 2009, with funds totalling 6.4 billion.

## Box 9.1 The Rescue of Fortis and Dexia

*Fortis*

Fortis, a banking insurance financial conglomerate, was one of Europe's twenty largest cross-border groups before the crisis. It was created in 1990 by the merger of the Dutch insurance group AMEV, the Dutch bank VSB and subsequently the Belgian insurance group AG, in Europe's first cross-border financial merger. In the years which followed, the group continued its strategy of acquisitions and growth, especially on the Benelux market, where it became leader, as well as outside this area.

The acquisition of ABN Ambro in a consortium with Royal Bank of Scotland and Santander, in 2007/2008, proved fatal for Fortis. This acquisition, at a total price of 71.9 billion (a figure judged to be too high given that the first signs of the crisis were already apparent), required Fortis to pay out 24 billion, 13 billion of this to be obtained from an equity issue, while the remainder was to be raised through the sale of assets, securitisation operations and the issue of hybrid securities. As the crisis worsened, this financial plan was no longer feasible, and Fortis's situation deteriorated dramatically in September 2008.

On 28 September 2008 the Benelux governments stepped in to save the group, with an initial investment of 11.2 billion, followed over the next few months by further investments which led to the nationalisation of the parent company *Fortis Banque Belgium*, (subsequently, 75 per cent of this company was acquired by the French bank BNP Paribas (BNP Paribas Fortis since May 2009), together with 25 per cent of the Belgian insurance business), *Fortis Banque Nederlands* and *Fortis Banque Luxembourg*, 67 per cent of which was subsequently sold to BNP Paribas.

*Dexia*

The Dexia group, one of the 15 biggest banking groups in the Euro area before the crisis, and a specialist in public sector loans, in which it is world leader, was formed in 1996 by one of the first European cross-border bank mergers, between Crédit Commercial de Belgique and the French bank Crédit Local.

The group's main operating units are in Belgium, France and Luxembourg. During the following yeas, the acquisition process continued both in Europe (including the acquisition in 1997 of a 40 per cent share of the Italian Crediop, subsequently increased to 70 per cent), and in other areas, especially the USA, where in 2000 it acquired Fsa Insurance, a leader in the insurance of local government bonds. Due to the deteriorating situation of Fsa as a result of the subprime mortgage crisis, in June 2008 Dexia granted its subsidiary a credit line of $5 billion for five years, renewable for further periods. The ongoing worsening of Fsa's situation finally threatened the stability of Dexia itself in September 2008.

On 29 September 2008 the governments of France, Belgium and Luxembourg intervened with a total amount of 6.4 billion, through a share issue underwritten for an amount of 3 billion each by the Belgian and French governments (in the case of France, 2 billion of the funds were provided by the state-controlled Caisse des Dépots et Consignations, CDC), and a new convertible bond issue of 376 million purchased by the Luxembourg government. A few days later, to deal with the group's liquidity crisis and assure its survival, the same governments provided collateral for new interbank and international loans to Dexia. Losses on loans to Lehman and the Icelandic banks, and finally involvement in the Madoff affair, further aggravated the situation. Fsa Insurance was sold on 14 November.

In the light of the picture outlined above, below we will describe the regulatory and control framework in which the crisis developed, and identify the possible routes being examined for the creation of a European framework consistent with the development of cross-border groups.

## 9.4   The common rules

The first aspect to be considered when assessing the suitability of the regulatory process for its purpose of safeguarding stability and protecting the financial markets is the drafting of rules.

In Europe, alongside the issue of directives, broken down by sector except for Directive 2002/87/EC on financial conglomerates, the so-called Lamfalussy approach has been adopted. Under this model, the regulatory process comprises four different levels, with the involvement of committees (hence 'Comitology'): regulatory, to assist the European Commission in the drafting of the regulatory guidelines, and supervisory, to participate in the drafting of the directives and oversee their subsequent implementation in the individual member states. The model initially envisaged the creation of two committees for the securities area only. Specifically, the Committee of European Securities Regulators (CESR) was assigned the task of setting guidelines (known as level 3) to be used by the competent national authorities when drafting the second-level rules placed under their responsibility by law, with the aim of reducing the sometimes very considerable degree of discretionality left to the national authorities by the directives. The Council resolution adopted by the ECOFIN on 3 December 2002 extended this approach to the banking and insurance industries, with the establishment of similar committees for the various sectors of business. The supervisory committees introduced are the Committee of European Banking Supervisors (CEBS) for the banking sector and the Committee of European Insurance and Occupational Pensions Supervisors (CEIOPS) for the insurance industry (Table 9.1). However, no supervisory committee is envisaged for conglomerates (Gualandri and Grasso, 2006).

Specifically, the function of the CEBS, comprising representatives of the supervisory authorities and central banks of the Union's 27 member states, is to advise the European Commission, work towards the convergent application of the common rules and supervisory practices, and encourage cooperation and information sharing between the supervisory authorities.[1] It must be acknowledged that the committee has played a major role, for example with regard to the application of the capital adequacy agreement, Basel II, and, more recently, in relation to the operating procedures for cooperation between authorities involved in the supervision of cross-border groups (CEBS, 2009a). In spite of this, the degree of convergence and uniformity in the application of the common principles, and to an even greater extent of supervisory practices, continues to be unsatisfactory, leaving unresolved the problem of asymmetries in the application of international

*Table 9.1*   The Lamfalussy process: regulatory and supervisory committees

|  | Securities | Banks | Insurance Companies | Financial Conglomerates |
|---|---|---|---|---|
| *Regulatory Committees Level 2* | European Securities Committee | European Banking Committee | European Insurance and Occupational Pensions Committee | European Financial Conglomerates Committee |
| *Supervisory Committees Levels 2 & 3* | Committee of European Securities Regulators | Committee of European Banking Supervisors | Committee of European Insurance and Occupational Pensions Supervisors |  |

standards and directives. There is no doubt that the core difficulty that has been affecting international standards for years, known in the literature as 'asymmetric application', or, in other words, the fact that each state can enforce these principles in a different way, with the risk of the familiar phenomenon of regulatory arbitrage, continues to be a major obstacle in this area. But it may be that the fear and panic on the markets will have some effect. The wind of crisis has spared no one, and in objective terms, these days there is less to be gained by bending the rules.

The surveys conducted amongst operators in the various states have highlighted the low level of impact of the committees' criteria, underlining the importance of achieving the common interpretation of rules. The need for measures to modify the committees' characteristics and the tasks assigned to them, and the Lamfalussy approach in general, clearly emerges. This mechanism's most obvious shortcoming is the committees' lack of any real power; trapped in a background role, they have proved unable to act quickly and effectively in response to the problems the crisis has gradually brought to light.

The need for a review of the committees' legal structure, changing their merely consultative, advisory nature, has been acknowledged above all in the work carried out by the group of experts appointed by the European Commission[2] to draw up an opinion on financial regulation and supervision. The group's final report, known as the de Larosière Report, proposes the establishment of a European System of Financial Supervision (ESFS), which will be discussed in greater detail below. This is an 'integrated framework of European financial supervisors working in tandem with level 3 committees allocated higher powers'. This regulatory framework involves the establishment of three new European authorities to replace the CEBS, CEIOPS and CESR, with the task of coordinating the application of shared supervisory standards and guaranteeing robust cooperation between national supervisory authorities.

The creation of a new European Union institutional structure, an independent authority, which would replace the Lamfalussy committees with stronger powers, is one of the recommendations of the Turner Review (Financial Services Authority, 2009, p. 102). As is stated by Turner (2009), the chairman of the Financial Services Authority (FSA): 'We recommend the creation of a new European institution into which the existing Lamfalussy Committees will fold, with legal powers in the area of regulation, and acting as a standard setter and coordinator in the area of supervision.'

To allow them to function effectively, these new authorities would need to have mechanisms which would at least enable them, on the one hand, to monitor the uniform application of the relevant rules by the individual authorities (CEBS, 2007) and, on the other, to act decisively and effectively in the event of divergence between the various authorities involved in the supervision of any one financial entity. Under the proposed system, the national supervisory authorities would continue to provide routine supervision of entities, retaining most of their current areas of jurisdiction, such as the granting of authorisations, monitoring of compliance with prudential supervisory requirements and the application of disciplinary measures. In fact, the ESFS would fulfil its role to a large extent through the activities of the committees of supervisory authorities, strengthened with the participation of representatives of the secretariat of the level 3 committees and observers from the European Central Bank and the European System of Central Banks (ESCB). The measures which establish this new body would need first and foremost to ensure its independence from political interference, together with the principle of responsibility for its activities and decisions, in relation to both EU and national political authorities, while also providing it with a clear mandate and tasks, supported by appropriate powers and resources.

## 9.5  Micro-prudential supervision

The second major aspect relates to the performance of controls. Hitherto, the dominant principle with regard to supervision within the EU has always been home country control. This rule is not being called into question; in fact, it is being confirmed as the keystone on which Europe is intending to restructure its system of controls over the financial market.

Amongst the specific rules on the supervision of firms organised into groups, there are two measures worth discussing briefly here: Directive 2002/87/EC on the additional supervision of financial conglomerates, and the Directive 2006/48/EC on the taking up and pursuit of the business of credit institutions. In the first measure, the EU lawmakers establish an authority 'responsible for the coordination and performance of supplementary supervision' on financial conglomerates (art. 10 Directive 2002/87/EC). This is the 'coordinator', a 'supplementary' control authority, the introduction of which makes absolutely no changes to the established structure of controls applicable to the individual entities concerned, with the consequent risk of both the duplication of costs and controls, and the evasion of the latter.[3] The gathering and dissemination of information are viewed as the key factors in supervisory activities, and are supported by the obligation on the coordinator to issue regular reports, at least once a year. However, coordinators are not backed up by any powers to demand information, or penalties they can impose in the event of failures to comply with obligations; nor are they granted any powers to perform mandatory inspections. The efficiency of the reporting system relies on the close cooperation between the authorities involved in the performance of supervision, which are to provide one another with 'any information which is essential or relevant' (art.12 (1)), and to 'have coordination arrangements in place' (art.11 (1)).

As well as supervision in terms of information, the coordinator is also required to perform a 'supervisory overview and assessment of the financial situation of a financial conglomerate', together with the specific 'assessment of compliance with the rules on capital adequacy and on risk concentration and intra-group transactions' (art.11 (1) (b) and (c)). The specific components of these regulations are to be determined by national law, and, to a lesser extent, by the rules issued by the coordinator itself, which is however always to act further to consultation with the 'relevant competent authorities'.

Finally, supplementary supervision also includes the conglomerate's internal control structure, organisation and system, while the member states are again to be responsible for setting the relevant mandatory requirements.

The limitations of coordination alone, not supported by an authority with suitable powers of regulation and intervention, have been underlined for some time (Vella, 2002; Andenas, 2003; Enria, 2006; Schulerr and Henemann 2005), especially with regard to supervision of large, multifunctional intermediaries operating at the cross-border level. Attention has been focused in particular on the risks intrinsic to this system: high 'negotiation' costs between national controllers, more intent on safeguarding national interests than on the overall stability of the entity controlled; the inability of coordination alone to deal quickly and effectively with pathological events; and the overlapping of areas of competence between authorities, leading to the duplication of controls and the unjustified increase in operating costs for intermediaries, as well as the creation of niches with potential for the evasion of controls.

Directive 2006/48/CE, on the taking up and pursuit of the business of credit institutions, aims to reinforce the role of the supervisory authority on a consolidated basis. To achieve this, it establishes a coordination model which combines home country control over the various spheres of activity and the presence of a consolidating supervisory authority, with the duties of gathering and disseminating relevant or essential information, as well as planning and coordinating supervisory activities, 'in going concern and emergency situations' (art. 129 (1)). Under this allocation of responsibilities, the national authorities with competence over the individual firms in the group 'cooperate closely with each other', communicate relevant information on request and essential information on their own initiative (art. 132 (1)) and consult each other before taking the most important decisions affecting the entity (art.132, (3)). However, this consultation stage may be omitted when the powers are exercised in emergencies, circumstances in which greater coordination may be necessary.

However, the provision of greatest interest, which can be viewed as the embryo of the approach subsequently developed in review proposals, is art. 131 of Directive 2006/48, which envisages written coordination and cooperation arrangements between all the authorities involved in the control process – the consolidating supervisory authority and the national authorities – in order to facilitate and establish effective supervision. These arrangements may extend the competence of the consolidated supervisory authority, and specify procedures for the decision-making process and for cooperation.

Moreover, the competent authorities responsible for the supervision of a subsidiary can delegate their supervisory responsibilities to the national authority which issued the authorisation to the parent company through bilateral arrangements, of which the Commission must be informed. This provision is a move towards the creation, even if on a voluntary basis, of a lead supervisor, as urged by the banking industry (Godano, 2009).

This is the picture as things now stand. Turning to prospects for the future, the latest draft directive on capital adequacy confirms that the responsibility for the prudential supervision of a banking organisation lies with the competent authority of the member state of origin, but amends art. 40 of Directive 2006/48 to specify that these authorities shall take into account 'the potential impact of their decisions on the stability of the financial system in all other member states concerned and, in particular, in emergency situations' (art. 40 (3)). This draft legislation clearly reflects the anxiety that independent, nonconforming decisions by member states may be damaging for the system as a whole, especially in crises. However, while underlining one highly crucial aspect, if adopted this proposal will not prove effective, since it does not state whether and how compliance with the requirement can be monitored, specify measures to be taken in the event of non-compliance with the rules, or define mechanisms for resolving any disputes between member states.

The principle of home country control is accompanied by an improvement in the efficiency of the supervision of cross-border groups, through the obligation to establish Colleges of Supervisors. Along the lines already indicated by art. 131 of Directive 2006/48, art. 131a (new) requires the consolidating supervisors to establish colleges of the national supervisory authorities, chaired by themselves. The EU legislators wish the colleges to have a consultative and driving role, assigning them the task of 'providing a framework' within which the authorities involved will carry out their tasks, without any change to the tasks and responsibilities assigned to the individual national authorities, although they may decide, on a completely voluntary basis, to delegate them. Specifically, CoS are required to encourage the authorities involved in the control of the organisation to optimise the exchange of information, increase the efficiency of supervision, partly by removing the unnecessary duplication of supervisory requirements, and achieve the consistent application of the directive's prudential requirements across all the entities in the group. CoS will also have the task of promoting the adoption of joint decisions on essential aspects of supervision (confirmation of IRB models under Basel II and definition of reporting obligations). The proposal does not provide detailed specifications of colleges' modus operandi, simply envisaging the need for the consolidating supervisory authority to make written arrangements in agreement with the national authorities, in accordance with the CEBS guidelines. The CEBS and the CEIOPS have since proceeded first to set a number of principles on which the colleges are to operate and then, more recently, to issue a series of 'good practices' for authorities to follow when drafting arrangements. These guidelines regulate subjects such as the structure of the colleges, their internal organisation, the exchange of information, and the possible procedures for assigning specific tasks to participants (CEBS, 2009b; CEBS and CEIOPS, 2009).

The consolidating supervisory authority is also required to continually inform the CEBS about the college's activities, including any decisions in emergency situations, and in all cases to provide the Committee with all the information required to develop uniform approaches in all the various colleges. Colleges of supervisory authorities are also to be established to supervise cross-border entities which do not have subsidiaries in other member states but do have systemically relevant branches.

## 9.6 Macro-prudential supervision: crisis prevention and management

The identification and management of risks, both within the individual entity and at the systemic level, is a focal point of the debate on the regulation and control of financial markets and an essential step in guaranteeing the stability of participants and the system overall. As became even more obvious during the current financial turmoil, the lack of awareness of the real risks present on the market was an obstacle to the prevention of systemic threats;[4] while the way in which the crisis was managed laid bare all the limitations of an approach which, except for a few fleeting episodes of coordination made necessary by the gravity of the moment, was not at all global, and was based on purely domestic measures.

On the subject of reform, the approach adopted by the de Larosière Report draws a clear dividing line between two separate problematical areas: on the one hand, the prevention and management of crises affecting individual financial entities (the task of micro-prudential supervision) and on the other, risk prevention and management for the system as a whole, known as macro-prudential supervision, different and separate from micro-supervision and thus assigned to a different authority. In actual fact, the two forms of supervision are closely connected, and in their document commenting on the proposal the three committees, the CESR, CEBS and CEIOPS, are in no doubt about the potential improvements it may bring, but also highlight the need for greater dialogue between the two levels of supervision, which will also prevent duplication (CESR, CEBS and CEIOPS, 2009).

As things now stand, the draft directive on capital adequacy already discussed contains a number of points which clearly acknowledge the close link between the two supervisory levels. This is particularly evident in art. 42a (new), which introduces the concept of the 'systemically relevant branch'. Branches are defined as systemically relevant further to an application, with reasons, from the host member state, which must be made with particular regard to whether the market share of the branch in terms of deposits is large (2 per cent), to its size and importance in terms of the number of clients, or to whether the suspension or closure of the operations of the credit institution might impact on market liquidity and the payment and clearing and settlement systems. The relative decision-making mechanism allows the competent authority of the host country, which made the application, to reach its own decision on the matter if no agreement is reached between those involved, such as the consolidating supervisory authority for the aspects under its control and the home member state authorities for the areas under their jurisdiction. Specifically, the authorities must do 'everything within their power to reach a joint decision' within two months of the application, and otherwise the applicant authority will decide within the next two months, taking views and reservations into account. A branch is designated as systemically relevant by means of 'a document containing the fully reasoned decision', transmitted to the competent authorities concerned, recognised as determinative and applied by the competent authorities in the member states concerned. This definition makes no changes to the approach and responsibilities with regard to supervision, but simply strengthens the exchange of information between the authorities involved, especially in 'emergency situations', in which it is particularly important for the multilateral exchange of information to take place without difficulties and obstacles (art. 42a (new) (2) and (3)).

In spite of the many opinions which identify the European Central Bank as the natural assignee of powers and responsibilities with regard to macro-prudential supervision (de Larosière Report, p. 42 s.), the proposal has been made for the creation of a new authority, called the European Systemic Risk Council (ESRC), operating within the ECB and with the participation of the central banks belonging to the ESCB. The proposed ESRC will consist of the chair – who will also become its chair – and deputy chair of the ECB, the 27 National Central Bank (NCB) governors, and the chairs of the CEBS, CEIOPS and ESRC, together with a representative of the European Commission (Figure 9.1). Moreover, in view of the different approaches to supervision adopted in the individual member states, the group is to 'interact closely with the supervisory authorities which are not part of the central banks', which will participate in discussions whenever necessary. In practice, therefore, the competent authorities for micro-prudential supervision in the individual states are not full members of the new body, with all the potential problems this may involve. The new authority is competent with regard to assessments and recommendations in the area of macro-prudential supervision, with a particular emphasis on risk warning and the issue of guidelines on prudential supervision. To enable it to function, the ESRC will receive a constant flow of compulsory information from the national central banks, and a mandatory follow-up from the national supervisory authorities in response to risk warnings. The ESRC also specifies who is to implement its recommendations,

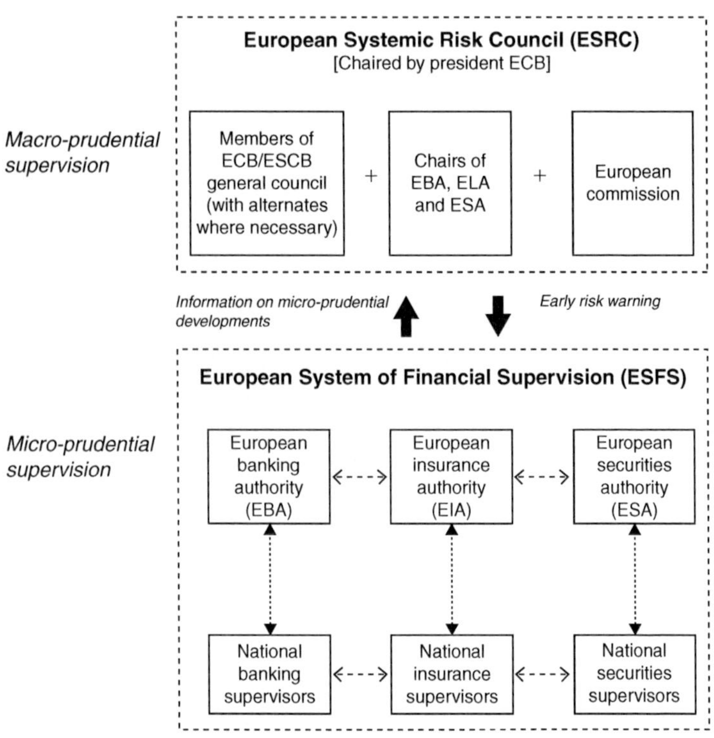


*Figure 9.1*   European Framework for Safeguarding Financial Stability

*Source*: The High Level Group on Financial Supervision in the EU, chaired by J. de Larosière (2009), Report, 25 February, p.56.

and if the response is inadequate, it notifies the Economic and Financial Committee (political authority).

The de Larosière Report's recommendations have met with general approval within the EU, although they are objectively only a compromise solution for those in favour of a more robust, better structured centralised supervisory system, with stronger powers over entities with systemically relevant size and characteristics. In the future, and this is already reflected in the debate underway at the EU level, it will be necessary to solve the problem of possible trade-offs between the areas of competence of the systemic controller and the fact that the costs for any bank rescue packages will still be met at the national level. This trade-off is itself symptomatic of the fact that once this option has been chosen, if it is to be effective European supervision will inevitably have to be combined with the centralisation of areas of competence and the uniformity of measures to be paid for by the taxpayer, only achievable with a high degree of political convergence between the member states; in spite of the current financial turmoil, there as yet no signs of this emerging.

## 9.7   Conclusions

The process of innovation which has affected the financial markets over the last decade has generated a new willingness on the part of intermediaries to internationalise both their business, which is becoming more and more inter-sectorial, and their ownership structures.

This transformed scenario made it essential to review the rules, which have accordingly began to reflect a desire for international regulation, in both the attempt to adopt rules shared by groups of states, and the introduction of mechanisms intended to facilitate the cross-border supervision of companies. However, the measures taken proved insufficient and the financial crisis overwhelmed intermediaries and markets, demonstrating the inability of a system still firmly anchored to a nationalistic approach to regulate a market which increasingly knows no borders.

The growth of cross-border groups, in particular, has inevitably amplified the effects a crisis hitting an intermediary can trigger on the market (and not just the market of the individual country but that of the single European market itself). The importance of what is at stake could not be more obvious, and all those involved on the European scene have come together in the common effort to achieve a reform which will strengthen the Europe-wide character of supervisory activities as soon as possible. The European Commission, the Council of Europe and the European Parliament are taking action in several areas, and all agree on the urgent need for a complete overhaul of the regulatory framework in the shortest possible term. However, there is no concealing the fact that the creation of a common purpose within the European Union always goes hand-in-hand with the member states' affirmation and defence of their specific national systems, and the thus the achievement of an agreement is often a matter of compromises and lengthy time-scales. It is unanimously acknowledged that the current circumstances demand a rapid response, and if the proposed schedule is complied with, the EU legislators will have accelerated the process to an impressive degree. However, even if the new measures are introduced considerably more swiftly than the reforms implemented so far, there is still the risk that they will prove to be too little, too late.

It is assumed, as the de Larosière Report also pragmatically accepts, that the proposed reforms will be compatible with the EU Treaty, and will therefore not involve the very lengthy procedure of constitutional reform.

The first in the raft of measures is about to be completed. It is expected that the revision of Directive 2006/48/EC will be definitely approved by the end of 2009. The European Parliament has recently accepted[5] the Commission's proposal for a number of amendments, which, however, do not clear up the doubts expressed about the efficacy of a system that still leaves all the power and responsibility of the home country supervisory authority intact, confirming the policy of maintaining the principle of home country control as the basis of the regulatory system, while acknowledging (preamble point 5, resolution of 6 May 2009) that 'it is essential that competent authorities coordinate their actions with other competent authorities and where appropriate with central banks in an efficient way, *including with the aim of mitigating systemic risk*'. The doubts persist concerning the usefulness of supervision which continues to be grounded merely on coordination and information exchange, without the creation of an authority with the powers to direct and issue guidelines for the process, or to resolve any disputes between the competent authorities involved, let alone to take rapid action if intermediaries are hit by crises which, by their very nature, must be dealt with through quick, targeted measures. On this last point, the issue of a Memorandum for financial stability, with the aim of improving coordination and introducing joint principles for the crisis management, proved insufficient to allow a rapid response to instability with implications for the entire system. The reform of the capital adequacy directive has the merit of making the intervention of the Colleges of Supervisors compulsory where the voluntary mechanisms previously adopted have proved inadequate, but its reinforcement of these bodies' role and area of jurisdiction is insufficient.

The heart of the ongoing reform is the new institutional framework which has taken shape over the past few months, starting from the recommendations of the de Larosière Report. We have seen that policy is moving towards the establishment of two pillars on which measures will be based: micro-prudential supervision, assigned to the European System of Financial Supervision; and macro-prudential supervision, to be entrusted to the European Systemic Risk Council.

The first criticism that can be levied at an approach of this kind concerns just this separation between the two levels of supervision, since the effective prevention and control of systemic risk is impossible without the consideration, assessment and control of individual institutions. Careful evaluation is thus required of both the assignment of areas of jurisdiction and roles, while effective mechanisms for the coordination of the two forms of supervision are also needed (Tarantola, 2009).

Moreover, as things now stand there is no clear identification of what can and must be considered 'relevant' for the containment of systemic risk. We have seen that art. 42b of the new capital adequacy directive introduces the concept of the 'systemically relevant branch'. The directive provides a number of guidelines to be used by the home country authority for the identification of branches in this category, but in our view they are ineffectual and too vague, since they consider the branch's market share in terms of deposits (with a 2 per cent threshold), its size and importance, its number of clients, and whether the suspension or closure of the operations of the credit institution might impact on the liquidity of the market, and the payment and clearing and settlement systems. One of the tasks to be assigned to the new macro-prudential supervisory authority is the identification and classification of potential risks to financial stability, but it is not given any legally binding powers. It will merely be enabled to issue alarms and recommendations, both of a general nature and addressed to individual member states, which will not be compulsory, although an 'act or explain' mechanism is envisaged to ensure that they receive due consideration. No solution is thus provided to the problem of how to deal with possible conflicts between supervisory authorities when it comes to the identification of systemically relevant branches.

According to the Commission,[6] micro-prudential supervision will continue to be the task of the national authorities, but the ESFS will have the power to issue technical standards binding on them, capable of ensuring consistent, uniform application with reference to a number of as yet unspecified sectors to be defined in EU law. At the same time, if discrepancies persist and conflicts arise, the new authority will be able to issue decisions binding on both the national authorities and the CoS, although only as *'ultima ratio'*, and this does provide at least a partial solution to the problems highlighted above. To be effective, the supervision of cross-border groups in particular requires, if not the introduction of a single regulator and supervisor (in our view the preferred solution), at least the adoption of mechanisms capable of ensuring that all the authorities involved follow the same rules of behaviour when it comes to controlling each individual organisation. For the time being, no solution is proposed to the need to ensure crises are dealt with through the immediate, effective intervention of a single, specific supervisory body, with powers appropriate to the needs arising from systemic risks.

# 10
## Consolidation in the Stock Exchange Industry

*Giusy Chesini*

## 10.1 Introduction

In the last two decades, the global stock exchange industry has grown significantly in scale; however, only in the twenty-first century has there been evidence of any far-reaching structural change, mainly because of consolidation driven by the new regulatory framework, advances in technology and new client demands.

The new regulatory framework introduced by the Markets in Financial Instruments Directive (MiFID) has brought significant innovation in market regulation by abolishing the concentration rule and providing for free market competition between various trading platforms. In general, MiFID has aligned the structure and operations of European exchanges with their US counterparts. The directive has also fostered consolidation among European exchanges and encouraged US exchanges to gain a foothold in Europe.

Thanks to advances in technology, it is well known that the processing power of information technology (IT) has doubled every two years for the last four decades. The exchange industry is inextricably linked to IT, and IT is becoming increasingly affordable for new entrants. Growth in processing capacity enhances the operational capacity of trading platforms; as unit transaction costs fall, the large exchanges with adequate IT systems reap a series of economies of scale that lower the overall costs of the platform, making it less expensive to put together new products at the margin that quickly become profitable. The overall profits of exchanges have thus risen rapidly in recent years, while transaction costs have fallen correspondingly fast (Hasan et al., 2003, pp. 1743–73). Ultimately, lower IT costs favour new entrants, who still however need to build the liquidity and the brand established by existing exchanges through years of stable trading.

Finally, as the result of new client demands, there is clear evidence of segmentation: clients now tend to diversify requests for services and facilities in relation to the type of order sent to the trading platform. Furthermore, over the years a distinction has arisen between broker-dealers that execute

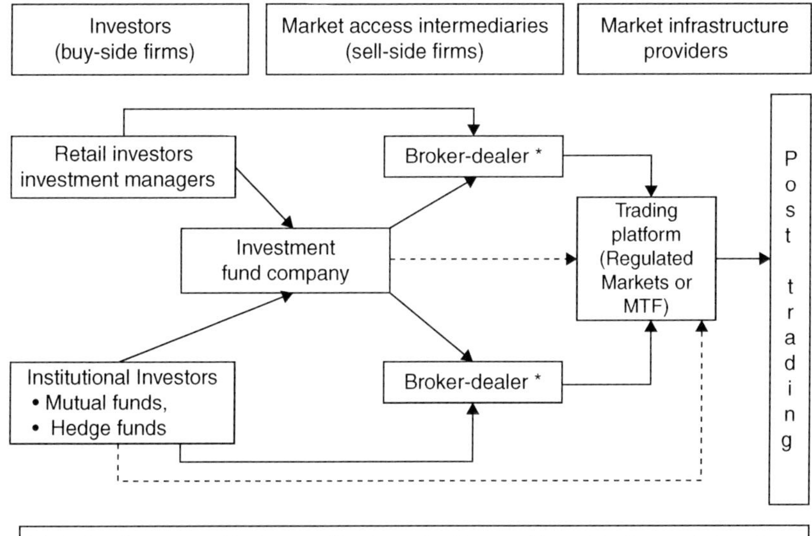



*Figures 10.1*   Trading: buy-side and sell-side operators
*Source*: Own elaboration.

progressively smaller orders, and perhaps parcel orders into smaller lots on the one hand, and those that trade large 'block' orders on less transparent platforms – 'dark pools' – to avoid distorting market prices on the other. As Figure 10.1 shows, investors, in other words the buy-side, send orders to the stock markets through broker-dealers or investment fund companies. In some cases, different regulations let institutional investors or buy-side investment fund companies send orders directly to the stock market. Owing to the variety of investors on the buy-side, specialist markets or dedicated market segments with separate tariff structures are starting to emerge.

On the sell-side, broker-dealers (the supply) act as retailers to large institutional investors on the buy-side (the demand) that submit large orders and act as wholesalers. Owing to this mismatch in the scale of operations, broker-dealers split block orders (either manually or via an algorithm) to execute them without distorting market prices.

In view of the unprecedented changes outlined above, exchanges have sought to defend their business and secure their future principally through the pursuit of growth strategies. Just like any other firm, exchanges may respond to change through internal growth, or pursue alliances or mergers to extend business along or even beyond a given value chain (Di Noia, 2001, pp. 39–72). However, in recent years, none of the major European exchanges has succeeded in establishing a position of continental leadership through internal growth. External growth through mergers and alliances has therefore represented the only way to achieve economies of scale and to deliver enhanced value to shareholders.

Even for market management companies, the success of a merger depends on the economic value of the parties and potential synergies in the form of a broader range of client services at a lower cost. The synergies of consolidation generally emerge in the long term, and the process is often more costly than initially forecasted; collectively these factors may undermine the results expected by shareholders. The advantages of consolidation are traditionally measured in terms of three types of economies (Chesini, 2007, pp. 146–60):

1. *economies of scale*, in particular those related to IT synergies. Traditional exchanges obviously have high fixed costs, so they pursue economies of scale in the face of a constant need for additional operating capacity and increasingly sophisticated operations. Growth is required to finance the modernisation of infrastructures;
2. *economies of product, process and geographical diversification* relating to the vertical extension down the supply chain of traditional stock exchange activities to integrate post-trading stages and processes;
3. *economies arising from network externalities:* an increase in liquidity flowing into an exchange permits a reduction in implicit trading costs. Following a merger between two or more exchanges, the expansion of the trading book creates a significant pool of liquidity, owing to the higher number of listed securities and the fact that brokers previously authorised to operate on one exchange can trade all listed securities on several exchanges. Furthermore, investor commissions decrease to reflect the lower brokerage costs. Obviously, companies intending to go public generally opt for the more liquid exchanges, in other words those with the highest number of listed companies, even if such exchanges are not in their home country; the same is true of brokers. At an industry level, exchanges therefore seek to attract the highest number of issuers and intermediaries, in order also to optimise sales of information services, that in many cases represent a significant source of profit.

In general, by exploiting economies of scale exchanges can increase volumes traded and lower the average trading commissions. Exchanges involved in consolidation activities should become more efficient since higher liquidity makes it possible to reduce bid–ask spreads and market volatility. Considering that a more efficient market is bound to attract dealers, a virtuous circle is likely to result and may produce further increases in volumes (Arnold et al., 1999, pp. 1083–107).

Exchanges that opt to remain independent – whether big or small – may decline in relative importance in the world exchange industry, and risk marginalisation. Therefore the relatively small exchanges have the greatest need to consolidate to withstand order fragmentation and to exploit economies of scale.

## 10.2 Market regulation and consolidation in Europe

MiFID came into force on 1 November 2007 and brought about far-reaching changes in stock market regulation in Europe. The aims of the directive were threefold: to offer greater protection to investors, to foster competition between trading platforms, and to increase transparency in the financial services sector.

Underlying the new approach to market regulation was the assumption that competition between diverse and competing trading venues could bring benefits to final investors, reduce transaction costs and increase market liquidity. In fact, by fostering competition between trading platforms MiFID set out to reduce the excessive transaction costs generated by virtual monopolies that allowed exchanges to make huge profits. MiFID's intended outcome is savings for investors and a greater incentive to operate on the securities markets, that should increase in size as a result.

To achieve these objectives, MiFID abolished the concentration rule on Regulated Markets (RMs) in favour of competition between alternative trading venues, and defined the regulatory framework for Multilateral Trading Facilities (MTFs), multilateral systems that do not offer listing services. MiFID also allowed certain intermediaries, known as Systematic Internalisers (SIs), to execute client orders autonomously. By paving the way for competition between different trading venues (RMs, MTFs and SIs), MiFID effectively made it possible for intermediaries to choose the most suitable platform for client orders to ensure best execution.

MiFID's definition of RM and MTF are closely aligned to reflect the fact that both venues offer the same organised trading function; in particular, in operating terms, both are authorised and functioning multilateral systems that bring together or facilitate the matching of multiple third-party buying and selling interests in financial instruments. Trades take place within the systems and in accordance with their non-discretional rules, and result in contracts relating to financial instruments admitted to trading.

In terms of organisational requirements, MiFID states expressly that not only authorised intermediaries but also exchanges can manage MTFs subject to verification, by the competent authority, of compliance with authorisation and operating requirements applicable to authorised investment companies and banks.

The loss of member states' rights to allow the concentration of trading and the establishment of new trading venues has resulted inevitably in the fragmentation of trades across venues. Fragmentation implies risks for investors and for the markets in general, in terms of lower liquidity in individual trading venues and a relatively less efficient process of price discovery. As far as price discovery is concerned, MiFID addresses the risks deriving from the fragmentation of trades by imposing rigorous pre- and post-trade transparency requirements. The directive aims to guarantee that investors are adequately informed of the prices of securities, regardless of whether trading takes place on RMs, MTFs, through SIs or away from these venues.

In terms of transparency of information for investors, MiFID sets out detailed pre-trade transparency requirements differentiated according to the structure of the market and the nature of the investor, as well as post-trade transparency requirements applicable to RMs, MTFs and SIs alike. In terms of pre-trade transparency, as a minimum requirement member states must ensure that trading venue operators (exchanges or MTFs) make public current bid and offer prices, and the depth of trading interests at such prices. This information must be disclosed to the public on reasonable commercial terms and on a continuous basis during normal trading hours. As far as post-trade transparency is concerned, MiFID requires member states to ensure that their national regulatory framework obliges stock exchanges and other MTF operators to disclose to the public the price, volume and time of execution of transactions concluded on their systems, on a reasonable commercial basis and as close to real time as possible. In short, the objectives of market efficiency and investor protection are based on a detailed system of pre- and post-trade transparency consistent with the principle of best execution that must be achieved on every client order.

In defining a common regulatory framework for transparency, MiFID was inevitably faced with a decision concerning the appropriate type and degree of transparency. This aspect is particularly relevant to competition between RMs and MTFs on the one hand, and SIs on the other. RMs and MTFs are typically order-driven and prosper in conditions of maximum pre- and post-trade transparency. SIs, on the other hand, being quote-driven, require some degree of opacity to justify their operation. MiFID substantially imposes the utmost pre-trade transparency on all trading venues, and then proceeds to identify transactions and operators that can benefit from derogations to this general principle (Gomber and Chlistalla, 2008, pp. 2–11). For example, a derogation is allowed for MTFs in the case of transactions larger in scale than normal market size: in this case, transparency requirements can be waived ex-ante. A similar waiver is foreseen for RM operators: public notification can be delayed for transactions larger in scale than those normally concluded in the same market for the same type of security. In operational terms, the derogation for MTFs has resulted in the creation of two types of trading platform: those with price discovery (light pools) and the dark pools described above, so-called because they lack the transparency of light pools.

Overall, even though the assessment of the full impact of MiFID will be possible only in the coming years, a number of significant changes have already become evident (Chlistalla and Gomber, 2007). In the USA, where different markets trading the same securities have long coexisted, the adverse effects of the dispersion of trades across multiple trading platforms have apparently been avoided by a system of consolidation that concentrates market information in a single virtual trading book. While European regulations do not provide for this type of instrument, they do recommend that mechanisms be put in place spontaneously to ensure consolidation of market information. The European market differs from the US market to the extent that in Europe, for many years, sales of pre-trade and post-trade information represented a substantial source of revenue for exchanges and trading systems. Furthermore, MiFID envisages possible differences in market information requirements among trading venues, making comparisons difficult for investors.

In terms of best execution, the inaccurate transposition of MiFID's best execution rule in certain national contexts allows intermediaries to inform clients on a one-off basis of the trading venue where orders are executed, thereby bypassing the requirement to compare on an order-by-order basis the conditions available on the market. In this way, only more sophisticated investors capable of gaining real-time access to different platforms are constantly in a position to exploit the best trading conditions; there is a real risk that retail investors will fail to reap many of the benefits envisaged by the new regulatory framework.

Early empirical data suggest that although in some markets MTFs have eroded traditional trading volumes, such as the London Stock Exchange (LSE), in other smaller markets, far from eroding trading volumes, traditional exchanges are receiving orders previously executed away from stock markets, and above all are benefitting from increased volumes generated by arbitrage opportunities.

## 10.3   European stock exchange consolidation

Although consolidation among exchanges seemed a natural and inevitable process as early as 1988, little merger activity was actually seen in Europe until 2006. In an attempt to speed up the process, the European Central Bank (ECB) and the European Commission (EC) underlined how cross-border trading costs were significantly higher in Europe than in the USA, and how the single currency alone was not sufficient to achieve the desired change: trading and post-trading structures needed to be more open than the existing facilities that were still confined within national borders (London Economics, 2002).

The opportunity for new trading venues to operate in Europe from November 2007 prompted traditional exchanges to seek partners in an effort to consolidate their market positions. Until 2006, only two significant mergers had been completed in Europe, those of OMX (1998) and Euronext (2000). In the many later successful mergers, the larger exchanges were involved: London Stock Exchange (LSE), Deutsche Börse and Euronext, all of which were listed in 2001 (Pagano and Padilla, 2005, pp. 229–67).

In 2006 the two main US exchanges, New York Stock Exchange (NYSE) and NASDAQ, expressed an interest in alliances or mergers with their major European counterparts; this news put an end to all prospective mergers in Europe, and alerted the attention of ECB and representatives of the governments of a number of European countries, who urged consolidation between European players to bolster Europe's financial system and reinforce the role of the euro (Schmiedel and Schonenberger, 2005).

In May 2006, the largest world stock exchange, NYSE and the pan-European exchange Euronext became the protagonists of an operation that would previously have been unthinkable. Following the NYSE–Euronext operation, two further mergers involving the major European exchanges were successfully completed: the NASDAQ–OMX merger, and the LSE–Borsa Italiana merger that culminated in the foundation of LSE Group. Another European exchange seen actively pursuing consolidation was Deutsche Börse, although at the time of writing it had yet to identify a suitable partner, despite supporting consolidation on smaller scale – albeit transatlantic in scope – between the derivates market Eurex and the US ISE.

From 2006–07, consolidation was seen at a global rather than a transatlantic level, as the United Arab Emirates exchanges began to acquire significant stakes in European and US exchanges.

Ultimately, in the current market climate, given the growth in size of exchanges, leadership at a continental level is no longer sufficient: for success, it is necessary to become a truly global competitor.

In media reports one of the main motives for consolidation cited by the exchanges was the growth in company size to ensure a larger critical mass of clients distributed across several continents. In addition, NYSE Group and Euronext reported a common strategic vision of technology and a preference for a horizontal business model. On the other hand, LSE and Borsa Italiana focused on operational gaps: in particular, Borsa Italiana brought into the new group a high degree of specialisation in the bond market thanks to the acquisition of Mercato telematico dei titoli di stato (MTS) the Italian government bonds wholesale electronic market, as well as a highly integrated business with efficient trading and post-trading structures. Conversely, Borsa Italiana benefitted from LSE's competence in the listing of small and medium-sized enterprises. Finally, for the NASDAQ-OMX Group, consolidation resulted in a technologically advanced transatlantic group; on their respective continents, both exchanges are the principal suppliers of technology to stock markets.

An entirely different case, though in the same context, was the merger between International Stock Exchange (ISE) and Eurex, the leading derivatives exchange in Europe jointly owned by Deutsche Börse and the Swiss stock exchange. The consolidation of the two exchanges led to the creation of a world leading equity and equity index derivatives exchange.

In the process of consolidation substantial investments were made by the exchanges: NYSE spent  7,780 million, London Stock Exchange  1,634 million and NASDAQ 2,363 million. The cash outlays required for these operations were justified to shareholders in terms of cost savings and increased revenues accruing from consolidation. In the case of NYSE Euronext, synergies worth 295 million were announced relating to cost reductions from the rationalisation of technology platforms and increased revenues from the creation of new products. As a result of the merger between LSE and Borsa Italiana, official press releases predicted annual revenue synergies of at least £20 million up to 2011 and annual cost synergies of at least £20 million until 2010. However, it was announced that one-off implementation costs of an estimated £40 million would effectively compensate the revenue and cost synergies for the first year at least. Finally, in the NASDAQ–OMX merger, total savings of 150 million were announced as a result of rationalisation of technology platforms and cost synergies.

The 2008 and 2009 annual accounts will confirm whether the synergies were achieved. At the time of writing, there is evidence of tension in all three of the newly merged groups, demonstrated by recent changes in senior management.

Clearly, stiffer competition had been accounted for in merger feasibility studies; significant erosion of trading volumes and a decline in the number of new listings due to the financial crisis had not. Nevertheless, competition has been stronger than expected, fostered by advances in technology that level the playing field and facilitate new trading venues (European Central Bank, 2007). Indeed, technological developments and MiFID have permitted new competitors of the likes of Chi-X, Turquoise, BATS Europe and others to join the industry. We shall turn our attention to these below.

Even though economies of scale and network externalities still have a centralising tendency that drives exchanges to seek consolidation opportunities, that tendency is weakening. Networks now extend beyond single markets and allow trading platforms to compete; a more technologically sophisticated competitor may surpass the economies of scale to be had from consolidation. It even seems that the greater the level of integration, the greater the degree of fragmentation (Stoll, 2006, pp. 153–74).

The financial crisis does not preclude further consolidation among stock exchanges; however, given that trading volumes are shrinking daily, in future the onus will be on the reduction of excessively high costs rather than the pursuit of leadership positions. Indeed, towards the end of 2008 news leaked of Deutsche Börse's unsuccessful attempt to merge with NYSE Euronext.

## 10.4   New competitors in the stock exchange industry

As we have seen, MiFID paved the way for greater competition in European stock markets; accordingly, exchanges took steps to secure internal growth, and pursued external growth through consolidation in a drive to improve their market position before MTFs became fully operational.

Prior to the entry of MTFs, the major European exchanges – Deutsche Börse, NYSE Euronext and the LSE Group – had handled virtually all trading in securities listed on their exchanges, earning substantial revenues from trade commissions and sales of market information. Initially, the exchanges declared that with continued investments in technology, new services and a competitive tariff structure to encourage order routing, competition from MTFs did not represent any particular threat. LSE was particularly quick to react, since the broker-dealers setting up Turquoise MTF were effectively LSE's major clients. By the summer of 2007, LSE had launched TradElect, a new trading platform that was ready to compete on an equal technological footing with MTFs (Alemanni et al., 2006).

Subsequently, the exchanges began to align their tariff structures with those of MTFs; for example, in early September 2008, just as Turquoise was reaching full-scale operation, LSE lowered its tariffs on trades used frequently in algorithmic trading.

Nevertheless, the competitive superiority of the major European exchanges was insufficient to stave off the arrival of MTFs, most of which were launched by the large investment banks actively engaged in trading that deemed the commissions applied by exchanges to be exorbitant.

At the beginning of 2009, 121 MTFs approved by various European authorities figured on the CESR list; most operated in the bond or derivatives markets, and some had yet to reach their full extent.

Table 10.1 provides a summary of the major MTFs competing with European exchanges in the equities market, managed by intermediaries or exchanges, in terms of transparency of pre- and post-trade prices.

Of the MTFs managed by intermediaries with complete price transparency, the first to start trading in Europe was Chi-X Europe Limited (Chi-X), a facility authorised by the Financial Services Authority (FSA) to provide services to investment companies in the European Economic Area (EEA). Chi-X was set up by the broker Instinet and started trading in European equities on 30 March 2007. Chi-X's strengths are the considerable number of pan-European shares traded, the speed of execution (nearly 10 times faster than traditional platforms) and the low cost (nearly 10 times cheaper than the exchanges). Orders on the trading book are executed anonymously and in order of time. Both visible orders and non-displayed orders can be entered and the system offers more innovative order types than traditional exchanges. Fortis Bank Global Clearing manages post-trading services. Another significant aspect is that Chi-X distributes market information free of charge directly to clients or third parties. At the start of 2008, this represented a far-reaching innovation, considering that traditional exchanges were charging hefty fees for such services.

The second MTF to enter the European market was Turquoise, whose launch was announced in November 2006. Turquoise was authorised to operate by the Financial Services Authority on 30 June 2008 and, like Chi-X,

*Table 10.1*   The major MTFs in Europe operating in the equities market

**MTFs with price discovery**

| MTFs managed by intermediaries (*) | | MTFs managed by exchanges | |
| --- | --- | --- | --- |
| Chi-X | 16 April 2007 | NASDAQ OMX Europe | 26 September 2008 |
| Turquoise | 15 August 2008 | NYSE Arca Europe | March 2009 |
| BATS Europe | 31 October 2008 | | |

**MTFs recognised as dark pools**

| MTFs managed by intermediaries | | MTFs managed by exchanges | |
| --- | --- | --- | --- |
| Liquidnet Europe | November 2002 | Euro Millenium (SWX, Nyfix) | December 2007 |
| ITG (POSIT) | 1998 | SmartPool (NYSE Euronext) | 2 February 2009 |
| | | NEURO Dark (NASDAQ OMX) | 11 May 2009 |
| | | Baikal (LSE) | Postponed until 2nd quarter 2009 |

*Note*: (*) As Table 10.2 below indicates, these MTFs have operated a dark book alongside their visible order book since their launch.
*Source*: Own elaboration.

is the holder of a MiFID passport and as such can offer trading services in every EEA member state. Trading began on a limited scale on 15 August 2008 (ten shares from two countries) but within one month, operations had expanded significantly. An independent company established by the major investment banks in Europe set up Turquoise to provide a trading platform accessible to all operators. In particular, as Table 10.2 shows, the first investors and founding members of this pan-European trading platform were nine financial intermediaries, later joined by other broker-dealers trading in European equities. Backed the main European investment banks, from the outset Turquoise obviously benefitted from a critical mass of natural liquidity. The facility runs a dark pool and a visible order pool that can interact to ensure swift and inexpensive execution of trades. In practical terms, the integrated order book combining dark and visible orders allows operators to obtain an excellent price for small orders and/or to negotiate large trades efficiently (Chlistalla et al., 2007, pp. 69–79). Clearing and settlement are performed by EuroCCP, a subsidiary of the US clearing provider DTCC.

In chronological order the third MTF to start trading in Europe was BATS (Better Alternative Trading System) Europe on 31 October 2008. BATS Europe is wholly owned by its US parent BATS, a facility headquartered in Kansas City that after only three years of operation on the US market has

*Table 10.2*   Key features of the main European MTFs

|  | **Shareholders** | **Market model** | **Clearing & Settlement** |
|---|---|---|---|
| Chi-X Europe | BNP Paribas, Citadel, Citigroup, Crédit Suisse, Fortis, Goldman Sachs, Lehman Brothers, Merrill Lynch, Morgan Stanley, Société Générale and UBS; Brokers: Optiver, Getco Europe. | Central Limit Order Book (CLOB). Visible and non-displayed limit order types). | Clearing: EMCF (Fortis) Settlement: local CSDs |
| Turquoise | Citigroup, Crédit Suisse, Deutsche Bank, Goldman Sachs, Merrill Lynch and Morgan Stanley, UBS, BNP Paribas and Société Générale. | Hybrid trading model consisting of a public limit order book and a non-public order book (dark pool) incorporating both displayed and non-displayed liquidity. | Clearing: EuroCCP Settlement: Citigroup (Global Transaction Services division) |
| BATS Europe | Investment banks: Citigroup, Crédit Suisse, Deutsche Bank, Merrill Lynch and Morgan Stanley; Brokers: Getco, Lime Brokerage and Wedbush. | CLOB (Visible and non-displayed limit order types). | Clearing: EMCF (Fortis) Settlement: local CSDs |

*Source*: Own elaboration.

a market share in excess of 10 per cent, and ranks third in the market by trading volumes after NASDAQ and NYSE. BATS was established as an Electronic Communications Network (ECN) in January 2006 but in November 2007 applied to the SEC for authorisation to operate as an exchange and began operating as such in November 2008. BATS Europe was the first European MTF to publicly disclose free of charge the market shares of exchanges and MTFs by volume and by value, virtually in real time, replicating the strategy pursued successfully in the US by its parent company. In the same way as the other two MTFs, BATS Europe operates a central limited order book (CLOB) in which visible and non-visible orders can be inserted. Post-trading is managed by a dedicated structure set up by Fortis, just as for Chi-X.

It is worth noting that a number of investment banks provided the capital for, and participated in the establishment of, the three main European MTFs. This can be seen from Table 10.2, which also illustrates clearly the evident need for more efficient and less costly facilities than exchanges, and confirms the rapid evolution of the sector. The fact that certain shareholders of Turquoise also have stakes in Chi-X and BATS Europe may be interpreted either as a form of 'coverage' in the event of one MTF being surpassed by the others and hence failing to achieve its objectives, or alternatively as a sign of confidence in the sector, considering that there is scope for at least three or four more MTFs in Europe.

Table 10.3 shows the market shares for the MTFs described above by market index. It is evident that the market shares of the three MTFs are proportionate to the length of time they have been operating, and that market share tends to increase over time. The most 'besieged' share index is that managed by LSE, followed by the Euronext index.

*Table 10.3*   Market share of the principal MTFs by market index (%)*

| MTF | AEX 25 | FTSE 100 | CAC 40 | DAX 30 |
| --- | --- | --- | --- | --- |
| Chi-X | 14.59 | 16.88 | 13.09 | 13.01 |
| Turquoise | 5.99 | 5.19 | 7.16 | 5.35 |
| BATS Europe | 1.23 | 2.13 | 1.35 | 1.47 |

*Note*: * Data at 27 February 2009.
*Source*: Press releases.

Chi-X's positive start to trading at the beginning of 2008 highlighted the need for exchanges to compete with MTFs on an equal footing by exploiting the possibility of managing their own MTFs. Basically, the exchanges established alternative platforms to avoid losing customers to their new rivals, and offered access at no additional fee above that already paid for the use of traditional platforms. During 2008, LSE, NASDAQ OMX, NYSE Euronext, and Deutsche Börse all announced plans to set up pan-European trading platforms akin to MTFs.

Note that the exchanges set up their dark pools first, in the form of negotiating platforms for the anonymous execution of block orders to avoid distorting market prices. In the autumn of 2007, LSE and NYSE Euronext both announced the launch of their respective pan-European dark pools Baikal and SmartPool.

The Baikal project, a joint venture between LSE and Lehman Brothers, was hard hit by the financial crisis. LSE was forced to reconsider the project following the bankruptcy of Lehman Brothers, which had been due to supply the algorithms and anti-gaming technology. The Japanese bank Nomura, which took over the European operations of Lehman Brothers, was willing to be a party to the joint venture; however, by that time LSE was seeking a small group of investors rather than a single partner to provide the necessary financial and technological support. Owing to these operating problems, the launch of Baikal was postponed until the second quarter of 2009.

SmartPool, on the other hand, was created following NYSE Euronext's decision to increase its trading venues to cater for block orders, in contrast with the market trend towards smaller execution sizes. The project was finalised by NYSE Euronext with the aid of BNP Paribas and HSBC. On 30 September 2008, JP Morgan became the fourth partner in the project. SmartPool is a dark pool that offers the advantage of a link with NYSE Euronext's light pool; it was established to execute block orders from institutional investors and sell-side firms that require an efficient platform with low latency and a level of information that does not distort market trends. SmartPool commenced operations on February 2009 following authorisation by FSA, and traded shares on 15 European markets during its first month of operation. Clearing of trades is handled for SmartPool by LCH.Clearnet or EuroCCP according to traders' choices.

Subsequently, the exchanges shifted their attention towards traders that submit high-frequency orders and require low latency, planning the launch of MTFs with price discovery and a 'maker taker' tariff structure, similar to the MTFs run by intermediaries. The maker taker system is designed to attract liquidity by rebating traders that submit orders (the makers) and charging only those that match orders (the takers). Generally, this preferential treatment is not applied to clients that use traditional regulated markets even though at times the two types of venue use the same technological platform.

NYSE Euronext in fact announced the launch of an MTF with a maker–taker pricing structure, NYSE Arca Europe, designed to attract orders from small investors who seek maximum transparency in trading. The initial intention was to trade blue-chip shares from 11 European markets, excluding Euronext markets, in other words the Paris, Amsterdam, Brussels and Lisbon official lists. However, the launch scheduled for November 2008 was postponed to March 2009 due to the negative market conditions brought on by the financial crisis.

The MTF with a price-discovering order book set up by rival NASDAQ OMX that started trading on 26 September 2008 under the name of NASDAQ OMX Europe was more successful. It was the first platform to connect European investors to pan-European routing. At the time of writing around 600 securities can be traded, including constituents of the main European indices, ETFs and other liquid instruments. The platform was built by Instinet's European subsidiary, Instinet Europe, while post-trading is managed by EuroCCP with a Fortis European Multilateral Clearing Facility (EMCF).

It is clear that competition is changing the face of the securities industry; all the players are eager to speed up trading and reduce latency times. The well-established exchanges seek to retain clients by adapting to changes in the market and by leveraging their reputation and proven track record in the provision of services.

On the post-trading front, exchanges are searching for the most efficient partner and offering a range of venues to operators; for example, NASDAQ OMX Europe's trades are cleared by EuroCCP, in the same way as Turquoise trades, while NYSE Euronext's SmartPool allows users to choose between the EuroCCP clearing facility used by Turquoise, and EMCF, the clearing facility set up by Fortis and used by Chi-X and BATS Europe. To remain competitive, LSE Group has also introduced choice in clearing: clients can opt whether to clear trades through X-Clear, a division of the Swiss stock exchange, or LCH.Clearnet.

Competition exists not only in trading but also in sales of market information on equity prices, both in real time and on executed trades, to clients and agencies that consolidate and distribute market information. The market information sector first seemed vulnerable to competition when the idea of a 'consolidated tape' – the US system that aggregates share prices on exchanges and Alternative Trading Systems (ATSs) – began to circulate in Europe. In January 2009, a group of MTFs based in Europe planned the launch of a free data service to allow traders to view selected share prices simultaneously across European markets, posing a serious threat to LSE's pay-for market data service. This initiative effectively opened a second front in the battle between new platforms and traditional exchanges. In any case, the MTFs all tend to provide their own market data service free of charge.

Some form of consolidated tape is likely to be realised in Europe by MTFs or by an agency specialised in the management and distribution of information. In January 2009, for example, Thomson Reuters launched a price information system containing data on exchanges and major MTFs.

## 10.5   The impact of the financial crisis

While increased competition fostered by the introduction of the new European regulations and advances in technology has certainly contributed to a reduction in the scale of the main European exchanges, the financial crisis has proved more detrimental to the health of the system.

As Table 10.4 shows, the market capitalisation of major exchanges decreased significantly in 2008, due to the financial crisis more than the other factors discussed above. The market capitalisation of European exchanges fell by 50 per cent, while that of US exchanges fell by just over 40 per cent. A drastic reduction in the share prices of companies listed on the main exchanges brought total market capitalisation down to levels recorded ten years earlier. At the end of 2008 and in the early months of 2009, US exchanges were forced to take urgent measures to stave off the automatic de-listing of shares that lost virtually all of their value during the financial turmoil.

The losses of market capitalisation were seen across the board and affected all the main exchanges in 2008. The principal cause was the financial crisis,

*Table 10.4*   Domestic market capitalisation (in millions of USD) (2006–8)

| Exchange | December 2006 | December 2007 | % change on 2006 | December 2008 | % change on 2007 |
|---|---|---|---|---|---|
| NASDAQ Stock Market | 3,865,003.6 | 4,013,650.3 | **3.8** | 2,396,344.3 | **−40.3** |
| NYSE Group | 15,421,167.9 | 15,650,832.5 | **1.5** | 9,208,934.1 | **−41.2** |
| BME Spanish Exchanges | 1,322,915.3 | 1,781,132.7 | **34.6** | 948,352.3 | **−46.8** |
| Borsa Italiana | 1,026,504.2 | 1,072,534.7 | **4.5** | 522,087.8 | **−51.3** |
| Deutsche Börse | 1,637,609.8 | 2,105,197.8 | **28.6** | 1,110,579.6 | **−47.2** |
| Euronext | 3,708,150.1 | 4,222,679.8 | **13.9** | 2,101,745.9 | **−50.2** |
| LSE | 3,781,358.5 | 3,851,705.9 | **1.9** | 1,868,153.0 | **−51.5** |
| OMX Nordic Exchange | 1,122,705.1 | 1,242,577.9 | **10.7** | 563,099.6 | **−54.7** |
| Total | 31,885,414.4 | 33,940,311.6 | **6.4** | 18,719,296.5 | **−44.8** |

*Source*: Own processing of World Federation of Exchanges (WFE) – Statistics.

so there was no direct effect on the world ranking of stock exchanges by market capitalisation.

Not only share prices but also the number of listings shrank on virtually all exchanges, with the exception of the Spanish Exchange which was comparatively unscathed (Table 10.5). The number of NYSE listings increased following the acquisition of American Stock Exchange (Amex) by NYSE, finalised on 1 October 2008, when 600 small to medium-sized enterprises listed on Amex joined NYSE Alternext US.

Table 10.6 summarises the value of share trading in the last three years on the main global exchanges. Nearly all the European exchanges lost value in 2008 due to operating difficulties exacerbated by competition and the financial turmoil; LSE recorded a particularly significant loss. On the other hand, the US exchanges grew, though a contributing factor to this superior growth was the exchange rate: in 2008, the US dollar rose five per cent against the euro and 37 per cent against sterling.

The 2008 annual accounts of the main European exchanges will presumably record significant falls in revenue in listing, trading and market data services. The erosion of trading volumes because of the financial crisis, and fierce price competition has forced exchanges to lower trading fees to avoid losing clients. There is a real danger that revenue from market data services may disappear entirely if a centralised market information system akin to the system already in place in the USA is established in Europe. The crisis has also affected listing services: many companies postponed listings

*Table 10.5*  Number of listed companies (2006–8)

| Exchange | 2006 | 2007 | % change on 2006 | 2008 | % change on 2007 |
|---|---|---|---|---|---|
| NASDAQ Stock Market | 3,133 | 3,069 | −2.0 | 2,952 | −3.8 |
| NYSE Group | 2,280 | 2,273 | −0.3 | 3,011 | 32.5 |
| BME Spanish Exchanges | 3,378 | 3,537 | 4.7 | 3,576 | 1.1 |
| Borsa Italiana | 290 | 307 | 5.9 | 300 | −2.3 |
| Deutsche Börse | 760 | 866 | 13.9 | 832 | −3.9 |
| Euronext | 954 | 1,155 | 21.1 | 1,002 | −13.2 |
| LSE | 3,256 | 3,307 | 1.6 | 3,096 | −6.4 |
| OMX Nordic Exchange | 791 | 851 | 7.6 | 824 | −3.2 |

*Source*: Own processing of WFE – Statistics.

*Table 10.6*  Value of share trading (in millions of USD) (2006–8)

| Exchange | 2006 | 2007 | % change on 2006 | 2008 | % change on 2007 |
|---|---|---|---|---|---|
| NASDAQ Stock Market | 21,792,852.4 | 28,116,428.2 | 29.0 | 36,445,906.1 | 29.6 |
| NYSE Group | 41,863,844.0 | 29,209,971.2 | −30.2 | 33,638,937.0 | 15.2 |
| BME Spanish Exchanges | 1,949,099.2 | 2,970,616.0 | 52.4 | 2,438,646.5 | −17.9 |
| Borsa Italiana | 1,379,875.5 | 2,311,826.9 | 67.5 | 1,526,237.2 | −34 |
| Deutsche Börse | 2,741,607.8 | 4,323,675.4 | 57.7 | 3,880,942.4 | −10.2 |
| Euronext | 3,858,672.4 | 5,648,451.9 | 46.4 | 4,454,415.2 | −21.1 |
| LSE | 7,582,149.4 | 10,324,334.6 | 36.2 | 6,473,611.6 | −37.3 |
| OMX Nordic Exchange | 1,330,531.8 | 1,863,306.8 | 40.0 | 1,335,003.0 | −28.4 |
| Total | 82,498,632.5 | 84,768,611.1 | 2.7 | 90,193,699.0 | 6.39 |

*Source*: Own processing of WFE – Statistics.

planned in the second half of 2008 until an improvement in market conditions. There has also been evidence of stiffer competition in the listing sector: for example, NASDAQ attempted to gain listings in Europe, and undermine LSE's dominant position by applying for FSA authorisation to operate as an exchange; imitating the strategy of the rival exchange NYSE, Euronext launched a service to make listing in Europe and the US more straightforward and cost effective.

The competitive environment has presented a serious challenge for the incumbent European exchanges, and the share prices of listed exchanges already reflect this negative trend (Otchere, 2006, pp. 926–53). Figures 10.2 and 10.3 show the share price trend of the main exchanges. In 2006 and 2007 the share prices of the listed exchanges rose considerably, particularly those of LSE and Deutsche Börse. However, in 2008 they fell dramatically: at

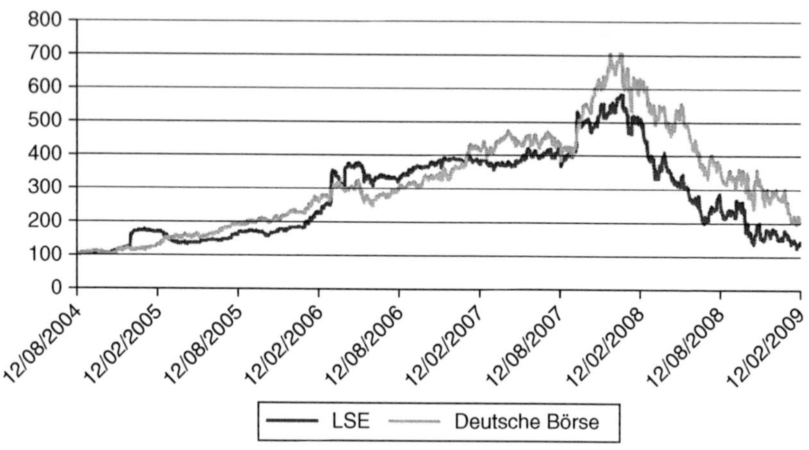


*Figure 10.2*    LSE and Deutsche Börse share price trend (2004–9)
*Source*: Own processing of Datastream Database.

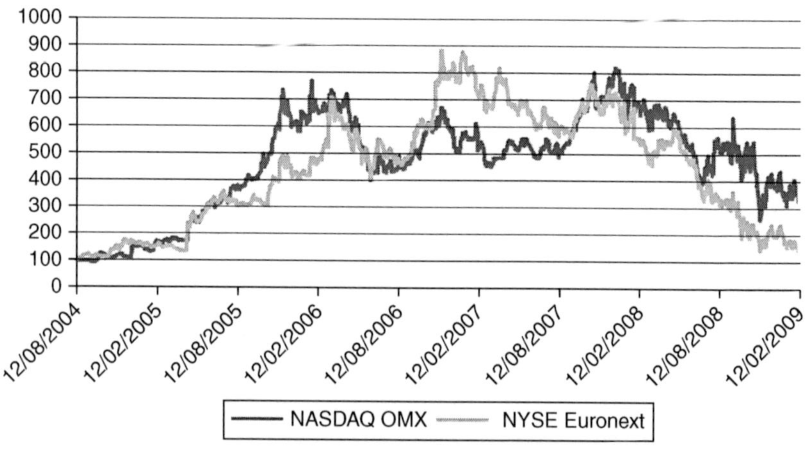


*Figure 10.3*    NYSE Euronext and NASDAQ OMX share price trend (2004–9)
*Source*: Own processing of Datastream Database.

the start of 2008, the LSE share price stood at £1.97, but it had plummeted to £0.50 by the end of the year; similarly, Deutsche Börse shares, priced at  130 at the start of 2008, fell to just  50 at the end of the year. Note also that a further drop in the share prices of both exchanges was seen in the first two months of 2009. For the transatlantic exchanges, until the beginning of 2008 growth was more erratic, particularly since consolidation in the US exchange industry (not considered in the present work), including the NYSE–Arca merger and the acquisition of Amex by NYSE, fuelled expectations of share price increases.

## 10.6   Conclusions

Even though there is a continuous process of consolidation in the stock exchanges industry, there may not be a significant decrease in the total number of exchanges since barriers to entry continue to fall. New competitors obtain authorisation to operate as MTFs, and some later apply to operate as exchanges, as in the case of BATS in the USA.

In general, the regulatory and operating framework has changed, and with it the characteristics required to gain a competitive edge. The key determinants have become competitively priced liquidity, ultra low latency and execution quality.

The financial crisis has not had a significant impact on forecasts, which were based on the new regulatory framework and advances in technology. However, the liquidity crisis has complicated the management of exchanges and exacerbated competitive pressure.

On the other hand, the financial crisis has not left MTFs unscathed. Their main shareholders – investment banks – have all been hard hit. Not surprisingly, the majority of MTFs postponed the start of operations. While the exchanges could have exploited this weakness in ownership structure to seek takeover opportunities, in fact they opted to set up their own MTFs.

In the present situation, the exchanges need to resolve a number of crucial issues concerning their market structure and their choice of market sector. While competition between exchanges and new trading platforms leads to fragmentation of trades on the one hand, on the other hand it should foster the emergence, at a European level, of efficient markets specialising in different types of financial instruments.

As a result of fragmentation, it is likely that more specialised markets will form, with client segmentation essentially guiding operations. Fragmentation of trades should thus bring about the spontaneous segmentation of trading markets.

# 11
# Measuring Value in Stock Exchanges' Mergers

*Josanco Floreani and Maurizio Polato*

## 11.1 Introduction

Measuring stock exchange value is a complex task, especially in consideration of the functions of public interest that are carried out by exchanges.

For many years the problem of value measurement was of secondary importance due to market segmentation and the monopoly conditions in which stock exchanges operated. However, stock-market privatisation and the fall of national trade barriers were to transform the exchange-industry structure. First of all, stock exchanges were converted into joint-stock companies, which were then listed. Secondly, in order to become more competitive, stock exchanges began a process of cross-border mergers.

The issue of measuring stock exchange value will be approached from two complementary viewpoints: earnings and governance.

In section 11.2 a literature-based framework is used to illustrate the problem of stock exchange pricing. Section 11.3 analyses trading-industry structure and incentives encouraging stock exchange mergers. Section 11.4 gives the results of an empirical study on the valuation criteria adopted in the most recent mergers. Value drivers are examined in section 11.5, in particular the relationship between operational exchange volumes and economic-financial dynamics. Finally, the pricing issue is related to the specific governance structure resulting from exchange mergers. Section 11.6 concludes.

## 11.2 Background and literature review

Consolidation in the exchange industry is a reaction to the growing competitive pressure that are being faced by incumbents. Innovations in technology and legislation have combined to break down the barriers that once protected stock exchanges, thus allowing for the entry of new players and the spread of alternative platforms.

Consequently, stock exchanges have to face the economic risk of profit margin erosion and the financial risk of needing to invest large sums on developing efficient trading platforms. From all points of view (economic, financial and operational) there is a strong incentive for stock exchanges to integrate their platforms so as to increase liquidity, share costs and develop synergies. Note that cash trading platforms are kept separate from derivatives platforms once mergers have been completed, though in some cases platforms have been integrated.

In order to reduce operational costs and their impact on economic dynamics, stock exchanges have taken part in mergers, invested in technology and diversified their production. As regards revenues, such policies have strengthened liquidity and the volume of exchange markets. Since liquidity derives from the number of listed issuers and the size of exchange volumes, it will affect listing and trading commission and revenues. Consequently, because of the cyclical nature of trading volumes, revenues are variable. As regards the effect of the policies on costs, an increase in volumes will cause a decrease in the level of average costs. Since investment in Information Technology (IT) is aimed at maintaining the efficiency of the trading infrastructure, it would be expected that such costs should make up a significant part of cost structure.

Exchanges faces risks associated with the cyclicity of trading following strategies of horizontal and/or vertical integration.

As regards the former case, exchange groups are able to establish trading revenues and related income, such as that deriving from the sale of market data, by:

- diversifying geographical presence in order to widen areas of liquidity;
- widening product range, for example to derivatives and Exchange Traded Funds (ETF's) in order to develop cross-selling opportunities.

It should be noted that exchanges' competitive strategies have implications for governance (Polato and Floreani, 2007). Stock exchange mergers generally lead to business diversification and involve profit-driven companies that are usually listed (the incentives for exchanges to list are analysed in Fleckner, 2006). Such mergers aim to widen production, strengthen oligopolistic control over order flows and develop network economies.

The goal of mergers is to support competition by developing direct and indirect network economies (Di Noia, 1999), thus regaining market share in terms of volumes exchanged and in the IPO market. The application of network theory to the stock exchange industry (Economides, 1993) shows that network economies result in an increase in liquidity and in the quality of price discovery. It is to be noted that the unfolding of network externalities is dependent upon compatibility and co-ordination (Economides and Flyer, 1997) among the constituent parts. Finally, several stock exchanges pursue vertical integration strategies with post-trading companies by taking advantage of:

- the recurrence of the relationship between stock exchange and post-trading companies;
- specific investment in the relationship;
- the divergence of interest among the parties, which can lead to opportunistic behaviour.[1]

The literature of industrial organisation identifies as incentives to integration-specific investment in the relationship (Williamson, 1985) and difficulty in drawing up contracts that will be able to meet all future contingencies (Grossman and Hart, 1986).

There has been much debate concerning the effects of integration on welfare and on the efficiency of company management, and the problem has often been analysed according to the former perspective.

In particular, Tapking and Yang (2004) examined industrial relations between exchanges and post-trading companies, especially as regards the effects of different trading and settlement industry structures on welfare. They observed that a strong tendency by investors to negotiate stocks issued by foreign companies favoured horizontal integration between post-trading companies operating under various national jurisdictions, rather than vertical integration with the stock exchange.

On the contrary, very few studies have examined the impact on stock exchange performance. One group looked in particular at exchange alliances in the broadest sense, ranging from mergers to forms of integration in which exchanges maintain their independent status. Models uniting investor utility functions and stock exchange profit curves have shown that exchanges operating under monopoly conditions are able to make supplementary profit from the trading services provided.

Shy and Tarkka (2001) modelled an alliance between two stock exchanges based on mutual access to the order flows of both exchanges on payment of an access fee. As long as the cost of access to stock exchange services remains high, the alliance is able to increase investor utility and raise the profits of exchanges and intermediaries.

Andersen (2005) added a further scenario to the analysis by considering a situation in which there is a monopoly stock exchange and by introducing the effects of network economies deriving from increases in liquidity. The hypotheses were supported by consolidation trends in the stock exchange industry resulting in the strengthening of monopolies. The findings showed that the consolidation of network externalities leads to an increase in the demand for trading services and a rise in profits for both stock exchanges and intermediaries. Moreover, the pricing of exchange services does not appear to be affected by network factors.

The cyclical nature of cash trading should lead logically to both product and process diversification. On the one hand, stock exchanges expand their business into high-growth segments and reduce revenue volatility; on the other hand, they aim to be the sole service suppliers in the trading value chain. In recent literature studies have examined the conditions in which stock exchange diversification policies are efficient.

Schmiedel (2001) assessed the conditions of economic efficiency in European stock exchanges between 1985 and 1999, while a year later the same author (Schmiedel 2002) examined gains in the productivity in the period 1993–9 of both stock exchanges that focus on their core business and those that also operate in derivatives and post-trading activities. On the contrary, Serifsoy (2007) adopted Farrel's (1957) notion of technical efficiency and applied his analysis to a sample of 28 stock exchanges using a non-parametric approach based on Data Envelopment Analysis. In particular, the author focuses on the vertical integration policies of stock exchanges. Findings do not give evidence that a vertically integrated business model leads to greater efficiency.

Overall, stock exchange value dynamics stem from a range of qualitative and quantitative parameters reflecting financial strength and business prospects (Standard and Poor's, 2006). The most significant parameters are:

- the level of liquidity and the depth of markets;
- diversification through the provision of a wide range of products for which the stock exchange can supply trading services (derivatives, ETFs), thus stabilizing operational income. Other business areas (data distribution, technology and post-trading services) enhance the effect of diversification;
- cost structure, investment in technology, cash-flow generation, debt service. The generation of cash flow is fundamental for technology investments and for debt service. Traditionally, a high level of cash-flow generation is evidence that stock exchanges have a limited need of finance through debt. On the other hand, acquisitions result in an increase in debt and absorb cash flow.

Our goal is to study evaluation criteria in recent exchange mergers and the relationship between profitability, liquidity and product diversification. Since stock exchanges deal in transaction-based business, revenues should increase in proportion to exchange volumes, and higher volumes should result in lower average costs.

We also assess the impact of various business areas on profitability. Being a high-profit, low-risk income spinner, the distribution of market data is a strategic operation for almost all stock exchanges. In addition, post-trading activities are important in many stock exchanges and guarantee an extra flow of income. Moreover, there is a tendency to combine cash markets with derivatives markets. We expect pricing taking into account both increased liquidity and synergies to be disgorged by diversifying the business model.

## 11.3   Exchange mergers: effects on governance and value

Stock exchange mergers began to occur after the demutualization and listing of the main stock exchanges. In Europe the Paris, Amsterdam, Brussels and Lisbon stock exchanges merged to form Euronext, while the OMX Nordic Exchange resulted from the merger of small northern European exchanges. However, the most significant mergers are those that have taken place most recently since they have involved the largest stock exchanges in the world and have linked up American and European finance. Finally, the main exchanges have built up relations with groups of purely financial investors (institutional investors, hedge funds) whose principal objective is to maximise profit and who often have the power to direct the strategic choices of exchanges.

The largest mergers were accomplished in successive stages of integration and included:

- the merger between the New York Stock Exchange (NYSE) and Euronext, which was announced in 2006 and completed in April 2007. The NYSE Group itself had originated from a merger between NYSE and Archipelago in 2006;
- the merger between the London Stock Exchange (LSE) and Borsa Italiana, which took place between June and October 2007, and gave rise to the LSE Group;
- the merger between NASDAQ and OMX, which resulted in the establishment of the NASQAQ OMX Group in February 2008;
- the acquisition of International Securities Exchange (ISE), an American options exchange, announced by the Deutsche Börse in 2007.

The most interesting case regards the NYSE–Euronext merger. One of the strategic development options considered by the NYSE was to transform itself from a non-profit mutual company into a for-profit business, which was regarded as being more suitable in facing this highly competitive sector. The choice to merge with Archipelago also allowed the NYSE to extend its business to the rapidly expanding equity options sector and to shift from traditional floor-based trading to electronic trading via the Archipelago platform. On the other hand, the objective of the subsequent merger with Euronext was geographical diversification.

The series of mergers resulted in the creation of a number of diversified groups with dominant positions in cash and derivatives markets (Figure 11.1 and Figure 11.2). Moreover, such mergers increased the level of market concentration around the major groups. However, concentration in the derivatives market is even stronger than in the cash market, and the products traded are more heterogeneous. The principal international players tend to concentrate in specific market segments.

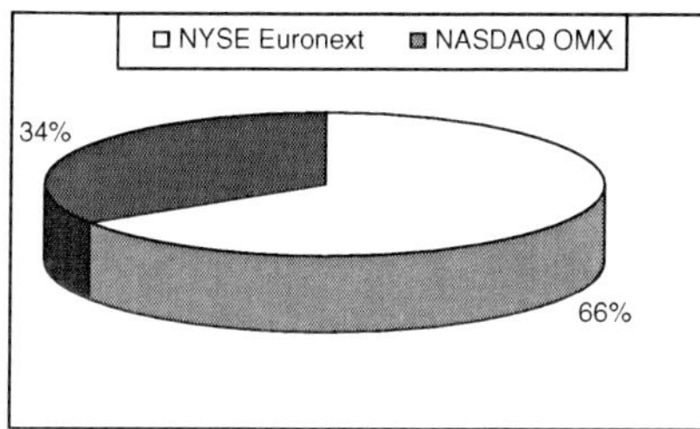


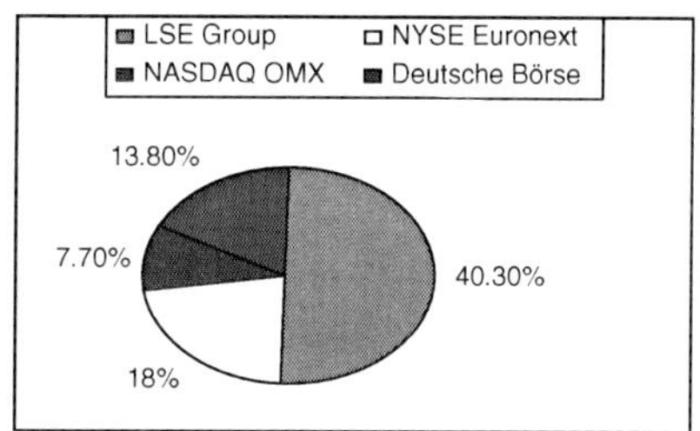


*Figure 11.1*   Share trading (left column: US markets; right column: European markets)
*Source*: Own processing of WFE (2007).

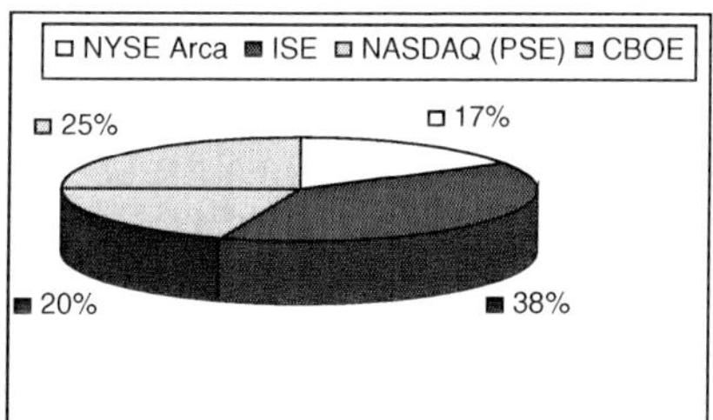


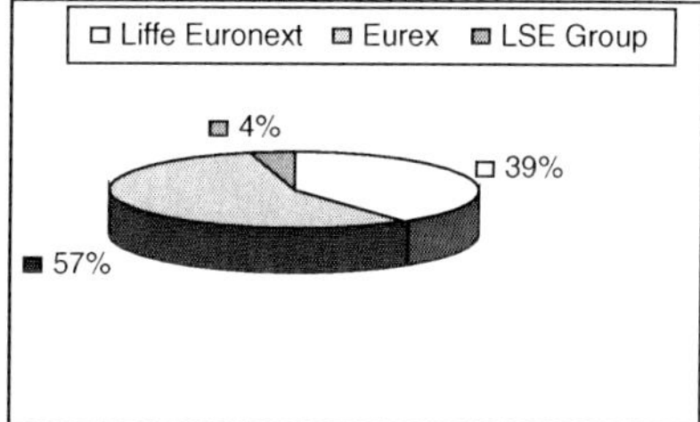


*Figure 11.2*   Equity derivatives (left column: US markets; right column: European markets)
*Source*: Own processing of WFE (2007).

In the USA there is a duopoly in which the NYSE Euronext Group and NASDAQ OMX make up almost the totality of exchange trading on the cash market. Recent mergers allowed both the NYSE Euronext Group and the NASDAQ OMX Group (through the Pacific Securities Exchange, PSE) to gain a significant share in the derivatives market, though limited to equity derivatives. At the same time, NYSE Euronext (through Euronext) has become co-leader in the European derivatives market, alongside Eurex. The three main European exchanges make up 72 per cent of trading volumes. It is also worth noting that the LSE Group has a strong international standing considering that 41 per cent of trading volumes involve foreign issuers. Deutsche Börse is pursuing a similar strategy to NYSE Euronext, though the focus is on the derivatives market. After the acquisition of ISE Deutsche Börse gained the largest market share in the US equity derivatives market.

Generally speaking, stock exchange performance appears to be linked to the following factors:

- the business model. Diversification affects value by widening the income base with several areas (for example, derivatives trading) having high income growth rates and high profit margins;
- corporate governance models affect value since management incentives will vary according to whether the organisation is a mutual company or a listed company;
- size, in terms of listed issuers and volumes traded on the stock exchanges.

*Table 11.1*   Distribution of revenues by area of business

| | Cash trading (%) | Derivatives trading (%) | Services (%) | IT (%) |
|---|---|---|---|---|
| NYSE Euronext | 47 | 16 | 29 | 8 |
| LSE Group | 64 | – | 34 | 2.3 |
| NASDAQ OMX | 88 | 12 | – | – |
| Deutsche Börse Group | 19.9 | 32.7 | 42.9 | 4.6 |

*Source*: Own processing of the financial reports of the stock exchanges considered.

At present, a focus on the core business is not the main feature of the competitive strategies of stock exchanges. Even British and American stock exchanges, which used to be the most focused on a specific sector, are now adopting business diversification strategies (Table 11.1). As for business diversification implications and competitive strategies for exchanges see Polato and Floreani (2008).

From a financial point of view, an analysis of cost structure, revenues and trading volumes reveals some interesting trends.

There is a strong correlation between revenues and trading volume, in so much as stock exchange revenues rises proportionately to the increase in market trading (Figure 11.3). This is particularly true in the case of derivatives. Moreover, derivatives trading continues to grow even when cash trading is in decline, especially during stock market crises, like the one that occurred in 2001–2 and the one that is unfolding at present. There would therefore appear to be little correlation between the derivatives sector and cash markets.

In most of the stock exchanges examined there is also little correlation between cost structure and trading volume, due to the fact that the majority of costs are fixed. However, in many US stock exchanges some components of cost are bound to volumes (rebates in favour of brokers). Table 11.2 shows the composition of cost structure in the main stock exchanges.

Therefore, mergers in the stock exchange industry aim to expand the revenue base and to develop economies of cost. Indeed, the greatest potential from synergies is related to the rationalisation of cost through the homogenisation of trading platforms.

## 11.4   What is the real value of exchanges?

Mergers currently taking place in the stock exchange industry highlight the need to identify the determinants of stock exchange value. However, it is not always easy to measure the fairness of the valuation. Exchange-industry transformation is redefining business models and is potentially capable of destroying some competitive advantages.

Our analysis aims to express some arguments regarding the process of consolidation that has led to the establishment of the main groups, starting

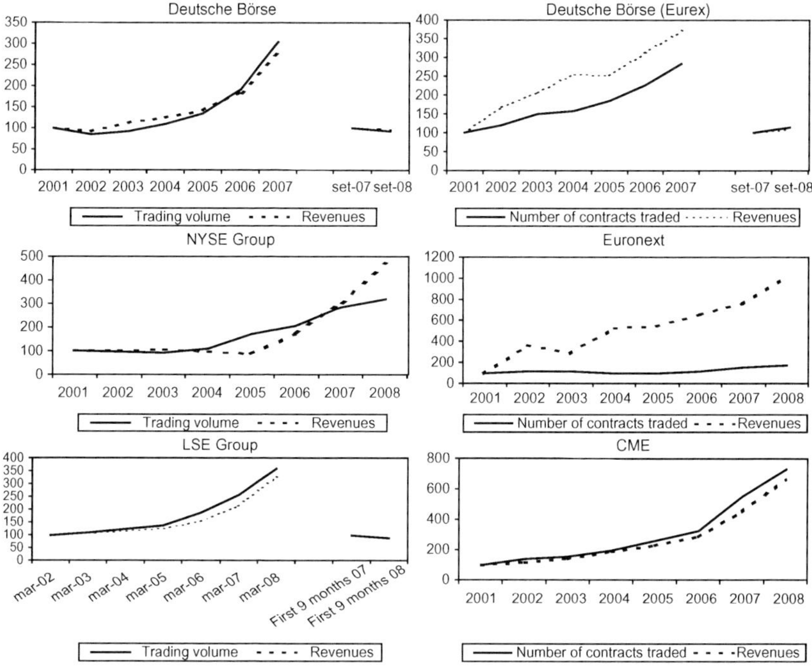

*Figure 11.3* Trading volumes and revenues in main cash (left-hand column) and derivatives markets (right-hand column)

*Source*: Own processing of exchanges' financial reports and WFE - Statistics.

*Table 11.2* Cost structure

|  | 2001 | 2002 | 2003 | 2004 | 2005 | 2006 | 2007 |
|---|---|---|---|---|---|---|---|
| **NYSE Euronext** | | | | | | | |
| Volume | 100 | 98.3 | 92.4 | 110.7 | 170.2 | 207.7 | 338.9 |
| Average Costs | 100.1 | 99.2 | 102.8 | 89.7 | 55.6 | 67.4 | 75.7 |
| **NASDAQ** | | | | | | | |
| Volume | 100 | 66.3 | 64.6 | 80.1 | 92.2 | 108 | 140.1 |
| Average Costs | 63.4 | 80.6 | 69.7 | 49.1 | 36.7 | 37.2 | 29.1 |
| **LSE Group** | | | | | | | |
| Volume | 100 | 88.5 | 79.8 | 114.3 | 125.6 | 167.5 | 228.6 |
| Average Costs | 47.4 | 52.6 | 70.9 | 55.3 | 53.2 | 41.8 | 31.8 |
| **Deutsche Börse** | | | | | | | |
| Volume | 100 | 85.2 | 91.3 | 108.3 | 134.6 | 192.3 | 303.8 |
| Average Costs | 146.3 | 194.3 | 152.2 | 126.8 | 105 | 75.3 | 67.9 |

*Notes*: Volumes traded equal to 100 in 2001. Average costs are expressed in US dollars for one million of volumes traded, employing the average exchange rate for the year.
*Source*: Own processing of exchanges' financial reports and WFE (2007).

from the analysis of multiples. This approach has been chosen in response to the immediate need to compare operations involving companies with different business models.

We are going to examine the implied merger multiples in a sample of deals that have taken place since 2005. A comparison among the multiples of the main deals, the multiples produced in comparable transactions and the multiples of comparable companies is also made.

Moreover combining two or more businesses may give rise to potential synergies deriving from cross-selling policies. Therefore, acquisition pricing should take account of the stand-alone value of the acquired company plus the expected synergies resulting from the integration.

Two problems arise from this calculation. First of all, stand-alone value is dependent on the business model adopted. Secondly, it is difficult to measure the impact of potential synergies.

In the former case, it is necessary to develop a method that is able to analyse the value of multi-business exchanges. Although there is no solid empirical evidence to support the view, derivatives trading is generally seen as being complementary to cash trading. In the latter case, it is necessary to identify synergies and suitable discount factors that account for the risk to which exchanges are exposed.

## Comparables and a sample of comparable transactions

There are a number of problems in defining the value of stock exchanges. It is evident that an analysis of comparables presupposes the identification of homogeneous peer groups in the exchange industry.

However, it is often difficult to identify stock exchanges that are directly comparable due to the fact that there may be considerable differences in terms of business models, strategic policy and size.

Several stock exchanges apply a competitive multi-business model in various forms. Generally speaking, diversification highlights the problem of evaluating different areas of business and defining their contribution to value.

The multiples of focused stock exchanges (both on cash and derivatives trading) can be used as benchmarks for the typical multiples of these two areas. The valuation of other types of business (for example market data sale) is difficult, either because the activity is not strictly related to conventional stock exchange business or because the activity is managed by divisions of the stock exchange or by non-listed companies belonging to the group.

Table 11.3 gives the average EV/EBITDA (Enterprise Value to Earning Before Interest Taxes Depreciation and Amortization) multiples for each group of listed stock exchanges for the period 2002–7.

The succession of mergers in the stock exchange industry provides a sufficiently large sample of deals to analyse. Moreover, a comparison of each case shows that there are substantial differences in merger multiples. Therefore, it would appear opportune to classify multiples according to the

*Table 11.3*   EV/EBITDA multiples

|  | 2001 | 2002 | 2003 | 2004 | 2005 | 2006 | 2007 | average |
|---|---|---|---|---|---|---|---|---|
| NYSE Euronext | – | – | – | – | – | 41.1 | 20.2 | 30.6 |
| NASDAQ | – | – | 26.3 | 11.9 | 27.5 | 19.7 | 15.7 | 20.2 |
| Euronext | 7.1 | 6.7 | 6.3 | 10.9 | 11.8 | 22.3 | – | 10.9 |
| London Stock Exchange | 13.8 | 6.97 | 7.8 | 9.3 | 16.2 | 15.8 | 11.3 | 11.6 |
| Deutsche Börse | 13.3 | 10.4 | 7.7 | 10.5 | 11.7 | 17.7 | 11.9 | 11.9 |
| CME | – | 7.1 | 9.6 | 19.2 | 23.4 | 25.5 | 30.7 | 19.2 |
| **Market data** | | | | | | | | |
| Thompson Financial Group | – | 9.9 | 13 | 11.7 | 14.2 | 15.6 | 11.4 | 12.7 |

*Source*: Own processing of the financial reports of the stock exchanges included in the table.

geographical area of the target exchange and to business sector focusing on stock exchanges operating in derivatives.

Table 11.4 summarises the sample mergers showing the bidder, the target company, announcement date and the EV/EBITDA multiple of the acquired company.

Table 11.5 gives the average and median values for the multiples associated to the transactions under consideration.

It can be seen that, on average, the values for US markets are higher than those for European markets. Moreover, since most of the deals in the US market involved derivatives exchanges, it can be deduced that the highest values refer to that particular market. In greater detail, figures reveal that:

- just considering public takeover bids for 100 per cent of the share capital (thus excluding the NASDAQ–Dubai Stock Exchange agreement) the European market multiples would fall to an average of 19 (19.5 median);
- the valuation issue is tied to some interesting corporate governance implications related to investment in stock exchanges. There is an increasingly strong relationship between broker-dealers and stock exchanges (for example General Atlantic's investment in NYMEX and the acquisition of the EBS Group by the broker ICAP). Then there are transactions that are clearly undertaken as part of a complex strategy to penetrate international finance centres (the acquisition of 28 per cent of LSE's share capital by the Dubai Stock Exchange at an implied multiple of 62 is emblematic);
- recent exchange industry mergers have taken place downstream of the production chain. Post-trading business is usually managed by unlisted

*Table 11.4*   A sample of comparable mergers

| Acquirer | Target company | Announcement date | EV/EBITDA target firm |
|---|---|---|---|
| OMX | Copenhagen SE | 1 December 2004 | 11.5 |
| NYSE Group | NYSE | 20 April 2005 | 37 |
| Australian Stock Exchange | Sydney FE | 27 March 2006 | 28.6 |
| General Atlantic | New York Mercantile Exchange (NYMEX) | 20 Sep 2005 | 9.2 |
| NASDAQ | LSE | 11 April 2006 | 19.5 |
| ICAP Plc | EBS Group | 21 April 2006 | 22.3 |
| Intercontinental Exchange | New York Board of Trade (NYBOT) | 14 September 2006 | 37.2 |
| Chicago Mercantile Exchange (CME) | Chicago Board of Trade (CBOT) | 17 October 2006 | 36 |
| NASDAQ | LSE | 20 November 2006 | 20 |
| Eurex | ISE | 30 April 07 | 27.6 |
| NASDAQ | OMX | 25 May 07 | 19 |
| Dubai Stock Exchange | OMX | 12 August 2007 | 23.9 |
| Dubai Stock Exchange | LSE | 25 September 2007 | 62 |
| NASDAQ | Boston Stock Exchange | 2 October 2007 | Neg. |
| NASDAQ | OMX | 12 October 2007 | 23.7 |
| NASDAQ OMX | Philadelphia SE | 7 November 2007 | 29.6 |
| Depository Trust and Clearing Corporation (DTCC) | LCH.Clearnet | 22 October 2008 | 2.74 |

*Source:* Own processing of financial reports of aforementioned exchanges and prospectuses related to the mergers considered.

*Table 11.5*   Average and median values for the transactions under consideration

| Total transactions | | European markets | | American markets | | Derivatives markets | |
|---|---|---|---|---|---|---|---|
| Average | Median | Average | Median | Average | Median | Average | Median |
| 27 | 23.9 | 25.3 | 20 | 28.5 | 29.1 | 27.6 | 28.6 |

*Source*: Own elaboration on data from Table 11.4.

stock exchange subsidiaries. Consequently, there are no value figures available for such companies. Recently, the DTCC bid €10 per share to acquire 100 per cent of LCH.Clearnet valuing the target company 2.7 times the EBITDA of 2007.

The fact that value tends to be higher on derivatives markets would suggest the need to valuate multi-business exchanges which operate important derivative markets with higher multiples.

## A method for analysing stock exchange value

In view of the above observations it would be reasonable to expect that value drivers should be related to the business model and to market share in each segment. Difficulties concern both the criteria used to determine stand-alone value and the value of expectations incorporated in the share price of the acquired company.

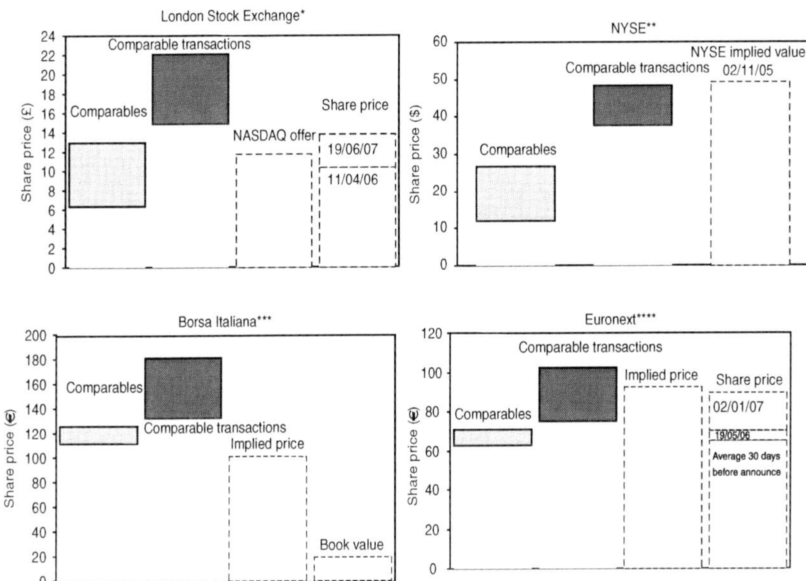


*Figure 11.4*   Stock exchange multiples

*Notes*: *Comparables: we assumed the 2005 NASDAQ and Deutsche Börse EV/EBITDA multiples. Comparable transactions: an EV/EBITDA range of between 25 (average multiples of transactions announced in 2005) and 37 (the NYSE's multiple) is assumed. **Comparables: an EV/EBITDA range between 9 (LSE multiple in 2004) and 20 (average NASDAQ multiples) is assumed. Comparable transactions: an EV/EBITDA range of between 19.5 (NASDAQ bid for LSE) and 28 (average multiple of deals involving American exchanges as target) is assumed. ***and****Comparables: an EV/EBITDA range between 16 (LSE multiple in 2006) and 18 (Deutsche Börse multiple in 2006) is assumed. Comparable transactions: an EV/EBITDA range of between 19.5 (the lowest multiple for transactions announced in 2006) and 26 (average multiple of all 2006 transactions) is assumed.

*Source*: Own processing of exchanges' annual reports and prospectuses.

Figure 11.4 illustrates the pricing problem in the cases of the LSE (NASDAQ bid), the NYSE (Archipelago bid), Euronext (NYSE bid) and Borsa Italiana (LSE bid). Firstly, an estimate of exchange value is made by applying the comparables and comparable transactions methods. Then a comparison is made with the implied value of the bids and with market prices.

A comparison between the NYSE and the LSE reveals some interesting findings. Table 11.6 sets forth the last price at which a NYSE membership was sold as of 19 April 2005 (the day prior the announcement of the merger with Archipelago) and as of 2 November 2005 (the date prior the issue of NYSE–Archipelago Joint Prospectus) and the implied equivalent value of each NYSE membership based on the standard NYSE consideration received by each member. The table also presents the NYSE value based on the implied equivalent value of the membership and the total number of members (1,366) and compares this value with the estimated value obtained applying the LSE's EV/EBITDA multiple.

The implied membership value on 2 November 2005 is made up of a 30 per cent premium on the membership price at the NYSE at the same date.[2] Since each NYSE member received a total consideration of $300,000 in cash and 80,177 shares of NYSE Group common stock, the implied value of the NYSE was $5.4 billion (here and after, billion refers to thousand of millions) on 2 November 2005 – 37 times the EBITDA.

It should be noted that as regards the NASDAQ bid, the LSE was valued less than the majority of multiples referring to transactions between 2004 and 2007 (Figure 11.4), and slightly more than the share price on the date of announcement. In the following months the LSE share price grew constantly. On 19 June 2007, just before the acquisition of Borsa Italiana was announced, the price of LSE shares was 18.4 per cent higher than the implied price of NASDAQ's bid. The LSE's management rejected the bid on the basis that the price offered was only just equal to the company's stand-alone value.

*Table 11.6*   NYSE valuation

| | Price of membership ($) | Implied price of membership ($)** | NYSE value | |
| | | | On implied price*** | Comparable |
| --- | --- | --- | --- | --- |
| 19 April 05 | 1,620,000* | 1,662,207 | 2.2 billion (15×) | LSE (9×) |
| 2 November 05 | 3,000,000 | 3,948,053 | 5.4 billion (37×) | 1.3 billion |

*Notes:* *Last price of membership at the NYSE before the announcement of the Archipelago merger.

**Implied price of membership at the NYSE based on the Archipelago average share price during the 10 trading days ending on the relevant date of measurement: $16.9 on 19 April 2005 and $45.5 on 2 November 2005.

***NYSE value based on the implied price of membership (in brackets the multiple in relation to the 2004 EBITDA).

As we have already mentioned, it is difficult to apply the comparables method to stock exchanges whose business is diversified. In order to do so, the contribution of each line of business to enterprise value needs to be determined.

When pricing two merging companies whose business model undergoes diversification, the various business segments should be taken into consideration. By observing the stock exchange as a portfolio of business activities, stand-alone value can be seen as the sum of the values of each business area. Therefore, the contribution of each sector is valued according to the typical sector multiples. We will analyse the above consideration by looking at the Euronext and Borsa Italiana cases (in Box 11.1 we report the merger conditions for Euronext and Borsa Italiana).

## Box 11.1 Merger conditions for Euronext and Borsa Italiana

*Euronext*

The implied Euronext share price based on the merger agreement was €93.06, corresponding to a multiple of 28.6 times Euronext's 2006 profits and an enterprise value of 23.5 times the 2006 EBITDA. Analyst estimates based on EV/EBITDA multiples are in line with those assumed in Figure 11.4.

The merger between NYSE Group and Euronext NV was based on a public takeover bid in which for every Euronext NV share the acquirer would offer €21.32 in cash and 0.98 NYSE Euronext shares. Subsequently, the NYSE Group merged with the new holding company by exchanging NYSE Euronext shares with NYSE Group shares at a value of 1 to 1. On the basis of the share exchange agreement proposed by NYSE Euronext, the French stock exchange's share price was set at €93.06, according to the share price of the NYSE Group on 2 January 2007. This implied price was slightly lower than the highest quotation reached between 3 January 2006 and 2 January 2007 (€95.85).

*Borsa Italiana*

In the LSE's acquisition of Borsa Italiana the latter was worth 4.9 LSE shares corresponding to 27.6 times the 2006 profit figure and to an implied enterprise value equal to 14.43 times the EBITDA.

At the time of the LSE's bid, Borsa Italiana's share capital was valued at €1,634 million (this figure results from a closing price of 1387 pence per LSE share at an exchange rate of €1.4815 per pound ) or €100.7 per share, while the book value was €19.6 per share.

*Table 11.7*    An estimate of the value of Borsa Italiana and Euronext

| | Cash trading | Derivatives trading | Market data* | IT** | Post trading | Value | Share price |
|---|---|---|---|---|---|---|---|
| Euronext | 11 | 19–27 | 12–17 | 12–15 | – | €6.7–7 bn | €59.5–62.1 |
| Borsa Italiana | 10 | 19–27 | 12–17 | 12–15 | 3 | €0.9–1.1 bn | €55–67 |

* The reference for this range comes from the multiples of Thompson and Reuters.
** These figures refer to the multiples of companies operating in IT services for finance, such as Fiserv, a NASDAQ listed company.

Our analysis (Table 11.7) is based on the following assumptions:

- cash trading services may be valued according to the past multiples of stock exchanges that have been traditionally involved in such business. Our benchmark is the LSE;
- as regards derivatives trading services, a range of between 19 times and 27 times the EV/EBITDA can be applied to Euronext's derivatives business unit, corresponding to the multiples recorded in the main derivatives markets over the last few years;
- the valuation of post-trading services can be based on the multiple attributed to Clearnet in its merger with DTCC.

Due to the low trading volumes of Borsa Italiana when compared to its competitors, a smaller range was applied for the EV/EBITDA multiple.

It can be seen that the estimated value for Euronext is similar to the company's market value at the time of the NYSE Group merger (on 31 May 2006 Euronext's share capital was €7.3 billion). In the same way, the value for Borsa Italiana ranges from €55 to €67 per share. The merger value for Borsa Italiana corresponds to an implied premium of 50 per cent with respect to the top figure in the range. The acquisition of Borsa Italiana by the LSE meant that Borsa Italiana shareholders would obtain a 28 per cent share of the post-merger LSE Group. On 19 June 2007 the LSE's share capital was worth €4.1 billion, while Borsa Italiana's value of €308 million was based on a book price of €19 per share.

In Table 11.8 we estimate the post-merger values of the two groups and the corresponding allotment of shares to Euronext and Borsa Italiana shareholders. To this end, the main difficulties are related to the valuation of synergies (see Box 11.2).

# Box 11.2 Expected synergies in NYSE–Euronext and LSE–Borsa Italiana mergers

The Euronext acquisition foresaw cost and revenue synergies of respectively $100 million and $275 million by 2011. The acquisition of Borsa Italiana by the LSE was expected to create synergies worth a total of €58 million by 2010. In both cases we estimate the incidence of synergies on the post-merger value assuming a P/E multiple of 25 at a 10 per cent discount rate. Such were the parameters adopted by the NYSE and Euronext when estimating the effects of synergies on value (NYSE Euronext, 2006).

*Table 11.8*   An estimate of the post-merger values of NYSE Euronext and the LSE Group

| | Low | High | | Low | High |
|---|---|---|---|---|---|
| NYSE Group per share price ($)* | 72.9 | 83.3 | LSE per share price (£)* | 17 | 19.7 |
| Exchange rate €/$ 20 Nov. 2006 | 1.2813 | 1.2813 | Exchange rate €/£ 19 Jun. 2007 | 0.6749 | 0.6749 |
| NYSE Group per share price (€) | 56.89 | 65 | LSE per share price (€) | 25.2 | 29.2 |
| Num. NYSE Group shares | 159.2 | 159.2 | Num. LSE shares | 207.1 | 207.1 |
| NYSE market capitalization (€) | 9.1 | 10.4 | LSE market capitalization (€) | 5.2 | 6 |
| Euronext per share price (€)** | 59.5 | 62.1 | Borsa Italiana per share price (€)** | 55 | 67 |
| Num. Shares Euronext | 112.6 | 112.6 | Num. Borsa Italiana shares | 16.2 | 16.2 |
| Euronext market capitalization | 7.4 | 8.7 | Borsa Italiana market capitalization | 0.9 | 1.1 |
| Cash distribution | −2.4 | −2.4 | Cash distribution | – | – |
| Synergies | 3.4 | 3.4 | Synergies | 0.6 | 0.6 |
| NYSE Euronext pro forma value | 17.5 | 20.1 | LSE Group pro forma value | 6.7 | 7.7 |
| Value for Euronext shareholder*** | 9.6 | 10.6 | Value for Borsa Italiana shareholder | 1.8 | 2.2 |

*(Continued)*

*Table 11.8   (Continued)*

|  | Low | High |  | Low | High |
| --- | --- | --- | --- | --- | --- |
| Premium on stand-alone value (%) | 29.1 | 21.6 | Premium on stand-alone value (%) | 105 | 100 |

*Notes*: Data are expressed in billions of € except for per share prices. Number of shares: millions.
* The estimate for NYSE Group value is based on an EV/EBITDA multiple ranging from 23.5× to 27.5×. The estimate for LSE value is based on an EV/EBITDA multiple ranging from 19 to 22.
** The estimates for Euronext and Borsa Italiana are based on the price intervals as in table 11.7.
*** Euronext shareholders held 41 per cent of the post-merger group's share capital. Borsa Italiana shareholders had a right to 28 per cent of the resulting group's share capital.
*Source*: Own elaboration.

In particular, it is necessary to estimate an appropriate discount rate that takes account of the risk to which stock exchanges are exposed. This task is made more difficult by the rapid structural changes taking place in the stock exchange industry, which reduce the level of future certainty.

Despite necessary precaution due to the methods of estimation used, examination of the two cases would appear to have produced rather different results. The NYSE's acquisition of Euronext resulted in an estimated shareholder premium (in relation to stand-alone value) of between 21 per cent and 29 per cent.

On 19 May 2005 (the trading day immediately prior to the announcement of the merger) the implied merger price had a premium of 0.4 per cent on Euronext's share price on the same day. On 2 January 2007, the premium on Euronext's share price rose by 31 per cent. Consequently, the implied value of Euronext on the same date was €10.3 billion. In the meantime, the increase in Euronext's share price brought the group's value close to the expected post-merger value.

In the case of the LSE's acquisition of Borsa Italiana the latter stock exchange's assets, as well as the contribution of potential synergies, appear to have been considerably over-estimated.

The start of merger procedures in 2005 coincides with a continuous series of share price increases, reaching a peak in the second half of 2007. Subsequently, share prices fell just as quickly. Such volatility certainly reflects the risk involved in the business model and competitive dynamics, but it is also due to speculation arising from the process of consolidation in the stock exchange industry.

## 11.5   Stock exchange value: a financial perspective

Stock exchange pricing should take both opportunities and risks into consideration. The oligopolistic structure of the stock exchange industry allows

*Table 11.9*   Main stock exchanges: trading volumes ($ billion)

|  | 2008 | 2007 | Var. (%) |
| --- | --- | --- | --- |
| NYSE Group | 33,639 | 29,210 | 15.2 |
| NASDAQ | 36,446 | 28,116 | 29.6 |
| LSE Group | 6,474 | 10,324 | −37.3 |
| Euronext | 4,454 | 5,648 | −21.1 |
| Deutsche Börse | 3,881 | 4,324 | −10.2 |

*Source*: Own processing of WFE (2008).

the main groups to take advantage of their high market share to increase revenues by means of product and process diversification. However, stock exchanges are exposed to risks related both to market cycles and to increasing competition.

As concerns the former risk factor, on 2008 the worsening crisis caused trading volumes to fall on European markets (Table 11.9). In the USA, on the contrary, trading volumes maintained the growth trends of previous years.

However, market trends in Europe are not homogeneous; trading volumes fell far more on the London Stock Exchange than on other exchanges.

As concerns competition, stock exchange mergers offer little protection. The rapid decline in stock exchange share prices appears to reflect expectations that business will deteriorate. Clearly, the trend results from a general market crisis and its probable impact on stock exchange revenues.[3] This decline, however, began in 2007, long before the start of the financial crisis, when stock exchanges were still announcing increases in trading volumes. More recently, market share and revenue/EBITDA margins have been threatened by new competitors.[4]

Stock exchange competitiveness is dependent on investment in innovation in respect of services supplied and the development of infrastructures. It is therefore crucial to generate sufficient cash flow. Indeed, debt growth has been identified as the greatest problem arising from the current trend in stock exchange mergers (Standard and Poor's, 2008).

Over the last few years, the analysis of stock exchange finances has shown a substantial increase in revenues and margins. Table 11.10 identifies indicators that act as stock exchange value drivers; namely, Earning per Share (EPS), Dividend per Share (DPS), leverage, EBITDA/Interest coverage, Debt/EBITDA, Free Operating Cash Flow (FOCF)/EBITDA. Table 11.11 shows trends in EBITDA margin, EPS and Operative Cash Flow per Share. Figure 11.5 depicts the incidence of IT costs on total costs and on Free Operating Cash Flow. A comparison between EBITDA margin and the incidence of interest expenses on EBITDA is also presented.

*Table 11.10*  Basic indicators

|  | EPS | DPS | Leverage (%) | EBITDA (%) | EBITDA/ Int.Cov. | Debt/ EBITDA (%) | FOCF/ EBITDA (%) | Cost/ Income (%) |
|---|---|---|---|---|---|---|---|---|
| NYSE Euron- ext Group | 2.7 | 0.7 | 36.1 | 27.9 | 9 | 151 | 60.7 | 78 |
| LSE Group | 0.7 | 0.2 | 43.4 | 61.7 | 6.6 | 143 | 52.7 | 38.3 |
| NASDAQ OMX | 4.5 | | 26 | 16.6 | 6 | 29 | 42.8 | 83.4 |
| Deutsche Börse | 4.7 | 2.1 | 41 | 55.2 | 12.5 | 126 | 57.0 | 49 |
| CME | 15 | 3.4 | 20.1 | 67.7 | 328 | 253 | 68.4 | 32.2 |

*Source*: Own processing of financial reports of the exchanges considered.

*Table 11.11*  Some basic indicators

|  | 2002 | 2003 | 2004 | 2005 | 2006 | 2007 | 2008 |
|---|---|---|---|---|---|---|---|
| **EBITDA %** | | | | | | | |
| NYSE Euronext Group | 0 | 40.4 | 34.7 | 9 | 15.6 | 27.9 | |
| LSE Group | 39.4 | 44.2 | 45.3 | 51.4 | 53.1 | 61.7 | |
| NASDAQ OMX | 25.5 | 5.5 | 15.6 | 20.5 | 17.2 | 16.6 | |
| Deutsche Börse | 33.3 | 17.3 | 13.6 | 10.4 | 9.8 | 10.5 | |
| BME | 49.6 | 50.6 | 56.7 | 62.9 | 66.8 | 74.9 | |
| CME | 43.5 | 43.5 | 43.5 | 43.5 | 43.5 | 43.5 | |
| **EPS ($)** | | | | | | | |
| NYSE Euronext Group | – | 0.52 | 0.26 | 0.35 | 1.38 | 2.72 | −2.8 (exp) |
| LSE Group | 0.29 | 0.39 | 0.46 | 0.48 | 1.07 | 1.45 | 1.1 (exp) |
| NASDAQ OMX | – | – | – | 0.68 | 1.22 | 4.47 | 2.3 (exp) |
| Deutsche Börse | 2.01 | 2.50 | 2.96 | 4.96 | 4.25 | 6.46 | 4.7 (exp) |
| BME | | 0.79 | 1.03 | 1.38 | 1.97 | 3.31 | NA |
| CME | 3.24 | 3.74 | 6.55 | 8.94 | 11.74 | 15.05 | NA |
| **Operating cash flow per share ($)** | | | | | | | |
| NYSE Euronext Group | – | – | – | – | 1.37 | 2.64 | |
| LSE Group | 0.47 | 0.65 | 0.56 | 0.85 | 1.34 | 1.28 | |
| NASDAQ OMX | | 1.34 | 1.49 | 1.08 | 1.39 | 1.14 | |
| Deutsche Börse | 4.12 | 5.40 | 4.89 | 8.61 | 5.36 | 5.96 | |
| BME | NA | NA | NA | 1.73 | 1.97 | 3.67 | |
| CME | 4.8 | 5.8 | 9.8 | 10.1 | 13.5 | 15.2 | |

*Note*: Expected EPS for 2008 comes from FactSet.
*Source*: Own processing of financial reports of the exchanges considered.

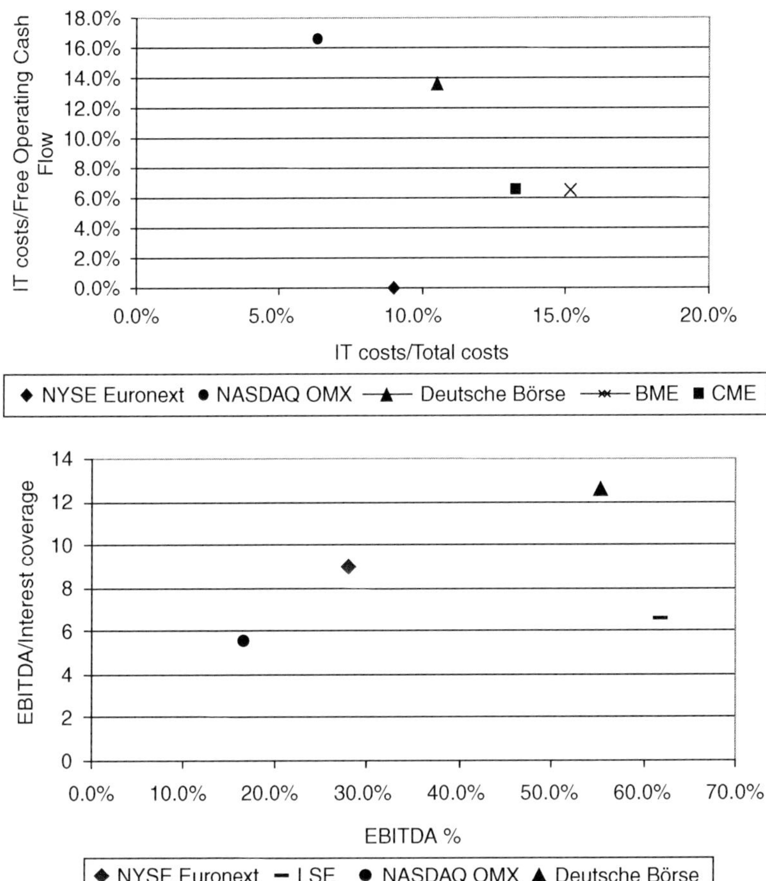



*Figure 11.5*   Some ratios (2007)

*Source*: Own processing of financial reports of exchange considered.

Mergers have resulted in increased debt for all the main exchanges, above all in the cases of Deutsche Börse, the LSE and NYSE Euronext. Actually, analysis of financial performance highlights that traditionally listed exchanges (that is the LSE and Deutsche Börse) tend to generate high revenue/EBITDA margins.

As regards the business model we observe that:

- derivatives trading is highly profitable. Both CME and Eurex have high revenue/EBITDA margins. However, the data do not confirm that the derivatives business is always superior. Xetra, Deutsche Börse's cash market, matches the profitability of Eurex (Table 11.12). Moreover, the margins of the LSE's cash division are growing constantly;

*Table 11.12*  Segment reporting

| LSE Group | Accounting period ending March 2008 | | | | First 9 months of 2007 | | | | First 9 months of 2008 (in brackets, change compared to the first 9 months of 2007) | | | |
|---|---|---|---|---|---|---|---|---|---|---|---|---|
| | Issuer services | Trading services | Information serv. | Post trade | Issuer services | Trading services | Informa-tion serv. | Post trade | Issuer ser-vices | Trading services | Informa-tion serv. | Post trade |
| Tot. revenues (£ bn) | 82,4 | 264,7 | 143,6e | 42,8 | 76,2 | 227,2 | 118,1 | 60,3 | 71,9 (−6%) | 215,9 (−5%) | 136,9 (+16%) | 77,6 (+29%) |
| EBITDA% | 49.3 | 66.8 | 59.1 | 64.3 | NA | NA | NA | NA | NA | NA | NA | NA |

| Deutsche Börse | Corporate year 2007 | | | | | First 9 months of 2007 | | | | | First 9 months of 2008 (in brackets, change compared to the first 9 months of 2007) | | | | |
|---|---|---|---|---|---|---|---|---|---|---|---|---|---|---|---|
| | Xetra | Eurex | Information services | Clears-tream | IT | Xetra | Eurex | Infor-mation services | Clears-tream | IT | Xetra | Eurex | Informa-tion serv. | Clear-stream | IT |
| Revenues (€ bn) | 435 | 713,9 | 179,6 | 777,5 | 497,7 | 329,9 | 547 | 124,7 | 570,9 | 75 | 306,8 (−7.5%) | 762,2 (+39%) | 136,4 (+9.3%) | 569,7 (−0.2%) | 71 (−5.3%) |
| EBITDA% | 59.8 | 64.4 | 50.7 | 55.3 | 26.7 | NA | NA | NA | NA | NA | NA | NA | NA | NA | NA |

| NYSE Euronext | 2007 | | 2008 | |
|---|---|---|---|---|
| | US Operations | European Operations | US Operations | European Operations |
| Revenues ($ bn) | 2,747 | 1,411 | 2,970 | 1,760 |
| EBITDA (%) | 13.6 | 39.7 | 11 | Neg. |

*Source*: Own processing of financial reports of exchanges considered.

- post-trading business still generates margins. Deutsche Börse's post-trading division has a 55 per cent[5] revenue/EBITDA ratio, while that of the LSE Group recorded margins of 64 per cent;
- stock exchanges that traditionally operate in the cash market are attracted by the high growth in volumes, revenues and margins offered by derivatives trading.

Finally, business diversification expands the stock exchange revenue base. Data have shown high revenue growth in all the main stock exchanges. Analysing each business segment individually, we can make the following observations:

- the cash-trading services segment appears to be affected by business cycles. In the European markets, cash-trading figures for 2008 showed a fall in tersm of both volumes and revenues. On the contrary, derivatives trading continued to grow. However, in the case of the LSE derivatives revenue growth was not able to compensate for the decline in cash-trading income;
- the revenues generated by other business segments appear to be more stable and less connected to trends in trading services;
- diversification by geographical area seems to be the most significant feature of NYSE Euronext. 37 per cent of revenues are produced in Europe and 63 per cent in the USA, with both areas recording growth. It is interesting to note that geographical diversification has enabled NYSE Euronext to compensate for the decline in volumes traded on the European cash market with a substantial increase in trading volumes in the USA. Moreover, derivatives trading has greatly contributed to revenue growth in Europe.

Evidence shows that cash trading is the sector that is most exposed to competition. Despite the high volumes of Over The Counter (OTC) trading, it is the derivatives market that has brought regulated markets a constant and substantial growth in trading volumes. As regards OTC derivatives transactions, it is worth noting that the financial crisis may generate opportunities for post-trading companies if they themselves internalise such transactions. Market data communication is also advantageous because revenues are generated through subscriptions and are not, therefore, directly linked to trading volumes.

In the past few years, stock exchanges have had to react to increasing competition through a general reduction in trading fees. As a result, stock exchange profitability will certainly be threatened independently of the effects of trends in the business cycle. Analysts now forecast a fall in profits per share (Table 11.11). Table 11.13 gives an estimate of capital costs and share prices for the NYSE Euronext Group, the LSE Group, Deutsche Börse and the NASDAQ OMX Group. The capital cost figures are based on beta calculated over the previous five years.

*Table 11.13*   Average weighted cost of capital

| | Leverage (%) | Cost of debt (%) (*) | Risk-free rate (%) (**) | ß | Equity cost (%) | WACC (%) (***) | Price(****) Dec. 08 | Target |
|---|---|---|---|---|---|---|---|---|
| NYSE Euronext | 36 | 5.3 | 2.8 | 0.75 | 11.6 | 7.5 | 27.4 | 16.6–29.8 |
| NASDAQ OMX | 26 | 3.7 | 2.8 | 1.4 | 13.9 | 11.3 | 24.7 | 8.1–10.8 |
| LSE Group | 25 | 6.4 | 3.6 | 1.6 | 13.2 | 12.3 | 1.9 | 1.8–2.3 |
| Deutsche Börse | 41 | 5.5 | 3.5 | 1.2 | 12.9 | 9.8 | 50.8 | 34.3–48.5 |

*Long-term cost of debt. ** The mid-December benchmark was referred to. *** 8 per cent risk premium considered. ****Prices expressed in local currency. Target price calculations (local currencies) based on a profit growth rate of between 2 per cent and 5 per cent.

The fall in stock exchange share prices has resulted in multiples declining to well below the usual value. The current crisis has led to a sharp decline in the rate of profit growth.

It is not easy to assess the impact of competition on the stock exchange industry, nor the suitability of the business models used to face it. However, cross-border mergers, especially between US and European exchanges, are coherent with a strategy of diversification. As concerns product diversification, the combining of cash and derivatives markets can lead to good results. As we have seen, volumes, revenues and earnings have increased constantly in the derivatives sector. It may be said that the integration of market-sector leaders enables stock exchanges to fully exploit the benefits of product diversification. In the case of the merger between the LSE and Borsa Italiana, the contribution of the Italian derivatives segment appears limited.

## 11.6   Conclusions

Stock exchange management needs to be placed in a wider context involving the system of relationships within the stock exchange industry. In other words, in what way does the post-consolidation structure of the industry affect synergies and competitiveness?

Observing the network of relations among actors (Figure 11.6) it is not difficult to identify problems in exploiting stock exchange industry assets.

Firstly, the development of a network structure has an impact on the strategic coherence of mergers, since it limits the exploitation of potential synergies. The LSE aimed to develop synergies with Borsa Italiana in the derivatives and post-trading sectors. In the derivatives business, the LSE had a joint venture going with OMX and EDX. In the same way, the development of synergies downstream in the production chain appear to be impeded

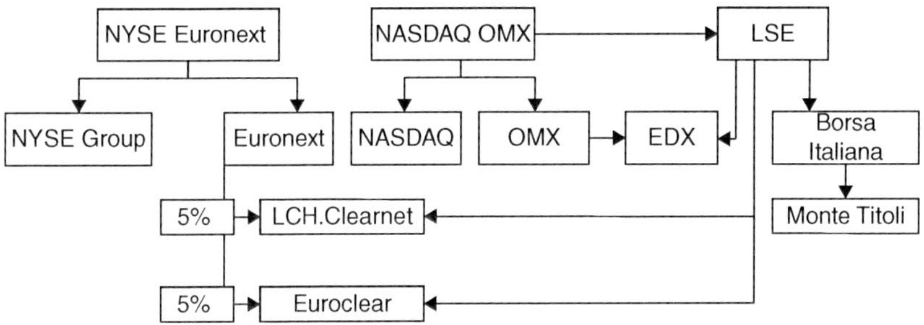


*Figure 11.6*   Exchange-industry ownership relations
*Source*: Own elaboration.

by the LSE's relationship with LCH.Clearnet and Euroclear, both as regards ownership and board representation. It is difficult to imagine how the new group can fully exploit post-trading assets when the trading of high-liquidity products is cleared and settled on the LCH.Clearnet/Euroclear network.

Secondly, there is no doubt that the development of a network structure will have a significant impact on governance, intended in a broader sense as the governance of relations inside the exchange industry.

Our study has raised some implications that should be of interest to the market and regulators. The first reflects the competitive strategies of exchanges, whose interaction helps shape the structure of the industry. These strategies are oriented by regulators' policies which have an important role in calibrating governance mechanisms. It could be argued that governance mechanisms are irrelevant in situations where the exchange has to face strong competition.

Indeed, change in ownership structure is the most problematic issue in respect of stock exchange governance, above all with regard to the listing of exchanges and to the network of interdependence resulting from the consolidation process. Not only should regulation assist the reconstruction of exchange-industry structure, but it should also promote non-discriminatory access to exchange-industry services.

Such an expectation should interest both service users and the actual stock exchanges. Indeed, exchanges have to face the threat of potentially losing their competitive advantage but can benefit from greater business opportunities resulting from cross-border expansion. In practice, non-discriminatory access regulations can be found in the codes of conduct of post-trading companies, as well as in the initiatives directed towards liberalizing access to trading services.

Cross-border convergence in the financial services sector raises the issue of mutual recognition based on minimal harmonisation and dialogue among regulators. This strategy is capable of maintaining regulation standards and supporting business opportunities resulting from increased market integration. For example, the Securities and Exchange Commission's proposal to negotiate a bilateral and selective system of substituted compliance with foreign supervisors could generate widespread benefits for European investment firms and exchanges by permitting access to the American market without the duplication of regulation costs (see Tafara and Peterson, 2007). This in turn implies that the American investor can have free access to services provided by an European exchange, thus effectively levelling the playing field. This development will clearly introduce further difficulties in the valuation of exchanges since the field of competition will be redefined. Moreover, it will be difficult to forecast at what level the trade off between threats and opportunities will be achieved.

Exchange mergers generate opportunities because trading volumes are increased and there is a consequent reduction in the level of costs. Moreover, product diversification creates further opportunities by stabilising revenues and developing synergies. However, stock exchange pricing raises a number of problems. There is a suspicion that opportunism may be behind many of the deals. Some major shareholders of exchanges embark on merger and acquisition operations for reasons of strategic interest. Often the value of the acquired exchange is overstated. As a result, the governance structure in the stock exchange industry has a substantial effect on the outcome of the consolidation process.

On the other hand, the network structure of the industry introduces some complexity to the governance issue and may be an impediment to potential synergies. The above considerations lead us to state that the consolidation process in the stock exchange industry is far from complete. It would be reasonable to expect regulatory bodies to stipulate further international agreements favouring mutual recognition among exchanges.

# 12
# Necessary Reforms for Book-entry Securities

*Alessandro V. Guccione*

## 12.1  Introduction

The increase in the volume of cross-border securities transactions has drawn the attention of EU and national lawmakers to the need for a regulatory system capable of ensuring a high level of market integration. The aim is to eliminate the considerable costs and hazards which arise when the parties to or objects of transactions are subject to more than one regulatory system, often with significant differences both in the rules themselves and in the concepts which underlie them.

While significant progress has been made in the trading sector thanks to the issue and implementation of Directive 2004/39/EC, there is still a high degree of fragmentation in the post-trading sector, and especially with regard to the settlement of transactions. Directives 98/26/EC and 2002/47/EC, relating to settlement finality and financial collateral arrangements respectively, have helped to increase uniformity, but the integration process is far from complete, due to both the sectorial nature of these regulations, and the considerable doubts concerning their interpretation.

This situation is a source of inefficiency and unjustified costs, as well as placing the European financial market at a competitive disadvantage compared to other markets (Legal Certainty Group, 2008). There is thus an urgent need to find reliable solutions to the legal problems hindering the full integration of cross-border settlement arrangements. The complexity of the crisis affecting intermediaries operating in a multiplicity of legal frameworks, and the Lehman Brothers affair in particular, have reflected the pressing need for appropriate forms of regulation (Van Duyn et al., 2008).

This survey examines the problems posed by the regulation of cross-border transactions undertaken by means of central securities depositories, and the international-civil law problems posed by the establishment or transfer of property rights to book-entry securities. The aim is to assess the proposals put forward for achievement of the highest possible degree of uniformity in the regulation of these areas, as a means to the sound regulation of post-trading activities, and thus the greatest possible consolidation of the financial markets.

## 12.2   Obstacles to cross-border settlement integration

Amongst the key obstacles to the efficient functioning of post-trading services for cross-border operations identified by the Giovannini Group (2001 and 2003) are those deriving from the differences in the legislation governing securities and the operation of the settlement and clearing systems. These rules involve aspects of fundamental importance for the individual legal systems (for example, the ways in which the ownership of goods or title to rights is transferred), with the consequence that whenever a settlement or clearing procedure assumes cross-border connotations, the reconstruction of the resulting regulatory framework becomes problematical (Committee on Payment and Settlement Systems, CPSS, and International Organization of Securities Commissions, IOSCO, 2001). The legal uncertainty generated restricts the efficient operation of regulatory systems, especially with regard to the identification of the holder of true title to the securities involved in the transactions, or any rights to them, in the event of disputes (Figure 12.1). For example, in the absence of harmonised rules it can be maintained that the law applicable to securities collateral arrangements is that of the state of residence of the intermediary with which the securities account has been

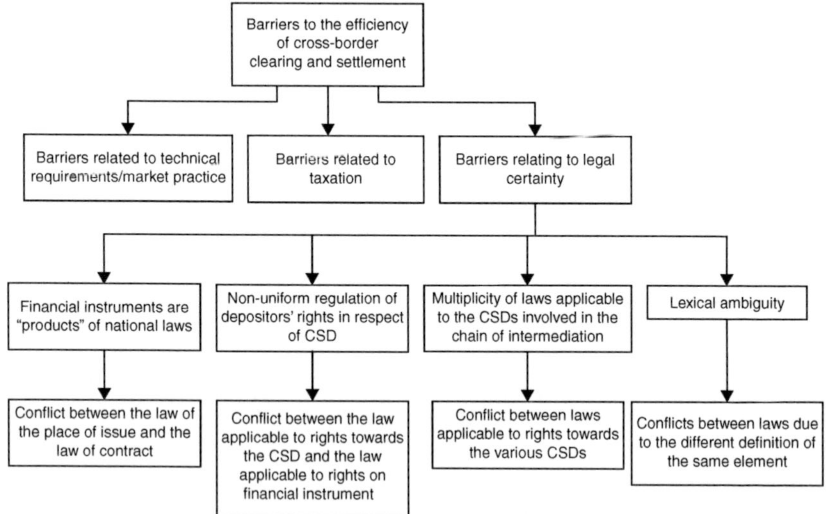


*Figure 12.1*   Barriers to the efficiency of cross-border post-trading – Legal barriers in particular

*Source*: Own processing of the Giovannini Group report (2001).

opened, or, with equal justification, that of the state in which the issuing company, or the manager of the centralised depository, is based. The consequences are particularly serious if one of the parties to the legal relationship concerning book-entry securities gets into financial difficulties, since the uncertainty with regard to jurisdiction may affect the hierarchy of creditors' claims, or the collectability of the receivables of the firm in difficulty.

The Giovannini reports recognised the adequacy of the solutions proposed by EU legislation to some of the questions posed by cross-border settlement, especially with regard to the regulation of settlement finality (Directive 98/26/EC), or netting (Directive 2002/47/EC). However, the criteria of the Place of the Relevant Intermediary Approach adopted by the above measures, under which the rights to securities are governed by the law of the place where the securities account is maintained, came in for some criticism. The reports thus put forward proposals for uniform regulation of the rights of the holder of the securities account in the event of the insolvency of the depositor itself, the intermediary or its counterparty, and in more general terms, in the event of proceedings against these rights by third parties in higher levels of the intermediation chain (upper-tier attachment), with a complex series of clarifications concerning the context of application of these rules.

The Giovannini Group's criticisms and proposals have not yet been fully incorporated into legislation, due to the complexity of an operation which would require the amendment of some of the principles on which the regulation of the transfer and constitution of the rights to securities are currently based in the legislation of the member states and the EU itself.

## 12.3   The Hague Convention

As well as by the EU legislation referred to above, the rights to book-entry securities are also regulated by the 'Convention on the Law Applicable on Certain Rights in Respect of Securities Held with an Intermediary' (the so-called Hague Convention), issued by the Hague Conference on Private International Law (2002) with the aim of reducing the legal and systemic risks, and the costs, of cross-border securities transactions. As of today, the Convention has been signed by three states (the USA, Switzerland and Mauritius), but it has not yet come into force since not all the necessary conditions have been met.

The Convention stipulates that the law applicable to proprietary matters relating to 'securities held with an intermediary', or in other words the 'rights of an account holder resulting from a credit of securities to a securities account' is the law chosen by the parties to regulate the account agreement. In order for this agreement to be admissible, the intermediary concerned must have at least one office in the state the legal jurisdiction of which has been chosen, established to perform one of the activities involved in the management of securities accounts (for example which effects entries to the account or undertakes operations relating to the exercise of the rights resulting from the security), or is identified by the system adopted within the state as maintaining securities accounts there. This condition is apparently intended both to prevent forum shopping and to put third parties in a position to identify the law applicable to the agreement. In the absence of specific agreements, the law envisages a series of additional criteria.

Clearly, in spite of the adoption of the place of the intermediary approach as the linking criterion, in practice the applicable law may be that chosen in the securities account agreement. This is in contrast with the criteria adopted by EU legislation, in which, although with many uncertainties with regard to interpretation, the applicable law is that of the state where the securities account is maintained.

## 12.4   The Legal Certainty Group's proposals

As things now stand, the problems relating to the legal obstacles to the correct operation of cross-border settlement arrangements identified by the Giovannini Group cannot be considered to have been solved, in spite of the regulatory measures outlined above. The lack of progress is due to the diversity of the legal traditions underlying national legislation on the transfer of property rights, as well as the complexity of the legal classification of book-entry securities.

The Legal Certainty Group's 'Second Advice on Solutions to Legal Barriers Related to Post-Trading within the EU' (2008) attempts to provide EU legislators with a pragmatic answer to this problem. Starting from the assumption that the central securities depository systems in operation today are basically founded on accounting relationships, and the efficacy of the rights the proprietor is able to exercise may depend, in the final analysis, on the actual functioning of the accounting relationship, the Legal Certainty Group proposes the adoption of standardised rules which guarantee the owners of book-entry securities a set of rights, regardless of the regulation of similar legal positions outside the central depository system (Table 12.1). The proposal (Recommendation 5) that European Union member states should recognise, within their own law, acquisitions or dispositions concerning book-entry securities rendered effective by 'crediting an account; debiting an account; earmarking book-entry securities in an account, or earmarking a securities account; concluding a control agreement; concluding an agreement with and in favour of an account provider' is particularly significant.

In spite of the eminent acceptability of the method adopted, the proposal of using accounting entries as the basis for the efficacy of the transfer of securities, or the constitution of rights to them, in relation to third parties, will inevitably come into conflict with the various national legal traditions

*Table 12.1* Legal effects of book entries – synthesis of Legal Certainty Group recommendations

| Recommendation | Subject | Synthesis |
| --- | --- | --- |
| 1 | Scope of future EU Legislation | The EU should take legislative action to address the legal effects of book entries in securities accounts for the purpose of the acquisition, disposal and creation of security interests over securities, and related aspects. |
| 2 | Core Elements and Terminology | EU legislation should recognise that today's securities holding systems operate through the relationship between account holder and account provider and book entries in securities accounts. |
| 3 | Core Role of Account Providers | The protection of the rights of account holders as well as the ability to ensure the continuity of the relationship between the issuer and the investors depend upon the careful and diligent exercise of a number of duties by the account provider. |
| 4 | Book-Entry Securities | The law of the Member States should confer upon account holders a legal position in respect of securities credited to the account holders' securities account. The legal position which is harmonised in its minimum content should be described by a common notion. The *Advice* uses the notion "book-entry securities". |
| 5 | Effectiveness of Acquisitions and Dispositions of Book-Entry Securities and Interests therein | Future EU legislation should require Member States' law to recognise acquisitions and dispositions which are rendered effective by one of the following methods: crediting an account; debiting an account; earmarking book-entry securities in an account, or earmarking a securities account; concluding a control agreement; concluding an agreement with and in favour of an account provider. |
| 6 | Effectiveness and Reversal | An acquisition or disposition using one of the methods set out in Recommendation 5 should be immediately effective *vis-à-vis* the |

(Continued)

212

*Table 12.1* (*Continued*)

| Recommendation | Subject | Synthesis |
| --- | --- | --- |
| | | account provider and against third parties, including the account provider's insolvency administrator and creditors in its insolvency proceedings. No further steps may be required by national law to render the acquisition or disposition effective. |
| | | Member States' law may stipulate that the effectiveness can be made subject to a condition agreed upon between account holder and account provider. |
| | | Member States' law should prescribe that book entries can be reversed under the following circumstances: in the case of consent of the account holder; in the case of erroneous crediting; in the case of unauthorised debiting, earmarking or removal of an earmarking. |
| 7 | Protection of Acquirers against Reversal | An account holder should be protected against reversal of a credit unless it knew or ought to have known that the account should not have been credited. |
| 8 | Priority | Interests in the same book-entry securities rank amongst themselves in chronological order. |
| 9 | Integrity of the Issue | An account provider has to maintain a number of book-entry securities that corresponds to the aggregate number of book-entry securities credited to the accounts of its account holders or held for its own account. |
| 10 | Instructions | An account provider is neither bound nor entitled to give effect to any instructions with respect to book-entry securities given by any person other than his account holder or a person legally entitled to do so. |
| 11 | Attachments | Creditors of an account holder may attach book-entry securities only at the level of the account provider of that account holder. |

whenever the problem of the validity of the disposition underlying the entry arises. Aware of this risk, the Legal Certainty Group proposes that accounting entries should be considered as valid even in the event of the invalidity of the underlying contract, leaving it to the common tools of law to adjust the consequences of the invalidity. Thus, for example, a vendor who had been the victim of misrepresentation would not be able to claim title to the book-entry securities sold; instead, he would have to sue the purchaser for unjustified enrichment or compensation of damages.

However, assigning such a definitive nature to book entries does not appear to be justifiable, because in the subject to which the Second Advice refers (the regulation of the relationship between the parties to a contract concerning book-entry securities) there does not appear to be sufficient collective interest to justify such a large sacrifice of the rights of the victim of the invalidity, which would be downgraded from the level of a claim to specific assets to that of an ordinary credit, with the consequent worsening of this party's position in the event of the insolvency of the party obliged to provide compensation.

## 12.5  Conclusions

The existing regulatory framework on matters affecting the regulation of cross-border transactions appears to be not only incomplete, but also incapable of providing a satisfactory level of certainty.

The place of the relevant intermediary approach is adopted in general terms in EU legislation, which however does not establish what 'the place where the account is maintained' actually means. To solve this problem, the 'Hague Convention on the Law Applicable on Certain Rights in Respect of Securities Held with an Intermediary' has adopted a criterion (of the law chosen by the parties to govern the securities account) which, in the case of securities accounts held through intermediaries with cross-border operations, could reduce the place of the relevant intermediary approach to an irrelevance. The regulation of settlement finality and financial collateral arrangements also appears to be incomplete. Directive 98/26/EC does not regulate the delicate matter of the relationship between the finality and the underlying legal relationships, which is left to the individual member states to define. In the attempt to offer a solution to a large number of problems, generally relating to the need to ensure the validity and efficacy of financial collateral arrangements as defined and regulated by financial contract practice, Directive 2002/47/EC neglects to consider the impact on the national legal systems of the rules it contains. As we have seen, there also seems to be little justification for the confidence the 'Second Advice on Solutions to Legal Barriers Related to Post-Trading within the EU' poses in the possibility of guaranteeing the correct operation of cross-border settlement arrangements without significantly affecting national legislation.

All the limitations described above seem to be due largely to the desire to avoid taking a clear position on the problem of the legal nature of book-entry securities. This cautious attitude, due to the fear of obstacles or resistance to the adoption of the necessary reforms by member states, might be reconsidered in view of the urgent need to deal effectively with the problems posed by the crisis hitting intermediaries working in a multiplicity of legal contexts, thus opening the way to truly standards, complete solutions for the regulation of cross-border settlements.

# Notes

## 2  M&As in Banking: A Literature Review

1. A problem that can often be observed while considering survey result in regard to M&As is connected to the historical difference based on market conditions, regulatory framework, technology, considered country, monetary union process, and so on. See Hasan et al. (2000).
2. This review could be incomplete because the number of the studies concerning M&As in financial sector is very high. Nonetheless the main papers have been reviewed.
3. See Franchini (2002), pp. 66–98.
4. The reasons of such results lie in the rigidity of certain costs: in particular, personnel costs. Especially in the past, incentives to leave, preretirement, hierarchical cutting or all those actions aimed at reducing employees and costs were not commonly used with reference to M&A operations.

## 3  M&As in Banking: Measurement of Some Effects

1. The authors wish to express their particular thanks to Mr Alessandro Figliuolo for his contribution to the chapter.
2. The most important works concerning this theme are: Jensen (1988), pp. 21–48; Vander Vennet (1996), pp. 1532–5; Berger et al. (1997); Dermine (1999), pp. 15–17; Llewellyn (1999), pp. 2–17.
3. About these aspects see: Sagari (1992), pp. 93–123; Borenstztein et al. (1998), pp. 115–35; Palmieri (2004), pp. 137–8; Focarelli and Pozzolo (2005), pp. 2435–63; Buch et al. (2005).
4. See Sullivan (1994), pp. 325–42; Slager (2005), pp. 16–22; Manna (2004). The indicator, by modifying its aggregates, can be calculated for different financial institutions.
5. The ratios could be obtained in terms of percentage weight of the 'external' division compared to the total figure (for example foreign loans to total loans) or by comparing the two figures (for example foreign loans to domestic loans). In both cases, an increase in the ratio would suggest a growing importance of the foreign division with respect to the internal one.
6. The main goal of this analysis is to obtain a discrimination based on the financial relevance of the covered regions. In this way, the comparison between companies characterized by an exclusive presence in underdeveloped economies and those operating in advanced financial markets, has to generate a discrimination that favours the latter.
7. It is also possible to simplify the considered classes, keeping at the same time a sufficient level of effectiveness. It is possible to aggregate several countries in homogeneous areas, obtaining a $\Omega$ set characterized by a lower number of elements. In particular, following macro areas could be considered: EU area, USA area, America (centre and south), Far East area (China, Japan, South Korea, India), rest of the world.

8. Several different aggregates (loans, deposits, etc.) to the total of the set could be considered as market share proxies.

9. The suggested solution does not measure the impact of web-based techniques, aimed at promoting, selling and managing products and services, on the internationalization level of an institution or financial group. The development of virtual channels makes it possible for the intermediary to serve customers everywhere, without remote operators physically present into the final market.

10. For these aspects, see Eisenbeis et al. (1984), pp. 881–92; Dubovsky and Varadarajan (1987), pp. 597–608; Zen (1994); Haubrich (1994); Klein and Saidenberg (1997); Zanotti (1998), pp. 30–46; Kwan and Laderman (1999), pp. 18–31; Laderman (1999); Cerasi and Daltung (2000), pp. 1701–26; Stiroh (2002); Minnetti (2002); Strahan (2006); Elsas et al. (2006); Mottura (2007).

11. See Winton (1999); Goisis (1999), pp. 407–26; Acharya et al. (2001); Landi and Venturelli (2001); Stiroh (2002); Acharya et al. (2004); Laeven and Levine (2007), pp. 331–67; Lepetit et al. (2007); Baele et al. (2006).

12. The scholar who created this index is C.E. Shannon, in fact it is often called Shannon Entropy (SE). With regard to the literature, see Jacquemin and Berry (1979), pp. 359–69; Hoskinsson et al. (1993), pp. 215–39; Raghunathan (1995), pp. 989–1002; Schwizer (1996), pp. 128–34; Behr et al. (2007).

13. Factoring, leasing, real estate and other instrumental companies (for example computational data centres).

14. By following Italian schemes, bank interest bearing assets are composed by loans, securities, equity investments, or better by the sum of the items 20, 30, 40, 50, 60, 70 and 100. With reference to insurance companies, the financial investments are represented by the sum of items C and D of the assets. With reference to asset management companies, the figure managed by the asset management company can be found in the explanatory note, section D – Other information, Section 1.2 – Information concerning managed wealth. Data about companies with merely instrumental activities are excluded.

15. In all cases, we try to define an aggregate able to express the economic margins of the core business and other revenues of strategic assets. With reference to insurance companies, there are several problems in defining the aggregate. First of all, the correct computation of the return belonging to mere insurance activities (premium reduced by services – claims) is influenced by the accountancy methods used for the balance sheet, or better by the adoption of IAS–IFRS principles (compulsory for listed companies and or consolidated balance sheet only). Then, concerning the life insurances, the item 'net claim costs' has to be depurated by those components that have financial nature, related to the variation of the reserve for amounts to pay and to the variation of mathematic reserves. See: Banca d'Italia (2005); Isvap (2005); Banca d'Italia (2006).

16. With regard this topic see: Bennet Stewart III (2000); Rappaport (1997); Guatri (1990); Velez-Pareya (2001); Pozza (2001), pp. 46–66; Magni (2001), pp. 94–119.

17. See, amongst the others: Uyemura et al. (1996), pp. 94–113; Panizza and Di Russo (1997), pp. 64–6; Peschiera (1998); Massari (1999); Birindelli and Del Prete (2000), pp. 105–17; AIAF (2003); Comana and Modina (2003), pp. 21–40; Fiordelisi (2004), pp. 339–66.

18. According to a bottom-up approach, NOPAT is obtained by the sum of following elements: net profit + interest charges on subordinated loans after tax +/– accounting changes. See Birindelli and Del Prete (2000), pp. 109–14.

19. According to a wide understanding of the invested capital, it should be computed taking in consideration issued securities and certificates of deposit. In this case, NOPAT should be increased by the interest charges paid on such debts after tax.
20. See Fuller and Farrell (1993), pp. 480–96.
21. This figure is considered to be correspondent to the effective capital in the balance sheet, or, to be more precise, that the entire capital is used to face the risks of different management areas.
22. The parameter used to define the benchmark could be represented by the size, the juridical category, the main competitors, etc.
23. With reference to the asset management companies, the general model of EVA measurement could be considered. Similarly, $TE_{pre}$ could be calculated as difference between the EVA of a specific company and the EVA of the benchmark, while $TE_{post}$ could be calculated as difference between the variation of the EVA of the conglomerate and the EVA of the previous benchmark. See AIAF (2001).
24. $RORAC > K_e$ has the same meaning of a positive EVA. In fact, if $CaR = Ec$ (Economic capital), and considering the expected profits (EP), then the previous formula can be written again as $EP/Ec > K_e$, from which $EP > K_e \times Ec$, that defines a positive EVA. See Kpmg (1997), pp. 160–5; Di Antonio (1998).
25. More in detail, overall marginal CaR is the sum of marginal CaRs of considered companies. These derive from the difference between the suggested risk capital, or the total CaR, and the partial CaRs, obtained by the combination of considered companies (for example, bank and asset management company CaR, bank and insurance CaR, asset management company and insurance CaR). See Sironi (2005), pp. 686–8.


# 4   M&As and Equity Risk in the EMU Financial Sector

1. In the general usage, 'abnormal returns' means returns above (or below) some market benchmark that is taken as representative of the price variations that would be expected for a given stock or portfolio if the event did not occur over the period of analysis.
2. The volume of M&A operations has been often observed to increase as prices on the equity market (or in some of its sectors) rise and to diminish with share values.
3. With the term 'market risk' we mean the sensitivity of the stock returns to market moves in a broad sense; for most of the surveyed studies, this is the slope coefficient (commonly called the stock's 'beta') in a market model regression.
4. Notice that Greece and Finland, that are located far from the core of the EMU area, are not involved in any cross-border operation. On this topic: European Commission (2007a).
5. The handbook by Bodie and co-authors (2005) contains a modern and clear description of the index model. All index data are retrieved from Thomson-Reuters Datastream. We carried out all analyses presented in this section using Morgan Stanley Capital International indices too, but did not find any appreciable difference in results.
6. It is unfortunate that data on asset values and on initial and final stakes are severely incomplete in the sample (as it is in the original list) since this hinders any further exploration of the M&A characteristics.

7. Available observations are generally about 65 trading days. We have used the same kind of index model as in section 4.4, which delivers consistent 'realized beta' estimates (Andersen et al., 2006). Standard errors have been estimated by the Newey&West method (Newey and West, 1987) to achieve robustness to autocorrelation and heteroscedasticity features that could arise because of market microstructure effects.
8. For all sample cases, the deal was announced in the same quarter when it was completed; therefore, our analyses do not distinguish between the impacts of the news and of the event on beta.
9. We have tested for positive or negative variations by the classical $z$-test procedure based on our robust estimates of beta standard errors.

## 9   Cross-Border Groups: Supervision after the Crisis

1. See European Commission (2009) 177 final, COMMISSION DECISION of 23.1.2009 establishing the Committee of European Banking Supervisors.
2. See The High-Level Group on Financial Supervision in the EU, chaired by J. de Larosière, Report, 25th February 2009, especially Recommendation 18, p. 52.
3. On the procedures for the appointment of the coordinator, his role and supplementary supervision, see Cotterli (2004), especially p. 276 and following pages.
4. See Vella (2009), which also provides full biographical references to the latest literature.
5. European Parliament Resolution of May 6, 2009, P6_TA(2009)0367.
6. Commission Communication COM(2009) 252 Brussels, 27.5.2009.

## 11   Measuring Value in Stock Exchanges' Mergers

1. The owners of listed stock exchanges, who are usually institutional investors, are particularly interested in fast, low-cost regulations, whereas post-trading companies wish to maximise profit.
2. On the day the Archipelago merger was announced, the value figure was 69 per cent higher than the estimated value based on a 19.5 times EBITDA multiple corresponding to NASDAQ's bid for the LSE.
3. Regulations introduced by the authorities, such as the banning of short sales, have intensified the trend.
4. In the third quarter of 2008, Chi-X recorded a market share of 22.7 per cent for stocks listed on the FTSE 100 index.
5. This percentage is very similar to the profitability of LCH.Clearnet, one of Deutsche Börse's main competitors (54 per cent in 2007).

# References


Abraham, J.P. and P. Van Dijcke (2003) 'La concentrazione finanziaria cross-border in Europa: l'Europa al bivio? Per eccezione, evoluzione o rivoluzione', in F. Cesarini (ed.), *Le strategie delle grandi banche in Europa*, Rome: Bancaria Editrice, pp. 179–269.

Acharya, V.V., I. Hasan and A. Saunders (2001) 'The effects of focus and diversification on bank risk and return: evidence from individual bank loan portfolios', Working Paper Series, Stern School of Business.

Acharya, V.V., I. Hasan and A. Saunders (2004) 'Should banks be diversified? Evidence from individual bank loan portfolios', Working Paper Series, Stern School of Business.

Affinito, M. and M. Piazza (2008) 'What are borders made of? An analysis of barriers to European banking integration', *Temi di Discussione*, Banca d'Italia, no. 666, April.

Agrawal, A., J.F. Jaffe, and G.N. Mandelker (1992) 'The Post-Merger Performance of Acquiring Firms: A Re-examination of an Anomaly', *The Journal of Finance*, 47: 1605–21.

AIAF (2001) *L'applicazione del modello EVA (Economic Value Added) alle compagnie di assicurazione*, Quaderno no. 103, April.

AIAF (2003) *La valutazione delle imprese bancarie: un approfondimento del metodo EVA*, Quaderno no. 114, July.

Akhavein, J.D., A.N. Berger and D.B. Humprey (1997) 'The effects of megamerger on efficiency and prices: evidence from a bank profit function', *Review of Industrial Organization* 12, 1: 95–139.

Al Sharkas, A., M. Kabir Hassan and S. Lawrence (2008) 'The impact of mergers and acquisitions on the efficiency of the US banking industry: further evidence', *Journal of Business, Finance & Accounting* 35, 1–2: 50–70.

Alemanni, B., G. Lusignani and M. Onado (2006) 'The European securities industry. Further evidence on the roadmap to integration' in G. Ferrarini and E. Wymeersch (ed.), *Investor Protection in Europe*, Oxford: Oxford University Press, pp. 199–234.

Altunbas, Y. and D. Marqués Ibàñez (2004) 'Merger and acquisitions and bank performance in Europe: the role of strategic similarities', ECB Working Paper Series No. 398, October.

Amel, D., C. Barnes, F. Panetta and C. Salleo (2004) 'Consolidation and efficiency in the financial sector: a review of the international evidence', *Journal of Banking & Finance* 28, 10: 2493–519.

Amihud, Y., G.L. DeLong and A. Saunders (2001) 'The geographic location of risk and cross-border bank mergers', Working Paper Series, Baruch College – Zicklin School of Business, September.

Amihud, Y., G.L. DeLong and A. Saunders (2002) 'The effects of cross-border bank merger on bank risk and value', *Journal of International Money and Finance* 21, 6: 857–77.

Andenas, M. (2003) 'Who is going to supervise Europe's financial market', in M. Andenas and Y. Avgerinos (eds), *Financial Markets in Europe: Towards a Single Regulator?*, London: The Hague, pp. xv–xxvi.

Andersen, A. (2005) *Essays on Stock Exchange Competition and Pricing*, Doctoral Dissertations, Helsinki School of Economics.

Andersen, T.G., T. Bollerslev, F.X. Diebold and J. Wu (2006) 'Realized beta: persistence and predictability', in T. Fomby and D. Terrel (eds.), *Advances in Econometrics: Econometric Analysis of Economic and Financial Time Series*, Amsterdam: Elsevier, Volume B, pp. 1–40.

Anderson, C.W., D.A. Becher and T.L. Campbell II (2004) 'Bank mergers, the market for bank CEOs and managerial incentives', *Journal of Financial Intermediation* 13, 1: 6–27.

Arnold, T., P. Hersch and J.H. Mulherin (1999) 'Merging Markets', *The Journal of Finance* 54, 3: 1083–107.

Ayadi, R. and G. Pujals (2005) *Banking Mergers and Acquisitions in the EU: Overview, Assessment and Prospects*, Wien: SUERF – The European Money and Finance Forum.

Ayala, A. (2005) 'Merger performance in the European banking industry: an integrated approach', Working Paper Series, University of Utrecht.

Baele, L., O. De Jonghe and R. Vander Vennet (2006) 'Does stock market value bank diversification?', *Journal of Banking and Finance* 30, 3: 915–45.

Balding, C. (2008) 'A portfolio analysis of Sovereign Wealth Funds', SSRN Working Paper, May.

Banca d'Italia (2005) *Il bilancio bancario: schemi e regole di compilazione*, Circolare 262, December.

Banca d'Italia (2006) *Istruzioni per la redazione dei bilanci degli intermediari finanziari iscritti nell'Elenco speciale, degli Istituti di moneta elettronica (IMEL), delle Società di gestione del risparmio (SGR) e delle Società di intermediazione mobiliare (SIM)*, Gazzetta Ufficiale 58, March.

Basel Committee on Banking Supervision – The Joint Forum (2003) *Operational Risk Transfer Across Financial Sectors*, Basel, August.

Basel Committee on Banking Supervision (2003a) *Sound Practices for the Management and Supervision of Operational Risk*, Basel, February.

Basel Committee on Banking Supervision (2003b) *The 2002 Loss Data Collection Exercise for Operational Risk*, Basel, March.

Basel Committee on Banking Supervision (2006) *International Convergence of Capital Measurement and Capital Standards*, Basel, June.

Beccalli, E. and P. Frantz (2008) 'Le aggregazioni bancarie: gli effetti sulla performance operative', in P. Gualtieri (ed.), *Le aggregazioni tra banche in Europa*, Bologna: Il Mulino – AREL, pp. 29–102.

Becher, D. A. (2000) 'The valuation effects of bank mergers', *Journal of Corporate Finance* 6, 2: 189–214.

Behr, A., A. Kamp, C. Memmel and A. Pfingsten (2007) 'Diversification and the banks' risk-return characteristics – evidence form loan portfolios of German banks', Discussion Paper 5, Deutsche Bundesbank.

Beitel, P. and D. Schiereck (2001) 'Value creation at the ongoing consolidation of the European banking market', Institute for Mergers and Acquisitions (IMA) Working Paper No. 5, September.

Beitel, P., D. Schiereck and M. Wahrenburg (2004) 'Explaining the M&A success in European bank mergers and acquisitions', *European Financial Management* 10, 1: 109–39.

Bennet Stewart III, G. (2000) *La ricerca del valore*, Milan: Egea.

Berger, A.N. (1998) 'The efficiency effects of bank mergers and acquisitions: a preliminary look at the 1990s data', in Y. Amihud and G. Miller (eds), *Bank Mergers and Acquisitions*, London: Kluwer Academic Publishers, pp. 79–111.

Berger, A.N. (2000) 'The integration of the financial services industries: where are the efficiencies?', *North American Actuarial Journal* 4, 3: 25–52.

Berger, A.N. (2003) 'The efficiency effects of a single market for financial services in Europe', *European Journal of Operational Research* 150, 3: 466–81.

Berger, A.N. and D.B. Humphrey (1994) 'Bank scale economies, mergers, concentration, and efficiency: the U.S. experience', Working Paper 94-25, Financial Institutions Centre, The Wharton Scholl, University of Pennsylvania.

Berger, A.N. and R. De Young (2000) 'The effects of geographic expansion on bank efficiency', Working Paper Series WP-00-14, Federal Reserve Bank of Chicago.

Berger, A.N., A. Saunders, J.M. Scalise and G.F. Udell (1998) 'The effect of bank merger and acquisition on small business lending', *Journal of Financial Economics* 50, 2: 187–229.

Berger, A.N., R. De Young, H. Genay and G.F. Udell (2000) 'Globalization of financial institutions: evidence from cross-border banking performance', Brookings – Wharton Papers on Financial Services 3, 23–158.

Berger, A.N., R.S. Demsetz and P. E. Strahan (1999) 'The consolidation of financial services industry: causes, consequences and implication for the future', *Journal of Banking & Finance* 23, 2–4: 135–94.

Berger, P. G. and E. Ofek (1995) 'Diversification's effect on firm value', *Journal of Financial Economics* 37, 1: 39–65.

Bianchi, T. (2001) 'Fusioni: una scelta sempre conveniente?', *Banche e Banchieri*, 1: 3–4.

Birindelli, G. and S. Del Prete (2000) *La creazione di valore nelle banche italiane*, Milan: Franco Angeli.

Bliss, R.T. and R.J. Rosen (2001) 'CEO compensation and bank mergers', *Journal of Financial Economics* 61, 1: 107–38.

Bodie, Z., A. Kane and A.J. Marcus (2005) *Investments*, 6th edition, New York: McGraw-Hill.

Borenstztein, E., J. De Gregorio and J.W. Lee (1998) 'How does foreign direct investment affect economics growth?', *Journal of International Economics* 45, 1: 115–35.

Boubakri, N., G. Dionne and T. Triki (2006) 'Consolidation and value creation in the insurance industry: the role of governance', Cahiers de Recherche/Working Paper 0626, CIRPEE, June.

Boyd, J.H. and S.L. Graham (1998) 'Consolidation in US banking: implications for efficiency and risk', in Y. Amihud and G. Miller (eds.), *Bank Mergers and Acquisitions*, London: Kluwer Academic Publishers, pp. 113–35.

Brewer III, E., W.E. Jackson III and J.A. Jagtiani (2007) 'Target's corporate governance and bank merger payoff', SSRN Working Paper, December.

Brewer III, E., W.E. Jackson III, J.A. Jagtiani and T. Nguyen (2000) 'The price of bank mergers in the 1990s', *Economic Perspectives* 24, 1: 2–23.

Bruner, R. (2002) 'Does M&A pay? A survey of evidence for the decision-maker', *Journal of Applied Finance* 12, 1: 48–68.

Buch, C. and G.L. DeLong (2004) 'Cross-border bank mergers: what lures the rare animal?', *Journal of Banking and Finance* 28, 9: 2077–102.

Buch, C. and G.L. DeLong (2008) 'Banking globalization: international consolidation and mergers in banking', IAW Discussion Paper 38, January.

Buch, C., J.C. Driscoll and C. Ostergaard (2005) 'Cross-border diversification in bank asset portfolio', ECB Working Paper Series No. 429, January.

Calomiris, C.W. (1999) 'Gauging the efficiency of bank consolidation during a merger wave', *Journal of Banking and Finance* 23, 2–4: 615–21.

Campa, J.M. and I. Hernando (2004) 'Shareholder Value Creation in European M&As', *European Financial Management* 10, 1: 47–81.

Campa, J.M. and I. Hernando (2006) 'M&A performance in the European financial industry', *Journal of Banking and Finance* 30, 12: 3367–92.

Campbell, R. and R. Kraussl (2006) 'Merger & Acquisition behaviour in European banking', Working Paper Series, University of Maastricht.

Caruso, A. and F. Palmucci (2005) 'Fusioni e acquisizioni di banche quotate: creazione e distruzione di valore nelle operazioni dal 1994 al 2003', *Banche e Banchieri*, 2: 119–40.

Cavallo, L. and S. Rossi (2001) 'Scale and scope economies in the European banking system', *Journal of Multinational Financial Management* 11, 4–5: 515–31.

CEA (2008a) 'European insurance in figures', Statistics, no. 36.

CEA (2008b) 'CEA disappointed at EU French presidency proposal on Solvency II', Press release, 20 November.

CEBS (2007) *Protocol on Review Panel of the Committee of European Banching Supervisors*, October.

CEBS (2009a) *Template for a Multilateral Cooperation and Coordination Agreement on the Supervision of XY Group*, January.

CEBS (2009b) *Good Practices on the Functioning of Colleges of Supervisors for Cross-Border Banking Groups*, April.

CEBS and CEIOPS (2009) *Colleges of Supervisors. 10 Common Principles*, January.

CEIOPS (2005a) 'Guidelines for Coordination Committees in the Framework of the Insurance Groups Directive', DOC-02/05, February.

CEIOPS (2005b) 'Answers to the European Commission on the second wave of Calls for Advice in the framework of the Solvency II project', DOC-07/05, October.

CEIOPS (2005c) 'Recommendation on possible need for Amendments to the Insurance Groups Directive', DOC-04/05, Cons. Paper n. 6, October.

CEIOPS (2006) 'Statement on the role of the lead supervisor in the context of supplementary supervision as defined by the Insurance Groups Directive', DOC-07/06, December.

CEIOPS (2007a) 'Guidelines on Information Exchange between Lead Supervisors and Other Competent Authorities', DOC-16/07, November.

CEIOPS (2007b) 'Policy on harmonisation of contents and formats for public disclosure and supervisory reporting, IGSRR-05/07', Issues Paper, November.

Cerasi, V. and S. Daltung (2000) 'The optimal size of a bank: cost and benefits of diversification', *European Economic Review* 44, 9: 1701–26.

CESR, CEBS and CEIOPS (2009) *3L3 Joint Contribution to the European Commission's Consultation on the Improvement of Supervison for the Financial Services Sector*, April.

Chesini, G. (2007) 'From demutualisation to globalisation: new challenges for Stock Exchanges', *International Review of Business Research Papers* 3, 5: 146–60.

Chlistalla, M. and P. Gomber (2007) 'MiFID – Catalyst for a new trading landscape in Europe?', in Pre-Conference Proceedings of the 1st Special Focus Symposium on "Market Microstructure: From Orders to Prices – Best Execution in the Age of Algo Trading and Event Stream Processing", 1st International Conference on Advances and Systems Research; Zadar, Croatia.

Chlistalla, M., P. Gomber and S.S. Groth (2007) 'The New Landscape: How MiFID Drives Changes Among European Execution Venues', *The Journal of Trading* 2, 4: 69–79.

Choi, S., I. Hasan and J. Kotrozo (2006) 'Diversification, bank risk and performance: a cross-country comparison', Working Paper, Rensselaer Polytechnic Institute, August.

Clifford Change (2008) 'Financial Institution Recapitalization – Global Comparison', Clifford Change LLP, November.

Comana, M. and M. Modina (2003) 'L'applicazione dell'EVA a un campione di banche italiane', *Banche e Banchieri*, 1: 21–40.

Connell, F. and R.L Conn (1993) 'A preliminary analysis of shifts in market model regression parameters in international mergers between US and British firms: 1970–1980', *Managerial Finance* 19, 1: 47–77.

Cornett, M.M., G. Hovakimian, D. Palia and A. Teharnian (2003) 'The impact of the manager-shareholder conflict on acquiring bank returns', *Journal of Banking & Finance* 27, 1: 103–31.

Cotterli, S. (2004) 'Forme e rischi dell'integrazione tra settori finanziari: dai gruppi ai conglomerati finanziari', *Banca Impresa e Società* 15, 2: 263–88.

CPSS and IOSCO (2001) *Consultative Report on Recommendations for Securities Settlement Systems*, Bank for International Settlements, Basle, November.

Cummins, J. D. and M. A. Weiss (2004) 'Consolidation in the European Insurance Industry: Do Mergers and Acquisitions Create Value for Shareholders?', Wharton Financial Institution Center Working Paper 04-02, University of Pennsylvania.

Cummins, J. D., S. Tennyson and M. A. Weiss (1999) 'Consolidation and efficiency in the US life insurance industry', *Journal of Banking & Finance* 23, 2–4: 325–57.

Cybo-Ottone, A. and M. Murgia (2000) 'Mergers and shareholder wealth in European banking', *Journal of Banking and Finance* 24, 6: 831–59.

Darlap, P. and B. Mayr (2006) 'Group aspects of regulatory reform in the insurance sector', *The Geneva Papers* 31, 1: 96–123.

Datta, D., G. Pinches and V. Narayanan (1992) 'Factors influencing wealth creation from mergers and acquisitions: a meta-analysis', *Strategic Management Journal* 13, 1: 67–84.

Davidson, W.N., S.H. Garrison and G. Henderson (1987) 'Examining merger synergy with the Capital Asset Pricing Model', *Financial Review* 22, 2: 233–47.

DeLong, G.L. (2001a) 'Focusing versus diversifying bank mergers: analysis of market reaction and long term performance', SSRN Working Paper, January.

DeLong, G.L. (2001b) 'Stockholder gains from focusing versus diversifying bank mergers', *Journal of Financial Economics* 59, 2: 221–52.

DeLong, G.L. (2003a) 'Does long term performance of mergers match market expectations? Evidence from the US banking industry', *Financial Management* 32, 2: 5–25.

DeLong, G.L. (2003b) 'The announcement effects of US versus non-US bank mergers: do they differ?', *The Journal of Financial Research* 26, 4: 487–500.

Demsetz, R.S. and P.E. Strahan (1997) 'Diversification, size and risk at bank holding companies', *Journal of Money, Credit and Banking* 29, 3: 300–13.

Dermine, J. (1999) 'The economics of bank mergers in European Union, a review of the public policy issues', Insead Fontainebleau Working Paper No. 35.

Di Antonio, M. (1998) 'Vecchi e nuovi indicatori di performance economico-finanziaria in banca: un inquadramento concettuale', *A.B.P. News* no. 3.

Di Noia, C. (1999) 'The stock exchange industry: network effects, implicit mergers and corporate governance', *Quaderni di Finanza*, CONSOB, 33, March.

Di Noia, C. (2001) 'Competition and integration among stock-exchanges in Europe: Network effects, implicit mergers, and remote access', *European Financial Management* 7, 1: 39–72.

Diaz, B., M. Garcia Olalla and S. Sanfilippo Azofra (2004) 'Bank acquisition and performance: evidence from a panel of European credit entities', *Journal of Economics & Business* 56, 5: 377–404.

Directive 2002/47/EC of the European Parliament and of the Council of 6 June 2002 on financial collateral arrangements (OJ L 168, 27.6.2002, p. 43).

Directive 98/26/EC of the European Parliament and of the Council of 19 May 1998 on settlement finality in payment and securities settlement systems (OJ L 166, 11.6.1998, p. 45).

Draghi, M. (2008) 'Combating the global financial crisis – the role of international cooperation' HKMA Distinguished Lecture, 16 December.

Dubovsky, P. and P.R. Varadarajan (1987) 'Diversification and measures of performance: additional empirical evidence', *The Academy of Management Journal* 30, 3: 597–608.

Economides, N. (1993) 'Network economics with application to finance', *Financial Markets Institutions and Instruments* 2, 5: 89–97.

Economides, N. and F. Flyer (1997) 'Compatibility and market structure for network goods', Discussion Paper, Stern School of Business, EC-98-02.

Eisenbeis, R.A., R.S. Harris and J. Lakonishok (1984) 'Benefits of bank diversification: the evidence from shareholder returns', *The Journal of Finance* 39, 3: 881–92.

Ekkayokkaya, M., P. Holmes and K. Paudyal (2009) 'The euro and the changing face of European banking: evidence from mergers and acquisition', *European Financial Management* 15, 2: 451–76.

Elango, B. (2006) 'When does cross-border acquisition of insurance firms lead to value creation?', *The Journal of Risk Finance* 7, 4: 402–14.

Elsas, R., A. Hackethal and M. Holzhauser (2006) 'The anatomy of bank diversification', Discussion Paper 1, University of Munich, August.

Emmons, R. W., R.A. Gilbert and T.J. Yeager (2001) 'The importance of scale economies and geographic diversification in community bank mergers', Working Paper Series 024A, Federal Reserve Bank of St. Louis.

Enria, A. (2006) 'Completamento del mercato Unico: le convergenze della supervisione nel settore bancario', in F. Passatelli (ed.), *Unione europea, governance e regolamentazione*, Bologna: Il Mulino, pp. 205–32.

European Central Bank (ECB) (2000) *Mergers and Acquisitions involving the EU Banking Institutions: Facts and Implications*, December.

European Central Bank (ECB) (2006) *EU Banking Structures*, October.

European Central Bank (ECB) (2007) *Financial Integration in Europe*, March.

European Central Bank (ECB) (2008a) 'Cross-border bank mergers & acquisitions and institutional investors', Monthly Bulletin, 10: 67–80.

European Central Bank (ECB) (2008b) *EU Banking Structures*, October.

European Central Bank (ECB) (2009) *Financial Integration in Europe*, April.

European Commission (EC) (1999) 'The review of the overall financial position of an insurance undertaking (Solvency II review)', EC-MARKT-2095-99.

European Commission (EC) (2005) *Cross-border Consolidation in the EU Financial Sector*, Commission Staff Working Document, SEC(2005) 1398.

European Commission (EC) (2007a) 'Merger & Acquisitions', NOTE no. 4, April.

European Commission (EC) (2007b) 'Proposal for a directive of the European Parliament and of the Council on the taking-up and pursuit of the business of insurance and reinsurance', Solvency II – COM(2007)-361 – amended in COM(2008)-119 final (2007/0143 COD), amended and approved in P6_TA-PROV(2009)0251.

European Commission (EC) (2009) 'Commission Communication COM(2009) 252', Brussels, 27.5.2009.

European Parliament (2009) 'Resolution of May 6, 2009,' P6_TA(2009)0367.

Evenett, S. J. (2003) 'The cross-border mergers and acquisitions wave of the late 1990s', NBER Working Paper No. 9655, April.

Farrel, M. J. (1957) 'The measurement of productive efficiency', *Journal of the Royal Statistic Society* 120, 3: 253–90.

Federal Reserve Board (2008) *Economic Research and Data*, December.

Federal Reserve System (2005) *Results of the 2004 Loss Data Collection Exercise for Operational Risk*, May.

Ferretti, R. (1995) *La gestione del capitale proprio nella banca*, Bologna: Il Mulino.

Ferretti, R. (2000) 'Le acquisizioni bancarie e la reazione del mercato borsistico: le analisi in USA, Europa e Italia', *Bancaria* 56, 10: 26–33.

Financial Service Agency and Bank of Japan (2007) *Results of the 2007 Operational Risk Data Collection Exercise*, August.

FSA (2009) *The Turner Review A Regulatory Response to the Global Banking Crisis*, March.

Financial Stability Forum (2009) *Report of the Financial Stability Forum on Enhancing Market and Institutional Resilience, Update and Implementation*, April.

Fiordelisi, F. (2004) 'La creazione di valore nelle banche: il contenuto informativo delle misure di performance', *Banca Impresa e Società* 23, 2: 339–66.

Fiordelisi, F. (2008) 'Il risultato delle concentrazioni bancarie: l'impatto sul valore creato per gli azionisti e sull'efficienza della banca', in A. Carretta and P. Schwizer (eds), *Le fusioni in banca. Gestire l'integrazione per creare valore*, Rome: Bancaria Editrice, 73–132.

Fleckner, A. M. (2006) 'Stock exchanges at the crossroad', *Fordham Law Review* 74, 5: 2541–620.

Floreani, A. and S. Rigamonti (2001) 'Mergers and shareholders' wealth in the insurance industry', SSRN Working Paper, March.

Focarelli, D. and A.F. Pozzolo (2000) 'The determinants of cross-border bank shareholdings: an analysis with bank-level data from OECD countries', *Temi di Discussione*, Banca d'Italia, no. 381, October.

Focarelli, D. and A.F. Pozzolo (2001) 'The patterns of cross-border bank mergers and shareholdings in OECD countries', *Journal of Banking and Finance* 25, 12: 2305–37.

Focarelli, D. and A.F. Pozzolo (2005) 'Where do banks expand abroad? An empirical analysis', *Journal of Business* 78, 6: 2435–63.

Focarelli, D. and A.F. Pozzolo (2008) 'Cross-border M&As in the financial sector: is banking different from insurance?', *Journal of Banking & Finance* 32, 1: 15–29.

Focarelli, D., F. Panetta and C. Salleo (1999) 'Determinanti e conseguenze delle acquisizioni e fusioni bancarie in Italia: un'analisi empirica (1984–1996)', *Banca Impresa Società* 18, 1: 63–92.

Franchini, G. (2002) *Concentrazione ed efficienza nell'industria bancaria italiana*, Milan: Franco Angeli.

Fricke, M. (2007) 'Performance analysis of merger & acquisition (M&A) activity in the German, Austrian, Swiss and United Kingdom (UK) banking sectors', Working Paper Series, Cranfield University, September.

Fritsch, M., F. Gleisner and M. Holzhauser (2007) 'Bank M&A in Central and Eastern Europe', SSRN Working Paper, February.

Fuller, R.J. and J.L. Farrel (1993) *Analisi degli investimenti finanziari*, Milan: McGraw-Hill.

Gascon, F. and V. Gonzalez (2000) 'Diversification, size and risk at Spanish banks', Working Paper, Universidad de Oviedo, June.

Giorgino, M. and C. Porzio (1997) 'Le concentrazioni bancarie in Italia: alcuni fattori interpretativi', *Bancaria* 53, 12: 32–47.

Giovannini Group (2001) *Cross-Border Clearing and Settlement, Arrangements in the European Union*, Brussels, November.

Giovannini Group (2003) *Second Report on EU Clearing and Settlement Arrangements*, Brussels, April.

Godano, G. (2009) 'La vigilanza bancaria europea. Problemi e prospettive', *Queste istituzioni*, gennaio-marzo, 152: 29–45.

Goergen, M. and L. Renneboog (2004) 'Shareholder Wealth Effects of European Domestic and Cross-border Takeover Bids', *European Financial Management* 10, 1: 9–45.

Goisis, G. (1999) 'Alcune considerazioni circa l'efficienza produttiva del sistema bancario italiano', *Il Risparmio*, 3–4: 407–26.

Gomber, P. and M. Chlistalla (2008) 'Implementing MiFID by European execution venues – Between threat and opportunity', *The Journal of Trading* 3, 2: 18–28.

Grossman, S. J. and O. D. Hart (1986) 'The Costs and Benefits of Ownership: a Theory of Vertical and Lateral Integration', *Journal of Political Economy* 94, 4: 691–719.

Group of Ten (2001) *Report on Consolidation in the Financial Sector*, January.

Gruson, M. (2004) 'Supervision of financial conglomerates in the European Union', *Journal of International Banking Law and Regulation* 19, 10: 363–81.

Gualandri, E. and A. G. Grasso (2006) 'Towards a New Approach to Regulation and Supervision in the EU: Post-FSAP and Comitology', *Revue Bancaire et Financière*, 3: 157–75.

Gualandri, E., A. Landi and V. Venturelli (2009) 'Financial Crisis and and New Dimension of Liquidity Risk: Rethinking Prudential Regualtion and Supervsion', *Journal of Money, Investment and Banking*, 8: 25–42.

Guatri, L. (1990) *La teoria di creazione del valore*, Milan: Egea.

Gupta, A. and L. Misra (2007) 'Deal size, bid premium and gains in bank mergers: the impact of managerial motivations', *The Financial Review* 42, 3: 373–400.

Hackbarth, D. and E. Morellec (2008) 'Stock Returns in Mergers and Acquisitions', *The Journal of Finance* 63, 3: 1213–52.

Hadlock, C., J. Houston and M. Ryngaert (1999) 'The role of managerial incentives in bank acquisition', *Journal of Banking and Finance* 23, 2–4: 221–49.

Hague Conference on Private International Law (2002) *Convention on the Law Applicable on Certain Rights in Respect of Securities Held with an Intermediary*, October.

Hannan, T. H. and S.J. Pilloff (2005) 'Will the proposed application of Basel II in the United States encourage increased bank merger activity? Evidence from past merger activity', Finance and Economics Discussion Series 13, Federal Reserve Board of Governors.

Hart, J. R. and V.P. Apilado (2002) 'Inexperienced banks and interstate mergers', *Journal of Economics & Business* 54, 3: 313–30.

Hartmann, P., A. Maddaloni and S. Manganelli (2003) 'The euro area financial system: structure, integration and policy initiatives', ECB Working Paper No. 230, May.

Hasan, H., A. Lozano-Vivas and J.T. Pastor (2000) 'Cross-border performance in European banking', Discussion Paper 24, Bank of Finland, December.

Hasan, I., M. Malkamaki and H. Schmiedel (2003) 'Technology, automation and productivity of stock exchanges: International evidence', *Journal of Banking and Finance* 27, 9: 1743–73.

Haubrich, J. (1994) 'Bank diversification: laws and fallacies of large numbers', Working Paper Series No. 9417, Federal Reserve Bank of Cleveland.

Hijzen, A., H. Gorg and M. Manchin (2006) 'Cross-border mergers and acquisitions and the role of the trade costs', European Commission Economic Papers 242, February.

Hoskinsson, R.E., M.A. Hitt, R.A. Johnson and D.D. Moesel (1993) 'Construct validity of an objective (entropy) categorical measure of diversification strategy', *Strategic Management Journal* 14, 3: 215–35.

Houston, J.F., C.M. James and M.D. Ryngaert (2001) 'Where do merger gains come from? Bank mergers from the perspective of insiders and outsiders', *Journal of Financial Economics* 60, 2–3: 285–331.

Huizinga, H.P., J.H.M. Nelissen and R. Vander Vennet (2001) 'Efficiency Effects of Bank Mergers and Acquisitions in Europe', Discussion Paper 01-088/3, Tinbergen Institute, October.

IAIS (1999) *Principles Applicable to the Supervision of International Insurers and Insurance Groups and Their Cross-border Business Operations (Insurance Concordat)*, December.

IAIS (2000) *Supervisory Standard on Group Coordination*, October.

IAIS (2002a) *Principles on Capital Adequacy and Solvency*, January.

IAIS (2002b) *Supervisory Standard on the Exchange of Information*, January.

IAIS (2003) *Insurance Core Principles and Methodology*, October.

IAIS (2008a) *Principles on Group-wide Supervision*, September.

IAIS (2008b) *Guidance Paper on the Role and Responsibilities of a Group-wide Supervisor*, October.

International Monetary Fund (2008) 'Sovereign Wealth Funds: A work agenda', IMF Working Paper, February.

International Working Group of Sovereign Wealth Funds (2008) 'Sovereign Wealth Funds. Generally Accepted Principles and Practice "Santiago Principles"', IWG Working Paper, October.

ISVAP (2005), *Regolamento concernente gli schemi per il bilancio delle imprese di assicurazione e di riassicurazione che sono tenute all'adozione dei principi contabili internazionali di cui al titolo VIII, capo I, capo II, capo III e capo V del Dlgs 7.09.2005 – Codice delle Assicurazioni Private*, Rome.

Jacquemin, A.P. and C.H. Berry (1979) 'Entropy measure of diversification and corporate growth', *Journal of Industrial Economics* 27, 4: 359–69.

Jensen, M. and R. Ruback (1983) 'The market for corporate control: the scientific evidence', *Journal of Financial Economics* 11, 1–4: 5–50.

Jensen, M.C. (1988) 'Takeover: their cause and consequences', *Journal of Economic Perspectives* 2, 1: 21–48.

Joint Forum (1999a), 'Supervision of financial conglomerates', Papers prepared by the Joint Forum on Financial Conglomerates, February.

Joint Forum (1999b) *Framework for Supervisory Information Sharing*, February.

Joint Forum (1999c) *Principles for Supervisory Information Sharing*, February.

Kane, E.J. (2000) 'Incentives for banking megamergers: what motives might regulators infer from event-studies evidence?', *Journal of Money, Credit, and Banking* 32, 3: 672–701.

Kern, S. (2007) 'Sovereign Wealth Funds: State investment on the rise', Deutsche Bank Research, September.

Kiymaz, H. and T.K. Mukherjee (2001) 'Parameter shifts when measuring wealth effects in cross-border mergers', *Global Finance Journal* 12, 2: 249–66.

Klein, P.G. and M.R. Saidenberg (1997) 'Diversification, organization and efficiency: evidence from bank holding companies', Economics Working Paper Series 97-2, Federal Reserve Bank of New York.

Kohler, M. (2008) 'Transparency of regulation and cross-border bank merger', Discussion Paper 08-009, ZEW-Centre for European Economic Research.

KPMG (1997) *Manuale di risk management*, Rome: Edibank.

Kusnadi, J. and A. Sohrabian (1999) 'The impact of insurance mergers on shareholder returns', *Cal Pomona Journal of Interdisciplinary Studies*, 12: 109–16.

Kwan, S.H. and E.S. Laderman (1999) 'On the portfolio effects of financial convergence – a review of the literature', *Federal Reserve Bank of San Francisco Economic Review*, 2: 18–31.

Kwan, S.H. and J.A. Wilcox (1999) 'Hidden cost reductions in bank merger: accounting for more productive banks', Working Paper Series 99-10, Federal Reserve Bank of San Francisco.

Laderman, E.S. (1999) 'The potential diversification and failure reduction benefits of a bank expansion into nonbanking activities', Working Paper Series, Federal Reserve Bank of San Francisco.

Laeven, L. and R. Levine (2007) 'Is there a diversification discount in financial conglomerates?', *Journal of Financial Economics* 85, 2: 331–67.

Landi, A. and V. Venturelli (2001) *The Diversification Strategy of European Banks: Determinants and Effects on Efficiency and Profitability*, EFMA Lugano Meetings.

Langetieg, T.C., R.A. Haugen and D.W. Wichem (1980) 'Merger and stockholder risk', *Journal of Financial and Quantitative Analysis* 15, 3: 689–717.

Lannoo, K. (2008) 'Concrete steps towards more integrated financial oversight: the EU's policy response to the crisis', CEPS Task Force Report, Brussels, December.

Legal Certainty Group (2008), *Second Advice on Solutions to Legal Barriers related to Post-trading within the EU*, Brussels.

Lepetit, L., E. Nys, P. Rous and A. Tarazi (2007) 'Product diversification in the European banking industry: risk and loan pricing implications', Working Paper Series, University of Limoges.

Lepetit, L., S. Patry and P. Rous (2004) 'Diversification versus specialization: an event study of M&As in the European banking industry', *Applied Financial Economics* 14, 9: 663–9.

Li, D., F. Moshirian and A. Sim (2003) 'The determinants of intra-industry trade in insurance services', *Journal of Risk and Insurance* 70, 2: 269–87.

Llewellyn, D.T. (1999) 'Le concentrazioni nell'industria bancaria Europea: tra ragioni economiche e luoghi comuni', *Bancaria* 55, 3: 2–17.

London Economics (2002) *Quantification of the Macro-Economic Impact of Integration of EU Financial Markets*, Executive Summary of the Final Report to European Commission – Directorate- General for the Internal Market, November.

Lorenz, J.T. and D. Schiereck (2007) 'Completed versus cancelled banking M&A transaction in Europe', Working Paper Series No. 3, Coventry University.

Lubatkin M. and H.M. O'Neill (1987) 'Merger strategies and capital market risk', *Academy of Management Journal* 30, 4: 665–84.

Ma, Y. and N. Pope (2003) 'Determinants of international insurers' participation in foreign non-life markets', *Journal of Risk and Insurance* 70, 2: 235–48.

Madura, J. and A. Picou (1993) 'Wealth effects of mergers in the insurance industry', *Journal of Insurance Issues* 15, 1: 63–78.

Magni, C.A. (2001) 'Scomposizione di sovraprofitti: Economic Value Added e Valore Aggiunto Sistemico', *Finanza, Marketing e Produzione* 19, 4: 94–119.

Malavasi, R. (2002) *The Effects of Mergers in Italy: a Quantitative Analysis for the Period 1990–1993*, Annali della Facoltà di Economia di Cagliari, 26: 31–60.

Mandelker, G. (1974) 'Risk and return: the case of merging firms', *Journal of Financial Economics* 1, 4: 303–35.

Manna, M. (2004) 'Developing statistical indicators of the integration of the Euro area system', ECB Working Paper Series No. 300, January.

Massari, M. (1999) 'La valutazione delle banche. Uno schema di riferimento', *La valutazione delle aziende* n. 13.

Mayer-Sommer, A. P., S. Sweneey and D.A. Walker (2005) 'Effect of bank acquisition on shareholder returns', *Bank Accounting & Finance* 18, 4: 11–16.

McGowan, J. R. and K. J. Carr *(2000)* 'International Dimensions of Insurance Coverage and Cross-Border Tax Issues', *International Tax Journal* 26, 2: 17–32.

Mediobanca, *Le maggiori banche europee nel 2008*, Ricerche e Studi, Milano, October.

Minnetti, F. (2002) *La diversificazione dell'attività bancaria nei servizi di intermediazione mobiliare*, Padua: Cedam.

Mørck, R., A. Shleifer and R. Vishny (1990) 'Do managerial objectives drive bad acquisitions?', *The Journal of Finance* 45, 1: 31–48.

Moshirian, F. (2008) 'Sovereign Wealth Funds and Sub-Prime Credit Problems', SSRN Working Paper, September.

Mottura, P. (2007) *Banche. Strategie, organizzazione e concentrazioni*, Milan: Egea.

Nail, L. and F. Parisi (2005) 'Bank mergers and their impact: a survey of academic studies', *Bank Accounting & Finance* 18, 4: 3–10.

Newey, W.K. and K.D. West (1987) 'A simple, positive definite, heteroskedasticity and autocorrelation consistent covariance matrix', *Econometrica* 55, 3: 703–8.

NyseEuronext (2006) *Creating the Global Exchange*, June.

OECD (1999) *Liberalisation of International Insurance Operations: Cross-border Trade and Establishment of Foreign Branches*, OECD Finance & Investment/Insurance & Pensions.

Otchere, I. (2006) 'Stock exchange self-listing and value effects', *Journal of Corporate Finance* 12, 5: 926–53.

Outreville, J. F. (2008) 'Foreign affiliates of the largest insurance groups: location-specific advantages', *Journal of Risk and Insurance* 75, 2: 463–91.

Pagano, M. and A.J. Padilla (2005) 'Efficiency gains from the integration of exchanges: lesson from the Euronext "annual experiment"', A report for Euronext, May.

Palmieri, S. (2004) *Fusioni e acquisizioni in Europa*, Rome: Ediesse.

Panizza, S. and T. Di Russo (1997) 'L'Economic Value Added (EVA): un nuovo indicatore di performance per le banche', *Bancaria* 53, 11: 64–6.

Peristiani, S. (1996) 'Do mergers improve the X-efficiency and scale efficiency of U.S. banks? Evidence from 1980s', Research Paper No. 9623, Federal Reserve Bank of New York.

Peschiera, F. (1998) 'La creazione di valore nel sistema bancario italiano. Applicazione della metodologia E.V.A. alle banche quotate italiane nel periodo 1995–1998', *A.B.P. News* no. 3.

Pesic, V. (2003) 'L'efficacia delle aggregazioni bancarie in Italia. Riflessioni ed evidenze empiriche', *Banche e Banchieri*, 6: 517–44.

Petrella, G. (2008) 'L'effetto ricchezza associato alle operazioni di aggregazione', in P. Gualtieri (ed.), *Le aggregazioni tra banche in Europa*, Bologna: Il Mulino, pp. 103–28.

Pfingsten, A. and K. Rudolph (2002) 'German banks' loan portfolio composition: market orientation vs specialization', Working Paper, University of Muenster.

Pilloff, S.J. (2004) 'Bank Merger Activity in the United States 1994–2003', Board of Governors of the Federal Reserve System, Staff Study 176, May.

Pilloff, S.J. and A.M. Santomero (1997) 'The value effects of bank mergers and acquisitions', The Wharton School, University of Pennsylvania, 97-07.

Polato, M. and J. Floreani (2007) 'Società di gestione quotate: organizzazione e governance nel nuovo assetto competitivo', *Banche e Banchieri*, 1: 5–20.

Polato, M. and J. Floreani (2008) 'Business diversification in the securities industry: Implications for exchanges', *Transition Studies Review* 15, 2: 281–8.

Power, M. (2003) 'The invention of operational risk', LSE Discussion Paper, 16, June.

Pozza, L. (2001) *La misurazione della performance d'impresa*, Milan: Egea.

Prosperetti, L. (2008) 'I processi di cambiamento nelle banche europee: fusioni, riorganizzazione, risorse umane', *Bancaria* 64, 5: 10–15.

Punt, L.W. and M.C.J. Van Rooij (1999) 'The profit structure relationship, efficiency and mergers in the European banking industry: an empirical assessment', Research Memorandum WO&E No. 604, December.

Raghunathan, S.P. (1995) 'A refinement of entropy measure of firm diversification: toward definitional and computational accuracy', *Journal of Management* 21, 5: 989–1002.

Rappaport, A. (1997) *La strategia del valore*, Milan: Franco Angeli.

Resti, A. (2001) *Decidere in banca con la matematica e la statistica*, Rome: Edibank.

Resti, A. and L. Galbiati (2004) 'Competitività e M&A: le aggregazioni bancarie creano valore? Il punto di vista del mercato', in G. Bracchi and D. Masciandaro (eds), *La competitività dell'industria bancaria*, Fondazione Rosselli, 9° Rapporto sul Sistema Finanziario Italiano, Rome: Edibank, pp. 209–44.

Rhoades, S.A. (1994) 'A summary of merger performance studies in banking, 1980–93, and an assessment of the "operating performance" and "event study" methodologies', Board of Governors of the Federal Reserve System Staff Economic Studies 167.

Rhoades, S.A. (1998) 'The efficiency effects of bank mergers: an overview of case studies of nine merger', *The Journal of Banking and Finance* 22, 3: 273–91.

Rhoades, S.A. (2000) 'Bank merger and banking structure in the United States 1980–1998', Board of Governors of the Federal Reserve System, Staff Study 174.

Roll, R. (1988) 'R²', *The Journal of Finance* 43, 3: 541–66.

Rosen, R.J. (2006) 'Merger Momentum and Investor Sentiment: The Stock Market Reaction to Merger Announcements', *Journal of Business* 79, 2: 987–1017.

Saccomanni, F. (2009) 'Nuove regole e mercati finanziari', *Bancaria* 65, 1: 31–7.

Sagari, S. (1992) 'United States foreign direct investment in the banking industry', *Transnational Corporation* 3, 1: 93–123.

Saita, F. (2000) *Il risk management in banca*, Milan: Egea.

Sarcinelli, M. (2009) 'La riforma dell'architettura di vigilanza europea', *Bancaria* 65, 1: 25–30.

Schmiedel, H. (2001) 'Technological development and concentration of stock exchanges in Europe', Discussion Paper, Bank of Finland, 21.

Schmiedel, H. (2002) 'Total factor productivity growth in European stock exchanges: a non-parametric frontier approach', Discussion Paper, Bank of Finland, 11.

Schmiedel, H. and A. Schonenberger (2005) 'Integration of securities market infrastructure in the euro area', ECB Occasional Paper Series, 33, July.

Schoenmaker, D., S. Oosterloo and O. Winkels (2007) 'The emergence of cross-border insurance groups within Europe with centralised risk management', *The Geneva Papers* 33, 3: 530–46.

Scholten, B. and R. De Wit (2004) 'Announcement effects of bank merger in Europe and U.S.', *Research in International Business and Finance* 18, 2: 217–28.

Schulerr, M. and F. Henemann (2005) 'The Cost of Supervisory Fragmentation in Europe', ZEW, Discusion Paper, Centre for European Research, no. 05-01.

Schwizer, P. (1996) 'La diversificazione dei gruppi creditizi: elementi per una verifica empirica', in P. Mottura, D. Previati, P. Schwizer, R. Borsato and F. Saita (eds), *Diversificazione e organizzazione dei gruppi creditizi*, Milan: Egea, pp. 128–34.

Scott-Frame, W. and W.D. Lastrapes (1998) 'Abnormal returns in the acquisition market: the case of bank holding companies 1990–1993', *Journal of Financial Services Research* 14, 2: 145–63.

Serifsoy, B. (2007) 'Stock exchange business models and their operative performance', *Journal of Banking and Finance* 31, 10: 2978–3012.

Shi, J., A. Samad-Khan and P. Medapa (2000) 'Is the size of the operational loss related to firm size?', *Operational Risk*, January.

Shy, O. and J. Tarkka (2001) 'Stock exchanges alliances, access fees and competition', Discussion Papers, Bank of Finland, 22.

Siems, T.F. (1996) 'Bank mergers and shareholders wealth: evidence from 1995's megamerger deals', Financial Industry Studies, Federal Reserve Bank of Dallas, August.

Sironi, A. (1996) *Gestione del rischio e allocazione del capitale nelle banche*, Milan: Egea.

Sironi, A. (2005) *Rischio e valore nelle banche*, Milan: Egea.

Slager, A. (2005) *Internationalization of Banks: Strategic Patterns and Performance*, Wien: SUERF Studies.

Standard and Poor's (2006) *Quantitative Rating Drivers: Exchange Methodology Put into Practice*, July.

Standard and Poor's (2008) *Industry Report Card: Exchanges and Clearinghouses Start 2008 on a Positive Note*, April.

Stiroh, K.J. (2002) 'Diversification in banking: is noninterest income the answer?', Staff Paper No. 154, Federal Reserve Bank of New York, September.

Stiroh, K.J. (2002) 'Do community banks benefit from diversification?', Working Paper Series, Federal Reserve Bank of New York, December.

Stoll, H.R. (2006) 'Electronic Trading in Stock Markets', *Journal of Economic Perspectives* 20, 1: 153–74.

Strahan, P.E. (2006) 'Bank diversification, economic diversification?', Federal Reserve Bank of San Francisco, Economic Research No. 10, December.

Sullivan, D. (1994) 'Measuring the degree of internationalization of a firm', *Journal of International Business Studies* 25, 2: 325–42.

Swiss Re (2000) 'Europe in focus: non-life markets undergoing structural change', *Sigma*, 3.

Tafara, E. and R. J. Peterson (2007) 'A Blueprint for cross-border access to U.S. investors: a new international framework', *Harvard International Law Review* 48, 1: 31–68.

Tapking, J. and J. Yang (2004) 'Horizontal and vertical integration in securities trading and settlement', Working Paper Series, European Central Bank, 387, August.

Tarantola, A. M. (2009) 'Causes and consequences of the crisis', Submission by Bank of Italy Deputy Director General, at the XXI Villa Mondragone International Economic Seminar, Rome, 24 June.

The High Level Group on Financial Supervision in the EU, chaired by J. de Larosière (2009) *Report*, 25 February.

Thompson, R.S. (1983) 'Diversifying Mergers and Risk: Some Empirical Tests', *Journal of Economic Studies* 10, 3: 12–21.

Turner, A. (2009) 'Turner Review Press Conference: Speaking notes and slides for the press', Financial Services Authority, 18 March.

UniCredit Group (2009) *Cross-border Banking in Europe: What Regulation and Supervision?*, Discussion Paper, March.

Uyemura, D.G., C.C. Kantor and J.M. Pettit (1996) 'EVA for banks: value creation, risk management and profitability measurement', *Journal of Applied Corporate Finance* 9, 2: 94–113.

Van den Berghe, L. A. A., K. Verweire and S. W. M. Carchon (1999) 'Convergence in the financial sevices industry', Tokyo Executive Seminar on Insurance Regulation and Supervision, Tokyo: Seminar 27–8 September.

Van Duyn A., D. Brewster. and G. Tett G. (2008) 'The Lehman Legacy', *Financial Times*, 13 October, 10.

Van Lelyveld, I., and K. Knot (2008) 'Do financial conglomerates create or destroy value? Evidence for the EU', DNB Woking Paper Series No.174, April.

Vander Vennet, R. (1996) 'The effect of mergers and acquisitions on the efficiency and profitability of EC credit institutions', *Journal of Banking and Finance* 20, 9: 1531–58.

Vander Vennet, R. (2002) 'Cross-border mergers in European banking and bank efficiency', Working Paper Series No. 152, University of Gent.

Velez-Pareya, I. (2001) 'Value creation and its measurement: a critical look at EVA', Working Paper Series, University of Bogotà, August.

Vella, F. (2002) 'Banca Centrale Europea, Banche Centrali Nazionali e vigilanza bancaria: verso un nuovo assetto dei controlli nell'area dell'euro', *Banca, borsa e titoli di credito* 55, 2: 150–65.

Vella, F. (2009) 'Il rischio: questo sconosciuto', *Analisi Giuridica dell'Economia-AGE*, 1: 161–78.

Wahlstrom, G. (2006) 'Worrying but accepting new measurements: the case of Swedish bankers and operational risk', *Critical Perspectives on Accounting* 17, 4: 493–522.

Williams, J. and A. Liao (2008) 'The search for value: cross-border bank M&A in emerging market', *Comparative Economic Studies* 50, 2: 274–96.

Williamson, O. (1985) *The Economic Institutions of Capitalism: Firms, Markets, Relational Contracting*, New York: The Free Press.

Winton, A. (1999) 'Don't put all your eggs in one basket? Diversification and specialization in lending', Working Paper Series No. 16, University of Minnesota, September.

World Federation of Exchanges (WFE) (2007) *Annual Report and Statistics*, Paris.

World Federation of Exchanges (WFE) (2008) *Market Highlights*, Paris.

Zadra, G. (2009) 'Per una riforma organica dell'architettura di vigilanza europea: le proposte dell'ABI', *Bancaria* 65, 2: 2–10.

Zanotti, G. (1998) 'Economie di scala e di diversificazione nel sistema bancario italiano', *Banche e Banchieri* 1: 30–46.

Zen, F. (1994) *La diversificazione produttiva nell'azienda di credito*, Turin: Giappichelli.

Zollo, M. and D. Leshchinkskii (2000) 'Can firms learn to acquire? Do markets notice?', Wharton School Center for Financial Institutions, University of Pennsylvania 00-01, January.

# Index